THE CENTER FOR CHINESE STUDIES at the University of California, Berkeley, supported by the Ford Foundation, the Institute of International Studies (University of California, Berkeley), and the State of California, is the unifying organization for social science and interdisciplinary research on contemporary China.

RECENT PUBLICATIONS

LOWELL DITTMER
Liu Shao-ch'i and the Chinese Cultural Revolution
The Politics of Mass Criticism

TETSUYA KATAOKA
Resistance and Revolution in China
The Communists and the Second United Front

SUZANNE PEPPER
Civil War in China
The Political Struggle, 1945-1949

EDWARD E. RICE
Mao's Way

FREDERIC WAKEMAN, JR.
History and Will
Philosophical Perspectives of Mao Tse-tung's Thought

JAMES L. WATSON
Emigration and the Chinese Lineage
The Mans in Hong Kong and London

Regional Government and Political Integration in Southwest China, 1949-1954

This volume is sponsored by the
CENTER FOR CHINESE STUDIES
University of California, Berkeley

DOROTHY J. SOLINGER

Regional Government
and Political Integration in
Southwest China, 1949-1954

A Case Study

UNIVERSITY OF CALIFORNIA PRESS
Berkeley   Los Angeles   London

University of California Press
Berkeley and Los Angeles, California

University of California Press, Ltd.
London, England

Copyright © 1977 by
The Regents of the University of California

ISBN: 0-520-03104-0
Library of Congress Catalog Card Number: 75-22662

Printed in the United States of America

CONTENTS

PREFACE

Regionalism—the phenomenon whereby distinct groups, living in discrete territorial enclaves within larger political communities, exert pressures for recognition of their differences—is a common problem in both new and old nations in the modern world. This study examines the problem in the provinces of Southwest China at the time of Communist takeover. It also analyzes the efforts of the People's Republic to overcome this regionalism and build a unified and integrated nation in the first five years of its rule. My focus is on the role played by regional government in achieving political integration in China.

I hope the insights here will prove useful to anyone attempting to understand the issues of regionalism and unification in other "new nations." Besides having a comparative perspective, the study deals with a period in the history of the People's Republic which has received relatively little attention in recent years; and it investigates an institution—the Great Administrative Region—on which no in-depth study has previously been made. Thus, the work offers new material for the China scholar as well as new hypotheses for the comparative analyst.

I wish to express my great debt to John Wilson Lewis in the preparation of this book. His constant efforts to help me to sharpen my thinking and clarify my concepts, and his insights and understanding were invaluable to the scholarly aspects of my work. In a broader sense his unfailing support and stimulation at all points along the way helped make the research purposeful and exciting for me.

I also would like to note my sincere gratitude to the Center for Chinese Studies at the University of California, Berkeley, both for the financial support I received under the Ford Foundation-funded "Young Scholars" program there during 1973-1974, and for the interest in my work shown by many individuals at the Center, particularly Joyce K. Kallgren and Chalmers Johnson. I also value the discussions I had at Berkeley with Hong Yung Lee.

My thanks also go to Michel Oksenberg for directing me to the topic; and to Robert C. North, Gabriel Almond, and Nobutaka

Ike for many valuable comments and suggestions in refining my original manuscript. I also wish to acknowledge the kind assistance of John Ma and David Tseng in locating materials in the East Asian collection of the Hoover Institution at Stanford University.

Many individuals who have read all or parts of this work helped me with useful advice at key points during my final revision, including the following: Eugene Dorris, Gardel Feurtado, C. Thomas Fingar, Malcolm Goggin, Harry Harding, Jr., Robert A. Kapp, John R. Shepherd, Seiichiro Takagi, James R. Townsend, and Wu Yuan-li. Thanks go to all of them. I wish, too, to thank Kippy Nigh for her preparation of the maps. I also appreciate greatly the help I received from the members of the staff of the University of California Press, who, besides everything else they did, found time to answer my many questions.

Finally, much gratitude goes to my husband, Joel Falk, for constant emotional support and encouragement; and for almost always being willing to listen to me think out loud and being ready with a new perspective or insight.

D.J.S.

Pittsburgh, 1976.

LIST OF TABLES, MAPS, AND FIGURES

INTRODUCTION

The juxtaposition of the two political phenomena central to this book—rule by regional government and the attainment of political integration—suggests two general questions. First, how were political integration and control over regional areas achieved in China through the use of regional governments? And second, why did the Communists' division of the country into six Great Administrative Regions immediately after the takeover foster rather than limit national unification and centralized political development?

In seeking answers to these questions this study inquires into the nature of the integration that took place during the early years of the People's Republic (1949-1954), while attempting to understand the role of the administrative region in this integration. The case of the Great Administrative Region in the Southwest, comprising the provinces of Szechwan, Yunnan, Kweichow, and Sikang, is the focal point.

Answers to more specific questions are also pursued: How did the Southwest, a separatist, isolated region, become a contributing member of the larger nation? How were the disconnected localities within this region made to relate to each other? What determined the central government's choice of strategy for achieving integration in specific problem areas and what was the Great Administrative Region's role in these strategies? What governed the form and level of integration adopted to deal with particular issues? What controlled the success or failure of given strategies? All of these questions bear on the larger problems of regionalism, political development, national unification, and integration.

I chose the Southwest area because as of 1949 it best illustrated the problems of regional diversity and separatism that thwarted political integration—it was both disunited internally and was poorly linked to the rest of China and the national center. I concentrated on the years 1949-1954 because it was then that regional governments (first called Military Administrative Committees and later simply Administrative Committees) existed.

My main data base was the Southwest China newspapers, so answers to my questions had to be found there. For the most part, accounts from the Chinese press have been taken at face value, for several reasons. First, for the period after 1951, when Westerners were expelled from China, there is no other source of data. Second, this press was prepared largely for domestic consumption: much of the reportage was geared toward explaining to cadres how to carry out their tasks. This applies especially to articles on administrative practice, governmental policy, and errors in work, which are the main types of reportage utilized here. On such matters there would have been no purpose in falsifying data. Third and finally, reliance on the Chinese sources gives the reader the official Chinese perspective of successes and problems in work; it lets the Chinese tell their own story.

The methodology used one case study, and research on this single case led to findings that pertain to Southwest China over the years 1949-1954. These are offered as propositions that delineate how a political system might deal with problems of development and centralization. Some of the more specific propositions describe how regional government was instrumental in this case (and might be in others) in overcoming regionalism and contributing to national political integration. These propositions are numbered as they appear in the text, according to the chapter in which they first appear. For example, the three propositions in Chapter Four are numbered 4.1, 4.2, and 4.3. All the propositions will be reviewed and discussed in the concluding chapter, since some are only implicit when first discussed.

The focus on one case allowed investigation in greater depth than might otherwise have been possible, and it permits one to see more clearly certain cause-and-effect relationships. The same relationships may or may not recur elsewhere, but by carefully specifying the pertinent variables in each proposition, the study has potential theoretical implications for other parts of China, and perhaps also for other third-world nations faced with problems of regionalism and challenges to centralization. Throughout, references will be made to the factors that conditioned the specific developments in Southwest China during the period under investigation, so that the limits of extending the propositions will be evident.

This book takes a new approach to the study of political

development and national integration. Most previous work on these problems has focused on how capabilities are accumulated at the central level—or, occasionally, on how society is transformed at the local level—during modernization.[1] Although many writers are aware of problems of regionalism in developing nations, few have directed their studies at particular regions, or dealt with the specific types of issues that arise in. regions in the course of integrating a nation. My discussion stresses the mechanics and dynamics of the integration process itself, the problems of territorial separatism that regionalism entails, and the specific ways these problems were tackled in the efforts to integrate the Chinese nation after 1949.

Several models will be presented, to explain the integration process in China from the perspective of the region and regional government,[2] and to clarify the interactions between the various levels of government in China.

Concepts and Conceptual Framework

The key terms of the analysis are these: region, regionalism, political development, integration, and political middlemen and intermediary structures. Throughout, the emphasis will be on the politics of regions and of regionalism. Further, the study will be concerned with the type of regionalism whose existence is a barrier to national political development.

Development will be discussed in terms of two distinct processes of integration. These will be labeled Integration I and Integration II. Most simply put, the former concerns the integration of large areas, such as the Southwest, into the nation; the latter deals with the integration of small localities into these larger

1. For example, on the central level, Gabriel Almond and G. Bingham Powell, *Comparative Politics* (1966); Leonard Binder, ed., *Crises and Sequences in Political Development* (1971); Cyril Black, *The Dynamics of Modernization* (1966); Lucian W. Pye, *Aspects of Political Development* (1966); A. K. F. Organski, *The Stages of Political Development* (1965); and Dankwart Rustow, *A World of Nations* (1967). On the local level, two examples are Daniel Lerner, *The Passing of Traditional Society* (1964); and Douglas Ashford, *National Development and Local Reform* (1967).

2. It is important to note here that the analysis has been undertaken from the point of view of the author, and that these models represent the author's interpretations of the Chinese experience.

areas. Taken together, these processes involve the control of regionalism and the attainment of political development. The crucial linkages between these two types of integration, decisive to achieving national integration, are the structures located at a level between the national center and the locality (here, the Great Administrative Region) and the elites or "political middlemen" at that level. These concepts will be discussed in more detail as follows.

"Region" in the generic sense—as opposed to the specific Southwest Great Administrative Region—will be used to mean "an area in which all places have certain characteristics by virtue of which it is distinct from the areas around."[3] In this sense, "regional groupings of places with similar or interrelated human attributes" or "regional associations" fall into three categories: economic, cultural, and political. Presumably, a total region would be comprised of regional associations of all three types.

An economic regional association reflects the limited spatial dimensions of economic systems and generally pertains either to production or commercial relations. A cultural regional association refers to territorial groupings of cultural factors. Such gross regional groupings mark off human populations from one another in terms of language, religion, custom, and social structure. Finally, a political regional association pertains to an historically unique set of political forces and relations that operate in a common geographic or spatial entity.[4] Here, "region" will be understood as a descriptive term, identifying an area in which there is homogeneity of social and economic forms and political outlook.[5] Thus, the existence of distinctive and common political, cultural, and economic attributes within a given territory is the test for the existence of a region.

Where the term "region" identifies an area in question, "regionalism" here will refer to the political, behavioral aspects of

3. Robert E. Dickinson, *Regional Ecology* (1970), p. 41.
4. *Ibid.*, pp. 77-87.
5. This definition of region coincides with what is generally known as a "uniform" region, or one that is homogenous throughout. Alternatively, "nodal" or "organizational" regions are those that have a focal area with surrounding areas tied to it by lines of circulation. See R. B. Vance, "Region," *International Encyclopedia of the Social Sciences* (1968), 13:379; and Dickinson, *Regional Ecology*, p. 78.

this area's relationship to its total political environment. Most writers on the topic agree that there are three basic aspects to regionalism. These are: distinctiveness from neighbors as to at least one important property (this aspect establishes that the criteria for a "region" are present); consciousness of this difference on the part of the local inhabitants; and attempts by these inhabitants to agitate and apply pressure for recognition of their differences. This pressure can be directed at obtaining special consideration for their common interests and traditions, economic favoritism, decision-making autonomy, a chance for greater expression, and fulfillment of shared demands and needs.[6]

The literature on regionalism is mainly addressed to situations in which the region is already an integral part of the national system. Thus the regional agitation studied by most scholars has only moderate political significance, for it merely seeks to obtain from the central government certain rights and powers the region currently lacks. My study deals with a more extreme case of regionalism. It remains concerned with local distinctiveness and consciousness, but it concentrates on a form of regionalism (in the Southwest area) in which there was an unusual degree of decision-making autonomy and a large amount of control over local economic and military resources. In other cases, achievement of some such autonomy and control has been an objective of regional demands. In the case researched here, however, the national unit had extraordinary problems in controlling the Southwest because the balance of power rested largely with the sub-units or mini-regions in the area.[7] When regional autonomy

6. R. Herberle, "Regionalism: Some Critical Observations," *Social Forces* 21, No. 3 (1943), pp. 280-286; R. B. Vance, "Region," pp. 377-382; Joseph L. Love, "An Approach to Regionalism"; Dickinson, *Regional Ecology*, p. 151. See also Peter Schneider, Jane Schneider, and Edward Hansen, "Modernization and Development: The Role of Regional Elites and Noncorporate Groups in the European Mediterranean," *Comparative Studies in Society and History* 14, No. 3 (1972), pp. 328-350, especially pp. 331-332, on the region as a political unit.

7. Chapter Two will show that in the Southwest before 1949, the pertinent "regions," as defined above, were localities below the level of the province. Thus, the word "localism" could be substituted for "regionalism" here. However, in keeping with the bulk of the literature on this topic, this study will use the term "regionalism." It is important to remember, however, that regionalism before 1949 in the Southwest was not based on the Southwest area (the future Southwest Great Administrative Region) as a whole unit.

is present to this extent, the urgent task in political development is to increase national control and integration.[8]

The concept of "political development" used here stresses centralized control and coordination.[9] Thus, political development relates to an increase in the competence of the central government to organize and control the entire territory of the state. Accordingly, in this book "political development" will refer to the central government's attainment of the capacity to coordinate and obtain access to the full range of resources of the nation, so that this government can pursue national goals.

Because the focus is on regionalism, the relevant aspect of political development here is the extension of authority throughout the entire national territory. Of the five crises Leonard Binder et al. say must be dealt with if political modernization is to proceed, it is the third one, "penetration," that best describes the concerns of this study.[10] All five, however, are present in the effort to enhance national-level control and coordination. The term penetration here refers to "changes in the degree of administrative and legal penetration into the social structure and out to the remote regions of the country."[11] Apparently a solution to the penetration crisis would entail administrative innovations and would result in increases in national unification.

But how does this process of penetration take place? What are the problems that must be overcome in unifying the national

8. As Weiner notes, the centrality of this task has been implicitly accepted by most social scientists, who have adopted the perspective of the elites they study. See Myron Weiner, "National Integration vs. Nationalism," *Comparative Studies in Society and History* 15, No. 2 (1973), p. 249. As Chapter One's discussion of the national political context will show, increasing the degree of national control and integration were indeed elite goals in China in the early 1950s.

9. Use of this sense of the term draws on the work of Organski, Black, Verba, and Coleman. See Organski, *Stages of Political Development,* pp. 6-7; Black, *Dynamics of Modernization,* Chapter Three; Sidney Verba, "Sequences and Development," in Binder, ed., *Crises and Sequences,* pp. 292-293; James S. Coleman, "The Development Syndrome: Differentiation-Equality-Capacity," in Binder, ed., p. 98. For an alternative and provocative treatment of the concept of political development with special reference to ethnicity, see Cynthia H. Enloe, *Ethnic Conflict and Political Development* (1973), pp. 9-11, 14.

10. Leonard Binder, "Crises of Political Development," in Binder, ed., *Crises and Sequences,* p. 67. The crises are: identity, legitimacy, penetration, participation, and distribution.

11. *Ibid.,* p. 53.

territory? These questions lie at the heart of the investigation of political development.

The literature on integration, some of which has a direct bearing on these problems, can be divided into three major types of work: those on supranational integration between developed countries; those on integration at the supranational level between developing nations; and those on integration within developing nations.

Works of the first type deal with the process of unification between sovereign and highly developed nations, and emphasize freedom of choice, decision, bargaining, and compromise as the bases of establishing the union.[12] They are concerned with relationships between equal political actors whose legitimate elites, power bases, and structures must be recognized by all political participants if the unifying process is to continue. Further, these works describe a process of gradualism in which economic cooperation tends to "spill over," in an almost automatic fashion, into demands for greater unification in other sectors. This type of alliance between equal industrial countries appears to provide little help in understanding the unification of regional areas within a developing nation attempting to centralize control.

The second group of writers, who focus on the integration between developing countries, perhaps stress even more heavily the importance of leaving existing national political elites and national sovereignty intact.[13] For in such areas as East Africa and Central America, newly independent regimes are often unwilling to surrender their recently won sovereignty for the sake of a coordinated union.[14] These writers maintain that political integration must rest largely on a shared ideology in these areas. Again, this kind of work also has little application to the problem

12. See Ernst B. Haas, *The Uniting of Europe* (1958); Amitai Etzioni, *Political Unification* (1965); and Karl W. Deutsch, *Political Community and the North Atlantic Area* (1957).

13. For example, L. Gordon, "Economic Regionalism Reconsidered," *World Politics* 13, No. 2 (1961), pp. 231-253; J. S. Nye, Jr., "Comparative Regional Integration," *International Organization* 22, No. 4 (1968), pp. 855-880; Nye, "Patterns and Catalysts in Regional Integration," in J. S. Nye, Jr., ed., *International Regionalism: Readings* (1968), pp. 333-349; Nye, *Pan-Africanism and East African Integration* (1965); Aaron Segal, "The Integration of Developing Countries," *Journal of Common Market Studies* 5, No. 3 (1967), pp. 252-282.

14. Nye, *Pan-Africanism*, p. 167.

of instituting a strong central government. Thus, works of these first two types deal with situations where centralized penetration, and a consequent control and coordination of the union, are thwarted to some extent by various degrees of autonomy among the members.

For this study, the theories of the third group of writers, those who address the problems of integration within developing nations, are most relevant.[15] They are concerned with cases where gaining national control and achieving penetration by the central government are the principal problems. Unification, according to these scholars, must be created by a central government along a variety of dimensions—political, economic, and often military.[16] Here the problem is generally one of undercutting, not compromising with, the autonomy of the elites and power structures among the member units. It is these authors who have most to offer in terms of understanding the relationship between integration and political development throughout most of the nonindustrialized states. The definition of integration they use approximates the concept of penetration.

Thus, several imply that the achievement of integration increases central coordination and that it is a matter of territorial ties and nationwide control.[17] One author distinguishes several facets of the process of integration, all of which are related to that "which holds a society and a political system together. . . . There are many ways in which societies may fall apart." One of these

15. As da Silva, Connor, and Enloe point out, similar problems of integration are also increasingly present among developed industrial nations. See Milton M. da Silva, "Modernization and Ethnic Conflict," *Comparative Politics* 7, No. 2 (1975), pp. 227-228; Walker Connor, "Nation-Building or Nation-Destroying?" *World Politics* 24, No. 3 (1972), p. 327; and Enloe, *Ethnic Conflict*, pp. 12-13.

16. Thus, we agree with da Silva, Connor, Melson and Wolpe, and Bates that "modernization" within a state, with its attendant increases in "social mobilization" and communications, does not necessarily or automatically produce integration. Rather, as Connor, Melson and Wolpe, Weiner, and Zolberg emphasize, creating an integrated state is a political and institutional problem that political elites must consciously handle. See da Silva, "Modernization," pp. 248-251; Connor, "Nation-Building," pp. 319-355, especially pp. 321 and 354; Robert Melson and Howard Wolpe, "Modernization and the Politics of Communalism," *American Political Science Review* 64, No. 4 (1970), pp. 1112-1130, especially p. 1130; Robert H. Bates, "Ethnic Competition and Modernization in Contemporary Africa," *Comparative Political Studies* 6, No. 3 (1973), pp. 457-484; Weiner, "National Integration," pp. 253-254; and Aristide R. Zolberg, "Patterns of National Integration," *Journal of Modern African Studies* 5, No. 4 (1967), p. 466.

17. See Black, *Dynamics of Modernization*.

facets, territorial integration, refers to "objective control over the entire territory."[18]

The body of literature on integration identified here as the third group focuses on cleavages in society and politics that pose obstacles to achieving national unification. These cleavages may be caused by alternative political centers competing for the allegiance and loyalty of relevant populations. They may also be created by social and cultural differences that cause barriers to grow up between different groups in the population. In such situations the problem is to find ways to eliminate these divisions or to lessen their power to obstruct national integration. This literature diagnoses the causes of these cleavages and in some cases suggests cures. Although our concern with regionalism means that we are particularly interested in territorial splits, this literature offers pertinent theoretical insights.

The most prevalent type of cleavage in developing societies has been characterized as the "conflict between civil and primordial sentiments" or between "communal and political loyalties."[19] "Primordial attachments" are those involving race, region, language, tribe, culture, kin, and religion. These attachments create social cleavages which may have the additional consequence of separating the "modernizing elite" from the "traditional mass."[20] Likewise, others speak of the "multiplicity of 'traditional societies' ";[21] "cultural-regional tensions and discontinuities";[22] and

18. Myron Weiner, "Political Integration and Political Development," *Annals of the American Academy of Political and Social Science*, No. 358 (1965), pp. 52-64. See also James S. Coleman and Carl J. Rosberg, Jr., *Political Parties and National Integration in Tropical Africa* (1964), pp. 8-11, on territorial integration.

19. Clifford Geertz, "The Integrative Revolution," in Clifford Geertz, ed., *Old Societies and New States* (1963), pp. 105-157.

20. Leonard Binder, "National Integration and Political Development," *American Political Science Review* 58 (1964), No. 3, pp. 622-631. See also Coleman and Rosberg, *Political Parties*, pp. 9-10; Weiner, "Political Integration," pp. 60-62; and W. J. Foltz, "Building the Newest Nations," in W. J. Foltz and Karl W. Deutsch, eds., *Nation-Building* (1963), pp. 117-131.

21. Ake, a Nigerian, emphasizes the divisions between various ethnic segments in society, rather than those between the masses and the leadership. He holds that, since politics in the new states is basically elitist and since the political loyalties of the masses are mainly determined by ethnic factors, political stability could be enhanced by increasing the group cohesiveness of the elites. He assumes that the masses would then follow the leaders and that group tensions would be lowered throughout society. See Claude Ake, *A Theory of Political Integration* (1967), p. 96.

22. Coleman and Rosberg, *Political Parties*, p. 8.

"parochial loyalties."[23] A last variation alludes to a separation between state and society: between the "highly differentiated politico-administrative superstructure . . . and the medley of fragmented elements in society over which it has been placed."[24] All these writers suggest that the problem of integration is the problem of finding a way to resolve these "primordial" or communal conflicts and of creating new, overarching attachments.

In short, the population's loyalties and activities must be focused upon one political center.[25] Ideally, in the broadest sense, closing gaps in all directions in a fully integrated society would involve two things: on a vertical dimension, the achievement of the capacity to control from above and the development of habits of compliance from below; and, on a horizontal dimension, the creation of cooperation between those living within one area. This study will focus on the construction of administrative mechanisms used in an attempt to build such a society.

How does this process of integration occur? This study deals with two sorts of integration processes, which I have labeled Integration I and Integration II. Both are primarily concerned with administrative integration and are predicated on the use of an intermediary structure to bridge and close the cleavages between competing political centers at the local and central levels, respectively. The first, Integration I, refers to the macro-level process by which the part—a part that intervenes between the center and localities, such as the Great Administrative Region— becomes tied in to the nation as a whole and thus more fully enmeshed in a national administrative structure. The second, Integration II, on a more micro level, pertains to the unification within this part—that is, to the integration of the localities within the Great Administrative Region, as they become administratively connected with each other.

23. Weiner, "Political Integration," p. 53.
24. Coleman, "Development Syndrome," p. 86.
25. Weiner, Connor, and Jackman all note that the process of national integration is above all a matter of increasingly directing political allegiances toward the national level over time, while local and other types of parochial allegiances are becoming less salient. See Weiner, "National Integration," p. 249; Connor, "Nation-Building," p. 336; and Robert W. Jackman, "Political Parties, Voting and National Integration," *Comparative Politics* 4, No. 4 (1972), p. 512.

Two alternative solutions to problems of separatism at the macro level (Integration I) can be gleaned from the literature. That is, there are at least two distinct ways in which a regionalistic enclave can be made to fit into the national system. One solution is based on establishing a cultural-ideological consensus or "psychological focus" throughout society. Some analysts believe that common values and normative agreement about politics will unify the nation.[26] Although we will not be concerned with the normative component of integration, the notion of creating a situation whereby the entire nation can be dealt with in similar terms has applicability to our analysis.

Alternatively, others have placed more importance on using institutions to deal with differences. For example, traditional ties can be adapted to the modern state "by channeling discontent arising out of their dislocation into political rather than parapolitical forms of expression."[27] Also, frameworks for constructive disagreement might be provided close to the citizen's field of observation, so that "consensus may rest on the multiplicity of frameworks and social differentiations through which disagreement is expressed."[28] In short, this viewpoint advocates the institutionalization of differences to integrate diverse sectors of society into the national system.

Broadly conceived, these two approaches represent alternate methods of attaining integration. The first is geared toward establishing a kind of uniformity—at least insofar as political matters are concerned—in order to integrate society. The second, on the other hand, recognizes the intractability of elemental bonds, and so is concerned with finding mechanisms for articulating differences in a way that can be combined with state-building.

These two conceptions—uniformity versus the articulation of differences—can be viewed as two separate components of Integration I. These components are not necessarily mutually exclusive; in fact, an effective integration would be likely to contain

26. E.g., Binder, "National Integration," p. 630; Ake, *Theory of Political Integration,* p. 96; Connor, "Nation-Building," p. 353.
27. Geertz, "Integrative Revolution," pp. 128, 154-157.
28. Douglas Ashford, *Perspectives of a Moroccan Nationalist* (1964); see especially Chapter 10.

aspects of each. It is hypothesized here that, in a nation lacking integration, a two-step process is effective in building an integrated state in the initial stages of national development. The first step would entail allowing for the articulation of differences. This can be done by recognizing territorial variations while integrating separate areas through similar institutions and policies on a geographical basis. This first step, then, prepares the way for a second one in which administrative uniformity across the country is achieved. It is hypothesized that this creation of uniformity involves integration on a functional basis, with functional sectors (economic, cultural, political) cutting across geographical boundaries (Proposition 1.1). Where this occurs, Integration I can be studied in terms of a shift from a geographic arrangement of administrative work to a functional one.

On the micro level, Integration II—within the part—can best be understood by focusing on particular issues which exemplify the lack of integration within that part. Thus, a study of Integration II involves analysis of the process by which separate localities become related to each other and to the intermediary structures uniting them with respect to these particular issues. Two model strategies for dealing with these policy areas will be posited—one direct and one indirect. The terms here—direct and indirect—are borrowed from Emerson's classic study on the direct and indirect rule of colonies by European imperialist powers.[29]

As used in this work, the direct approach refers to a strategy that seeks to install outsiders to the region in positions of power within the region or to rotate officials frequently to avoid favoritism toward the local population. It erases traditional "natural" administrative boundaries or replaces them with new demarcations, thus shaking up old and habitual administrative patterns. Finally, it imposes a uniform policy toward substantive issues in all localities, regardless of local conditions.

29. According to Emerson, direct rule makes use of a European administrative framework to reach directly every person in the community through officials appointed from above. Indirect rule, on the other hand, is often a temporary measure by which a small number of European officials are used to ensure the natives' obedience and to carry out necessary reforms. Most states under this second type of rule are permitted to survive intact or nearly so under traditional political forms and elites until machinery is available to absorb them. See Rupert Emerson, *Malaysia* (1964), pp. 3, 6-8.

The indirect model refers to a strategy that entails retention of old personnel and traditional administrative boundaries, and entrusts to these officials the adaptation of national policy to circumstances in the localities. The aim here is to raise local initiative, enthusiasm, and, consequently, allegiance through permitting locals to participate actively in their own governance. Such participation, of course, is authorized only within a centrally controlled mandate.

It is hypothesized that the strategy chosen for achieving integration in relation to a particular problem within an area is a function of the following factors: the degree of local cultural differences associated with the problem; the degree of threat the problem poses to the new regime and its goals and values; the perceived capacity the group in question has for supporting the new regime and the value of its support to the regime; and the resource costs of controlling the problem. The nature of the integration achieved is related to the strategy—direct or indirect—used in achieving it.

These models and hypotheses afford a sense of the separate dynamics involved in two complementary and interrelated processes of integration. What is the vehicle or vehicles that serve to connect Integration I, the process going on between the center and the intermediate level, with Integration II, during which small localities are being related to each other at this intermediate level?

Here several pertinent concepts can be borrowed from the field of political anthropology. First, the term "political middleman" refers to an individual who is "the local leader to the local community as against the higher politicos, and the national party or government worker to both these audiences or publics."[30] His (or her) function is to "interrelate and anticipate the needs, aspirations, resources, and traditions of his local village or tribe to the corresponding demands, supplies, resources, and jural order of the province and nation." Such persons can have a crucial role to play in integrating isolated regional enclaves into a national system.

30. Marc J. Swartz, *Local-Level Politics* (1968), pp. 199, 203. In this volume see also Hugh Tinker, "Local Government and Politics, and Political and Social Theory in India," pp. 217-226; Paul Friedrich, "The Legitimacy of a Cacique," pp. 243-269. See also F. G. Bailey, *Stratagems and Spoils* (1969), p. 167.

Administratively, these middlemen tend to occupy "inter-hierarchical roles." They uphold "positions in which distinct levels of social relations, organized in their own hierarchies, gear into each other. Those occupying these roles stand in positions where "there are major discontinuities in the total hierarchy and the sets of social relations become radically different."[31] At such points in the administrative system, the clash between the values and goals of the locality and those of the wider system must be resolved.

These concepts—of political middlemen and inter-hierarchical roles—can be taken to refer to mediating individuals as well as to the structures within which they work. In the case studied here, these roles were filled by the Great Administrative Regions and their personnel. Those in such positions provide possible mechanisms for bridging the gaps between competing political centers in the developing nation during Integration I, in the attempt to allow for the articulation of societal differences while striving for an ultimate uniformity administratively. Thus, such intermediary structures and individuals can serve as channels for the aggregation of local interests and their communication upward. They are a means for relating subnational differences to the larger political arena. Once a developing national center has used such structures to penetrate the localities, it may be necessary to eliminate these structures, in order to attain a more total integration, a more complete unification.[32] Consequently, we would expect their role to be more crucial during the geographical, or first, phase of Integration I than it would be later on.

In terms of Integration II, in managing separatist tendencies within a part of the nation, intermediary structures can serve as institutional means of aggregating regional differences at the highest level where they are relevant. Thus such structures can isolate local problems into territorial compartments, and integrate them at a subnational level until they are solved. In this manner too, national policy can be related differentially to local areas in a manner applicable to their special traits even as these local characteristics are being adapted to fit national goals.

31. Max Gluckman, "Inter-Hierarchial Roles," in Swartz, *Local-Level Politics*, p. 71.
32. Bailey notes that integration occurs when the local populace learns to make its own connections with the center, bypassing the intermediate leaders, and/or when the higher-level power decides it will no longer tolerate the middlemen's existence. See Bailey, *Stratagems*, pp. 175-176.

In short, political middlemen and intermediary structures can provide means for creating linkages as a step on the road toward integration. And, taken all together, the two forms of integration, interconnected by these linkages, constitute the penetration aspect of political development referred to above—the extension of authority throughout the entire national territory through administrative changes.

Structure of the Study

The chapters in this book will closely follow the analytical framework described above. The first two chapters will provide the background information essential to an understanding of the later analysis. Chapter One will focus on the historical, ideological, and legal issues connected with the regional administrations used in ruling China from 1949 to 1954. Chapter Two deals with the Southwest during the Republican era and will begin to apply the conceptual framework outlined here. By the presentation of historical, geographical, cultural, political, and commercial data, this chapter will show that neither Integration I nor Integration II existed in the Southwest before 1949. The area had few ties with the central government or with the rest of China; in short, Integration I was absent. Moreover, many of the Southwest localities were relatively separate and self-sufficent entities in terms of politics, trade, and culture, which meant that Integration II was absent. The analysis in Chapter Two suggests that political development and unification vis-à-vis this Southwest area would have to be effected through the creation of linkages between the localities and the center. These linkages could then be instrumental in achieving these two forms of integration.

Chapters Three and Four will explicate the process of Integration I in the Southwest. Both will posit that this aspect of national integration was a two-step process, involving first a geographical and then a functional focus in the organization of work. That is, solution of local problems preceded the solution of national problems (Chapter Three); and regulation of the local (Southwest) political and economic situations by the Great Administrative Region laid the foundation for a greater central government control (Chapter Four). Chapter Three will examine the events in the Southwest and the changing focus of the regional leadership's concerns over time. It will show that the local leadership gradually enlarged its range of vision to concentrate more on national and less on local problems. Chapter Four will investigate the changing functions and powers of the regional administration over time, and analyze the steadily decreasing role of this administration relative to other bodies in its environment—the center, the regional Party apparatus, and the provinces. Both chapters, then, highlight the fact that attention to and institutionalization of local differences preceded nationwide administrative uniformity and control.

Following the insights afforded by the "middleman" literature, Chapter Five will examine the backgrounds of the personnel in the Southwest administration and the new military units instituted for control there. It will illustrate how the backgrounds of the officials and the organizational ties of the military units enabled the regional regime to play a mediating role between center and locality.

Chapter Six will deal with Integration II. Here hypotheses will be presented pertaining to the strategies—direct or indirect—adopted in the attempt to achieve an integration of the localities within the Southwest. Data from the Southwest press will be used to illustrate the procedures specified for handling local problems. This data will be analyzed to show how the strategies mandated were related to the nature of particular local problems and determined the way these problems were to be solved. This chapter will also consider changes in the forms of local integration in the Southwest over time and posit that central decisions and local events both had an impact on the direction which integration took in the Southwest.

Chapter Seven will evaluate problems in integration from the perspective of the Chinese leadership. Here difficulties in work, as recounted in the local press, will be related to problems in the administrative and personnel system set up in the Southwest. The effect on integration produced by popular reactions to regime policies will also be assessed.

In conclusion, Chapter Eight will analyze from several perspectives the success of the regional organs in achieving integration. First, it will reinterpret the framework outlined in this introductory chapter in terms of the data presented in Chapters Two through Seven. Second, it will consider the dynamics involved in this case of integration by reviewing and reformulating the propositions interspersed throughout the study; and it will discuss their broader relevance. Finally, it will offer some general reflections on regional government and political integration in China as well as in other developing nations.

CHAPTER I

The Historical, Ideological, and Legal Background of the Great Administrative Regions

The Great Administrative Regions, set up in the wake of Communist takeover in December 1949 at a level between the provinces and the center, were an attempt to deal with a traditional problem in Chinese politics: how to implement national policy over a large and complex area dotted with regional enclaves. In fact, two key themes of this study—regionalism and the administrative imposition of structure to achieve control—have been recurrent motifs in Chinese history.

Regions, Regionalism, and Administration in Traditional China

Several writers have pointed out the strength of regional loyalties throughout Chinese history and related tendencies toward disintegration and separatism.[1] One historian has calculated that there have been nine identifiable periods of division or loss of central control since the Eastern Chou period (which preceded the unification of China under the Ch'in dynasty in the third century B.C.). He reports that these periods add up to a total of almost 1,350 years of division out of some 3,000 years of history.[2]

1. J. B. R. Whitney, *China: Area, Administration and Nation-Building* (1970); Jean Chesneaux, "The Federalist Movement in China, 1920-1923," in Jack Gray, ed., *Modern China's Search for Political Form* (1969), pp. 96-137; Martin Wilbur, "Military Separatism and the Process of Reunification under the Nationalist Regime, 1922-1937," in Ho Ping-ti and Tsou Tang, *China in Crisis* (1968), 1:203-276; Franz Michael, "Regionalism in Nineteenth-Century China," in Stanley Spector, *Li-Hung-chang and the Huai Army* (1964); Chi Ch'ao-ting, *Key Economic Areas in Chinese History* (1936).
2. Wang Gungwu, "Comments," in Ho and Tsou, *China in Crisis*, 1:264-270.

Analyses of the causes for the periodic breakdown of the Chinese state vary. One author attributes the oscillation between unity and disunity to a permanent instability in the Chinese system. This instability has resulted from an interplay between "the centralizing predilections of the rulers," growing out of the magnitude of the tasks with which they must deal, and "the decentralizing dictates of the environment," related to the complexity of peoples and environments across the country.[3] Another emphasizes the particularism and individuality of the provinces and the typical feeling among the people of a given province of "belonging to one's 'little country' . . . an awareness of the distinctive features of each province."[4]

Chi Ch'ao-ting notes that provincial groupings in Chinese history have for centuries been combined into self-sustaining and highly independent geographical regions based on topographical divisions. He holds that the outlines of these regions were particularly emphasized in times of disturbance and divided rule.[5] His analysis relies on the concept of the "key economic area" to explain that an economic factor underlay the alteration of unity and division over time.[6] Basically, control of such an area as a place of mooring and source of grain supply was essential for the unified domination of regional territories. Historically, he maintains, China was held together by military and bureaucratic domination through the control of a key economic area. But this unity could not be enduring; and as soon as the supremacy of one area was challenged, the ruling power lost its base. Then division and chaos would ensue until a new power rooted itself in a new area and was able to use it to reestablish unity.[7]

Finally, two historians of modern China discuss the militarists of the late-nineteenth and early-twentieth centuries, respectively. They both stress the importance of central control over finances and armies in maintaining national unity. They note that central loss of this control in the aftermath of the T'ai-p'ing rebellion of the mid-nineteenth century left a power vacuum which regional

3. Whitney, *China*, p. 166.
4. Chesneaux, "Federalist Movement," pp. 100-102, 135.
5. Chi, *Key Economic Areas*, p. 4.
6. *Ibid.*, especially Chapter 1.
7. *Ibid.*, pp. xii-xiii.

elites, through a gradual accumulation of powers, were able to fill.[8] One also calls attention to such "latent factors" as differences in topography and climate which have resulted in varying cultural adaptations; China's size and poor communications; an ethic of particularistic loyalties; and separate historic traditions in the different regions.[9] And the other also attributes the deterioration of central control he is describing to the discrediting of Confucianism as an ideological cement, along with a shift in the political role of its traditional gentry supporters.[10] Both trace regionalism after 1850 to the creation of provincial or regional armies in the 1850s and 1860s, and to the modernization of these armies beginning around 1880. For both see in the ensuing development of regional politico-military administrations the future bases of autonomous power.[11] All of the above writers emphasize the difficulties of sustained political unification in China.

The regrouping of territory to achieve control over power centers at lower levels is an ancient trick of administration in China. The process of adding echelons to the hierarchy of administrative areas, as was done in 1949 in creating the Great Administrative Regions, has recurred time and again in Chinese history. One analyst cites instances in which the number of echelons was increased, generally to cope with emergency situations that incumbent local officials and their administrative areas had been unable to handle. Here he refers to the thirteen *chou* of the Eastern Han, the fifteen *chou* of the Sui, the ten *tao* of the T'ang, and the supraprovincial *tsung-tu-ch'ü* of the Ch'ing.[12] He then notes that power tended to shift from the center to these newly created regions with this amalgamation of lower-level units into higher-order entities. He illustrates this by pointing to the difficulty the Republican government had in attempting to abolish the *tsung-tu-ch'ü* of the Ch'ing. In fact, several of these multiprovince groupings later became the territories of the warlords or militarists of the Republican era whose power seriously limited the functioning of the central government.[13]

8. Michel, "Regionalism," pp. xxxii-xxxv; Wilbur, p. 205.
9. Wilbur, "Military Separatism," pp. 217-218.
10. Michel, "Regionalism," p. xli.
11. Wilbur, "Military Separatism," p. 218; Michael, "Regionalism," p. xxi.
12. Whitney, *China*, pp. 80-81.
13. *Ibid.*, p. 83.

Other administrative devices were used by central governments in China to exert control over component territories. For example, the Liang state (during the Five Dynasties between the T'ang and Sung) tried to cut down the power of the military governors of the T'ang by diminishing the amount of territory under the jurisdiction of each and appointing loyal military commanders for the vacated areas.[14] Alternatively, during the Southern Sung, areas under the control of certain village leaders were enlarged to draw these men out of the arenas where they had established networks of power.[15]

Neither regionalism nor experimentation with administrative forms in attempting to combat regionalism were new phenomena in twentieth-century China. Moreover, the Chinese Communist Party (CCP) had its own history of experience with the use of administrative forms in the control of territory.

The CCP's Experience with Regions before 1949

Base Areas

The CCP's use of administrative forms to control territory dates back to the earliest years of its existence. The particular organizational form its members utilized was the base area, first adopted at the time of the founding of the Red Army. Following the Autumn Harvest uprising in late 1927, P'eng Pai, who for some five years had been working with the peasantry in the Haifeng and Lufeng area near Canton, first established organized political power on a territorial base and set up the first Chinese soviet government. In the same winter, Mao and Chu Teh created the first revolutionary base at Ching-kang-shan on the Hunan-Kiangsi border, combining principles P'eng Pai had used—peasant militia, a soviet government, and a policy of land division and burning land deeds—with a favorable terrain and techniques of warfare.[16] These early bases were to serve as prototypes for the local military-political organizations that later

14. Wang Gungwu, *The Structure of Power in North China during the Five Dynasties* (1963).
15. John W. Lewis, "Memory, Opportunity and Strategy in Peasant Revolutions" (1973).
16. Benjamin Schwartz, *Chinese Communism and the Rise of Mao* (1966), pp. 102-103; Stuart Schram, *Mao Tse-tung* (1966), pp. 78-79, 126.

cropped up during the long years of civil and anti-Japanese war in the border or liberated areas.

As new revolutionary armed forces grew up, each retreated to the countryside and set up its own base. By early 1930 such strategic territorial organizations existed in many areas, covering parts of Kiangsi, Fukien, Hunan, Hupei, Anhwei, Honan, Kwangtung, Kwangsi, and Chekiang. These bases organized the peasantry around issues of democratic government, army and party building, and land redistribution, and they concentrated forces to counter the enemy. It was hoped that the bases could eventually be used to bring about a nationwide revolutionary upsurge.[17]

The second thrust in building bases occurred in the late 1930s just after the outbreak of the war against Japan. These areas were designed to wage guerrilla warfare independently from small, isolated centers. The first to be established was the Shansi-Chahar-Hopei military zone, created in autumn 1937.[18] By 1945, nineteen wartime bases or liberated areas had grown up behind the Japanese lines in isolated areas and mountainous terrain on the borders between several adjacent provinces. The isolation and poor communications that sheltered these units rendered military and administrative coordination difficult.[19] Problems of geography, the instability of guerrilla warfare, and the absence of a central government led to a situation in which relative autonomy reigned in individual base areas in matters of military technique and pace of expansion.[20]

Under these circumstances, the Party played a central role in effecting what unification existed between the scattered bases. The Central Committee, through its three regional departments or branch bureaus—in Northwest, North, and Central China—attempted some minimal coordination.[21] Unavoidable decentral-

---

17. Ho Kan-chih, *A History of the Modern Chinese Revolution* (1959), pp. 207-211.

18. *Ibid.*, pp. 328-334.

19. Boyd Compton, trans., *Mao's China* (1952), p. xix. Whitson states that there were twenty-three military regions at some point during the Anti-Japanese War. William W. Whitson, *The Chinese Communist High Command* (1973), pp. 158-159. And Van Slyke shows that as of 1944 there were sixteen military regions, though he notes that accuracy is difficult since the areas constantly fluctuated in size and location. Lyman Van Slyke, ed., *The Chinese Communist Movement* (1968), pp. xii-xiii and 129-130.

20. Compton, *Mao's China*, p. xxvi.

21. *Ibid.*, p. xxxi.

ization, however, paved the way for local Party initiative and
taught the importance of relying on intensive indoctrination and
training to link up separate areas on an ideological basis.[22]

By the end of March 1949, however, successes in warfare
allowed the once isolated border regions north of the Yangtze to
be merged into new regional groupings. The expansion of conquered territory led to linking up the different regions, and it was
both possible and necessary to establish more solid territorial
blocs, thereby facilitating trade and administration.[23] By September of that year, Shanghai's *Hsin-wen jih-pao* reported the creation
of a scheme that divided China into six regional governments and
an Inner Mongolia Autonomous Region.[24] Within three more
months, on December 16, 1949, the "Organic Law of the New
Regional Government Councils" was promulgated, effecting the
final division of China into six Great Administrative Regions
along with the Inner Mongolia Autonomous Region.[25] These
final regions had evolved directly from the earlier bases, both in
concept and in form.

Doctrines

Over the long years of the Communists' struggle for power, the
experiences of the Party and the People's Liberation Army (PLA)
informed a set of doctrines concerning administrative relationships and structures. The notion of "democratic centralism" was
used in the efforts to standardize the implementation of general
policies. And the attempts to organize territory to fit the crucial
functions of rule at a given point in time produced a theory about
the size and numbers of administrative units.

22. *Ibid.*, p. xxvi.
23. H. R. Lieberman, "On Conditions in North China; Territory Divided into
Six Administrative Regions," *New York Times,* April 4, 1949.
24. "Chinese Reds Plan Six Regional Rules," *New York Times,* September 12,
1949. This scheme did not include Southwest China, which had not yet been
liberated at that time.
25. "Organic Law of the New Regional Government Councils," *Current
Background* [hereafter *CB*], No. 170 (1952), pp. 19-22. The Regions were the
North China Central Control Area, the Northeast People's Government, the
Inner Mongolia Autonomous Region, and the East, Central-South, Northwest,
and Southwest Great Administrative Regions. The governing organs in the
Great Administrative Regions were initially called Military Administrative Committees. In North China, the organ was initially titled the Ministry of North
China Affairs and operated from the start as a ministry of the central govern-
ment.

Map 1. The Six Great Administrative Regions and the Inner Mongolian Autonomous Region, 1949-1954. Note: Although Tibet is included in the Southwest Region according to this map, after it was liberated in May 1951, a separate military administrative committee and a military area headquarters were set up for Tibet.

The principle of "democratic centralism," initially a Leninist concept of decision-making and life within the Party, has ramifications for policy-making and its implementation in governing subordinate areas. The essence of the principle lies in the resolution of the contradiction between democracy, meaning the freedom of opinion that precedes final decision-making, and centralism, meaning the consensus and unity achieved after discussion. In administrative practice, this contradiction is manifested in a dichotomy between the control implicit in a general policy made at the center as against the pluralism which must crop up in attempting to fit this policy to concrete situations in the regions or localities below the center.[26] This principle appears in

26. Franz Schurmann, *Ideology and Organization in Communist China* (1966), pp. 86-87.

Mao's belief in the need to combine national unification with local
initiative in governing regions below the central level.[27]

A piece on the relationship between tasks of governance at a
given point in time and the size and number of administrative
units used to carry out these tasks appeared in the Chinese press
in late 1956. It presented a theoretical account of the reasons
behind various changes made by the Communists in the division
of administrative areas. It contrasted the organizational forms
used during the period of revolutionary war with those adopted
during socialist construction. According to this analysis, wartime
called for a multiplicity of levels to grant flexibility of action to
different areas. It also required a multiplicity of administrative
units on any one level, since under conditions of war, scattered
bases were inaccessible and leadership had to be locally centered.
Large-scale, planned socialist construction, on the contrary, demanded a strengthening of centralized and unified leadership,
and therefore required the use of fewer levels and fewer units on
each level.[28]

These principles—dictating the combination of centralized
control with flexibility for the localities, and calling for administrative measures that mesh with the outstanding work tasks of a
given period—continued to inform Chinese Communist policy
after 1949. These tenets, then, are relevant in analyzing the
nature of the Great Administrative Regions, their creation, and
their abolition.

Regions under the People's Republic of China, 1949-1954

*The National Political Context
and Rationale for Dividing the Country*

In late 1949 when the People's Republic was established, its
new rulers had a vision of effecting centralized control and rapid

27. For example, see "On the Ten Great Relationships," in Jerome Ch'en,
ed., *Mao* (1969), pp. 74-76.
28. Chang Li-men, "Special Features in the Changes of Administrative Areas
in China," *Cheng-ta yen-chiu*, No. 5 (October 2, 1956). Translated in *Excerpts from
Chinese Mainland Magazines*, No. 57 (1956), pp. 1-14. A similar line of analysis is
given in Chou Fang, *Wo kuo kuo-chia chi-kou* [My Country's National Organs]
(1955), p. 81.

modernization in China.[29] However, they were confronted with a nation variegated in economic condition and in degree of military challenge, infested with local loyalties, and undeveloped in the vital sinews of communications and transport.

The load on the center was heavy, and its leaders' goals were great. Key documents of the takeover period reveal five tasks the new regime set for itself.[30] These were: economic recovery and consolidation of economic control, including the control of inflation, communications, taxation, water conservancy, agriculture, industry, and commerce; the centralization of power in the hands of the Party, the first step of which was to expand the area of control to include all of China's territory through use of the army, the police, courts, and propaganda; elimination of the enemy, both within China and abroad; becoming a first-class world military power; and carrying out land reform. On top of these initial aspirations, the Korean War broke out just a year after takeover in October 1950. This put further strain on the already debilitated Chinese economy, and added to the military responsibilities of the army, which was still concentrating on internal pacification at that time.

29. Unification of control and centralization of power have traditionally been goals of Chinese rulers. However, at this point in time, the example of the Soviet Union and its centralized model of administration was also before the eyes of the new leadership and probably played a large part in determining this leadership's designs for regional government. As the following discussion and Chapters Three and Four will show, the regional layer of administration was never meant to have a large degree of independence; rather, its development followed a course of increasing subordination to the center, especially after 1952. This reliance on the Soviet model is alluded to in Schurmann, *Ideology and Organization,* pp. xlii, xliii, and 13; in Richard L. Walker, *China Under Communism* (1955), pp. 22-23, 275; and S. B. Thomas, *Government and Administration in Communist China* (1955), pp. 75-76. Most simply, the Soviet model involves a hierarchical, bureaucratic structuring of the state system. The government of each administrative unit is subject to local control and also is strictly subordinated to the next higher level. Few matters are left exclusively within the jurisdiction even of the republics, the highest level in the local or subcentral governmental hierarchy. See Leonard Schapiro, *The Government and Politics of the Soviet Union* (1967), pp. 132-133; John S. Reshetar, Jr., *The Soviet Polity* (1971), pp. 228, 253, 260; and Robert Conquest, *The Soviet Political System* (1968), pp. 32-34.

30. Walker, *China Under Communism,* pp. 4-6. He based this assessment on Mao's "The People's Democratic Dictatorship," Mao's report to the Third Plenary Session of the Seventh Party Congress of the CCP (June 6, 1950), the "Common Program of the Chinese People's Consultative Conference," and other documents.

Since the work tasks before the new government were so formidable, there was a definite need for reliable and strong governments at the lower levels of the administrative hierarchy to help bear the burden. Also, many of the tasks were to be carried out in the form of mass campaigns—against landlords, counter-revolutionaries, intellectuals, businessmen, traditional marriage customs, and the bureaucracy—which could only be directed by lower-level organs. But, as indicated above, the environment throughout the country was varied, and Communist power was unevenly distributed. Takeover had occurred in different places at different times, so that each broad area of the country was at a different stage of "social reform" by early 1950. Moreover, military control problems varied greatly from region to region.[31]

Also, while the need to depend on the lower levels for assistance was great, the Communists were well aware of the tradition of provincial separatism and autonomy that had marked the warlord years to a greater or lesser degree throughout the period from 1911 to 1949. Accordingly, some have viewed the main objective of the central government in creating regional administrations as being the attainment of closer control over the provinces. In this analysis the regions were meant to be "bulwarks to defend the central government against possible treachery by turncoat provincial warlords and ex-Kuomintang (KMT) generals whose 'deals' with the Communists accounted for the sweeping expansion of Red forces in the winter of 1949-1950."[32]

The Communists' own interpretations take account of some of these factors. Thus, Chou Fang, writing in 1955, explained: "because in the period after liberation the conditions in the various regions were complicated, and the developments in work uneven, political organs were set up at the Great Region level.

31. Thus, though economic restoration was in full swing in the Northeast and land reform was long since completed there, and while agrarian reform was being carried out in the East, Central-South, and Northwest regions, in the Southwest the movement for suppressing bandits, fighting despots, reducing rent, and refunding deposits, which was the precursor to land reform, was just in progress. See *Survey of China Mainland Press* [hereafter *SCMP*], No. 841 (1954), pp. 35-37. See also John Gittings, *The Role of the Chinese Army* (1967), p. 270.

32. For example, see H. A. Steiner, "New Regional Governments in China," *Far Eastern Survey* 19, No. 11 (1950), p. 112. Also *CB*, No. 170 (1952), p. 3; and Norton S. Ginsburg, "China's Administrative Boundaries," *Far Eastern Economic Review* [hereafter *FEER*] 10, No. 4 (1951), p. 107.

They were to facilitate local initiative under the center's united leadership."[33] In early 1953 Chou Fang had already pointed out that "as the degree of work was different in various places, a strong leadership organ capable of representing the central government had to be depended on in the Administrative Regions for timely and properly guiding local governments concretely and thoroughly to implement the unified programs and policies of the central government."[34]

Western observers have suggested several other possible explanations to account for the division. One calls attention to the fact that this system "made the most efficient use of the few capable administrators and bureaucrats and kept them under the eyes of Party stalwarts and military men."[35] In fact, the less than twenty men who completely controlled the political and military situation at the regional level were almost all also members of the Party Central Committee and of the Central People's Government Council.[36] Thus, the abilities of a few key individuals were stretched to take command over the crucial posts at both the national and regional levels across the country.

Military control was also a paramount objective in establishing regions. The final campaigns of the civil war had sketched out certain broad areas associated with the separate field commands, and so each region became more or less the preserve of the Field Army command which took it over.[37] Some see the "military exigencies of the moment" as being the "raison d'être" of these regions.[38]

Still another factor was the unexpectedly rapid liberation of the whole country. This left no time for the elaboration of a new system of administration;[39] and the previously existing border regions provided a ready model that could be grafted on to the areas of occupation resulting from the war. In yet another interpretation, the new regions merely endorsed a de facto state of

33. Chou Fang, *Wo kuo,* p. 81.
34. *SCMP,* No. 494 (1953) , p. 37.
35. Robert W. McColl, "The Development of Supra-Provincial Administrative Regions in Communist China, 1949-1960," *Pacific Viewpoint* 4, No. 1 (1963), p. 54.
36. *CB,* No. 170 (1952), p. 2.
37. *Ibid.,* p. 3. For details here, see Whitson, *High Command,* and Chapters Three and Five below for the takeover of the Southwest.
38. McColl, "Supra-Provincial Regions," p. 56.
39. *China News Analysis* [hereafter *CNA*], No. 43 (1954).

affairs, based on the CCP branch bureaus and the military areas of the PLA left over from wartime.[40]

Finally, one geographer sees in the establishment of the regions an attempt to break up the traditional North-South division of China, and thus break down local regional feelings. He adds one more suggestive explanation: that provinces with an ideological alliance with the center—that is, .those provinces where Communist feeling was relatively strong—were linked up in regions with other provinces that did not have such an alliance.[41] For example, Shantung, long a stronghold of Communism in the North, was put together with provinces in East China traditionally more favorable to the KMT.[42]

Some of these ideas will be considered in more detail at a later point. Here it will suffice to note that all these factors—distrust of the provinces, disparities between different areas, a shortage of cadres, military deployment, an unexpectedly rapid takeover, and a divide-and-rule strategy—were involved to a certain extent in the decision to split up the country for administrative convenience.

Original Conceptions, and Constitutional Rights and Duties of the Regional Organs

The interplay between democracy and centralization discussed earlier is reflected in Mao's thinking on the regions. Thus he is aware of a possible contradiction between local initiative (*yin-ti-chih-i*) and unification. When the Great Regions were instituted in late 1949, he advocated combining these two tendencies:

China is big. . . . We must establish this kind of level of forceful local organ; only then can we manage affairs well. What ought to be unified must be unified . . . [there] absolutely cannot be administration by each of its own affairs without coordination with the others, but we must combine unification and local expediency. Under the people's political power, the historical conditions giving rise to the warlord system have been destroyed. Thus, a suitable division of labor between center and locality will be beneficial.[43]

40. Steiner, "New Regional Governments," p. 114.
41. Ginsburg, "Administrative Boundaries," p. 106.
42. Norton Ginsburg, "China's Changing Political Geography," *Geographic Review* 42, No. 1 (1952), p. 107.
43. *Jen-min jih-pao* [hereafter *JMJP*], December 4, 1949, p. 1.

Mao apparently believed that under the People's Republic of China (PRC) both tendencies could coexist without conflict. However, in his confidence that the localities would not be recalcitrant, it seems that it is unification which is to be the primary factor in this combination. Six-and-one-half years later, in discussing the "Ten Great Relationships" in socialist China, Mao's emphasis is similar:

We must have both uniformity and individuality. For the development of regional enthusiasm, each region must have its individuality congenial to its local conditions, which is at the same time conducive to the interests of the totality and to the strengthening of the unity of the country. . . . What can be made uniform and should be uniform are to be made uniform; what cannot or should not will not forcibly be made uniform.[44]

Again, it appears that the dichotomy may have to be resolved in the direction of unification: whatever can be made uniform is to be made to conform.

The "Common Program of the Chinese People's Consultative Conference," promulgated on September 29, 1949, also explained the division of power between the center and regions in these terms in its Article 16: "The jurisdiction of the Central People's Government and local people's governments shall be defined according to the nature of various matters involved, and shall be *prescribed by decrees of the Central People's Government Council* so as to satisfy the requirements of both national unity and local expediency." (Emphasis added.)[45] Here, despite the emphasis on combining the two principles, it was the central government which decreed just how they were to be combined.

Another facet of the thinking on regions as of 1949 was that, though regions themselves were meant to persist, the organs governing them were not to retain their original form. According to the Common Program, the present regional organs would be temporary bodies, pending the establishing of local people's congresses. Article 14 reads: "In all places where military operations are completely ended, agrarian reform thoroughly carried out and people of all circles have been fully organized, elections based on universal franchise shall be held immediately for the

44. Ch'en, *Mao*, pp. 74-76.
45. Albert P. Blaustein, *Fundamental Legal Documents of Communist China* (1962), p. 41.

purpose of convening local people's congresses."[46] Thus, after preliminary pacification and reforms, local elected congresses would take over the tasks of rule.

The "Organic Law of the New Regional Government Councils," passed by the Government Administrative Council on December 16, 1949, also calls attention to the transitory nature of the initial regional organs, set up principally for military purposes. It states that: "For enforcing military control and establishing revolutionary order at the initial phase of liberation, there shall be established military and administrative committees." It goes on to note that:

In administrative regions where military action has been concluded, agrarian reform thoroughly carried out, and people of all circles fully organized, popular elections shall be held, and regional people's congresses called for the formal election of *regional* people's government councils. After the establishing of regional people's government councils, the Military Administrative Committees shall be wound up.[47] [Emphasis added.]

Here there is an allusion to the specifically military nature of the Military Administrative Committees, which would cease to exist at some point in the future, even though regional government would persist.

A last aspect of the regional councils was noted by the Organic Law. It states that they were to have a dual nature: to be "the highest local administrative authority of the provinces [or municipalities] in the region concerned *and* the Government Administrative Council's representative organ directing the work of the local governments."[48] Thus they were to serve as intermediaries between base and center.

In sum, these were to be temporary organs, exercising local initiative under the rubric of central control, with military functions outstanding. They would be dual in nature, having some powers of their own; however, as agents of the center, their use of these powers was to be subject to central review and supervision.

These were the original conceptions of the regional regimes. What were the rights and duties bestowed on these organs? The

46. *Ibid.*, p. 38.
47. Translated in *CB*, No. 170 (1952). This reference is to p. 19.
48. *Ibid.*

Committee was to have the following seven functions and powers:

1. Transmitting Government Administrative Council decisions and orders to provinces and municipalities under its jurisdiction, and within the scope of its functions and power, issuing decisions and orders and review of their implementation.

2. Drawing up provisional laws and regulations relative to local administration for submission to the Government Administrative Council for ratification or record.

3. Requesting the Government Administrative Council to appoint and dismiss or ratify the appointment and removal of, or asking the Government Administrative Council to request the Central People's Government Council to ratify all the officials of any importance in the Great Region, province, city or *hsien* governments.

4. Appointing and removing or ratifying the appointment and removal of lesser figures in provinces, cities, and *hsien* under its jurisdiction.

5. Within the scope of overall state budgetary estimates or budgets, preparing the administrative region's budgetary estimates or budgets for submission to the central government for approval, and approving budgets and financial statements of the provinces, cities, and *hsien* under its jurisdiction and transmitting these to the central government for ratification.

6. Connecting, unifying, and directing coordination between its various committees, departments, administrations, banks, bureaus, and offices, their internal organizations and work in general.

7. Guiding the working of provincial, municipal, and *hsien* governments under its jurisdiction.[49]

Thus, these organs were to serve as administrators and coordinators of the affairs in their regions. But at the same time they were accountable to the Government Administrative Council for the bulk of their actions.

In relation to the Government Administrative Council their duties were as follows:

1. The Military Administrative Committee must report after disposal of important work and request approval in advance in the case of work with national effect.

2. The Military Administrative Committee must forward all official requests from provinces and municipalities and *hsien* below it.

3. Copies of communications between the Government Administra-

49. *Ibid.*, pp. 19-20.

tive Council and provinces and muncipalities must be sent to the Military Administrative Committee.

4. Ministries and departments under the Government Administrative Council may deal directly with offices under the Military Administrative Committee only on business management and technical points; where the whole region is affected, copies of the documents must be sent to the Military Administrative Committee.[50]

According to these specifications, the overall nature of these organs was determined by their mediating function between the Government Administrative Council and the localities. Thus, legally the Great Regions were to have no privileged position nor any autonomous rights or powers; there was no important distinction between their powers and those of the provincial governments. They were essentially to be conveyor belts between the center and the localities; their acts were subject to annulment or alteration by the Government Administrative Council.

However, the fact that military control was paramount in the initial conception of these governments meant that generally speaking each area was made the territory of one of the PLA's five Field Armies. Thus many of the rulers at this level were revolutionary generals used to independent command.[51] Further, each area had its particular political, economic, and cultural traits. This called for an adaptation of the general policies emanating from Peking. Here the Committees had the function of fitting the orders from the capital to the situations in the localities.[52] Finally, the chaotic nature of the takeover called for improvisation and expediency. This situation unavoidably led to delegation of a greater measure of autonomy to the Field Army staffs than might have been desirable otherwise. All these factors may have meant that the regions were ruled somewhat independently, especially at first.

Looking back on the period of the regions, Teng Hsiao-p'ing noted in 1956 that "in the first few years after the founding of the PRC, the Central Committee gave local organs extensive powers to deal with problems independently."[53] And in late 1952 it was

50. *Ibid.*
51. *CNA,* No. 43 (1954), p. 6.
52. *Ibid.*
53. Teng Hsiao-p'ing, "Report on the Revision of the Constitution of the Chinese Communist Party," in *Eighth National Congress of the Chinese Communist Party* (1956), 1:189.

conceded that "in land reform and other movements, under the unified policy of the Central People's Government, certain regulations of a local nature were drawn up at the regional level out of necessity."[54] Thus, local initiative apparently had a significant role to play, at least in the beginning.

The activities of the regions, then, were circumscribed legally but expanded somewhat in practice. It is possible, consequently, to view the interactions between the central government and the regions from 1949 to 1954 as occurring within a context of experimentation. This is related to a central ambiguity that existed in the thinking on the regions suggested above. That is, the regions were expected to remain as a level in the governmental hierarchy, but the eventual functions of their organs were left unclear. The history of their existence seems to indicate central-level uncertainty as to how much and what kinds of powers these regional organs needed to possess in order to make them a viable level of administration. For the purposes of this discussion, the two levels of government—the center and the region—will be considered separate and distinct levels, ignoring for the time being that in fact many of the same individuals operated on both levels, as mentioned above.

Center-Region Interaction in a Context of Experimentation, 1949-1954

This discussion is limited by the fact that few interchanges between the central government and the regional Committees have been published. In fact, information has been located on only five occasions when powers were either added to or subtracted from the regions. The first two instances, in 1950 and 1951 respectively, concerned taxation powers; and the third, in 1951, pertained to powers of appointment. On the fourth occasion, in 1952, the overall powers of the regions were reduced; and on the fifth, in 1954, the regions were altogether abolished.

The first interchange occurred on March 3, 1950, when the Government Administrative Council passed a decision on the unification of national financial and economic work.[55] This provided for centralized management of national finances, and had

54. *SCMP*, No. 460 (1952), pp. 29-30.
55. *Hsin-Hua yüeh-pao* [hereafter *HHYP*], No. 6 (1950), pp. 1393-1395 and 1329-1330.

four principal goals: to centralize control over national revenue and expenditure; to plan on a nationwide basis the use of materials and resources; to unify the control over currency; and, most important, to unify the tax collection system.

The act demanded that all grain, taxes, and storage goods, and a part of the profit of public-operated enterprises and of the money set aside to replace depreciated machinery (*che-chiu chin*) should go to the nation. Thus it deprived the Great Regions of much of their material wealth. Moreover, the national financial organs had to approve all items of expenditure under the state budget. Local needs were admittedly secondary; national priorities were to come first.

Just over a year later, on March 29, 1951, however, the Government Administrative Council promulgated a new decision on financial management.[56] This decision changed the direction of economic work, in calling for "unified leadership with different levels dividing up the responsibilities" (*t'ung-i ling-tao, fen-chi fu-tsu*). The principle here was that, under the central government's leadership, actions could be based on local expediency and a division of labor would be practiced. This involved the sharing of control between the center, the regional governments, and the provinces.

According to this decision, certain taxes became central income; certain other taxes were allotted to the center and to the locality on a proportional basis; and certain other income sources belonged to the region or the province. Administrative expenses were divided up, so that the center and locality could disburse them separately.

The rationale behind the change is hinted at in references to "certain hardships in the localities." Also, "the country is big, the people many, the situation complicated; concentrating everything in the center must make the central organs' administrative work too heavy." Further, a discussion in the press which followed the decision notes that "due to a development of local initiative, the center's leadership will be more consolidated." Here it appears that in the crucial area of financial affairs, the regional organs were given powers beyond the original intentions of those who had first fashioned these organs. Presumably this

56. *HHYP*, No. 18 (1951), p. 1358.

was done either because of the strength of regional pressure or because of certain incapacities at the center.

Then, on November 5, 1951, in a third decision on the regions, the Central People's Government Council passed a new "Provisional Regulation on Appointment and Dismissal." This repeated the Government Administrative Council's "Ordinance on Appointments and Dismissals" of November 1949, but changed one key point: "provisionally," it read, "the prefects, subprefects, and council members of the *hsien* are to be named by the Great Region governments."[57] Thus, in another critical area of local government, the Military Administrative Committees had won powers not initially assigned to them; it may be concluded both that their political power had grown over two years of local rule, and that they emerged from this new decision either with greater powers than before or with legal recognition of a de facto situation.

The next historical data published in regard to the powers of the Military Administrative Committees came in late 1952, when the Military Administrative Committees' title was changed to Administrative Committee, and the original dual nature of the organs was removed.[58] Thus, where the Military Administrative Committees had been both local power organs and central agents, they were now merely central agents. Further, the various departments (*pu*) under the regional authorities were reorganized as bureaus (*chü*) or offices (*ch'u*), and some of these were to be taken over by the concerned ministries of the Central People's Government. Though it was never mentioned which ministries would be so transferred, it can be assumed that these were chiefly economic and financial ones, since the decision was justified in terms of the need "to meet the new tasks of nationwide large-scale and planned economic construction."[59]

The decision was publicly stated to be based on the belief that large-scale economic construction called for strengthening central unification and concentrating leadership, to expedite national planning. Cutting down the regions' powers was seen as

57. *JMJP*, November 8, 1951.
58. "Decision on Change in the Structure and Tasks of the People's Governments of the Administrative Regions," translated in *CB*, No. 245 (1953), pp. 9-11. See also *SCMP*, No. 460 (1952), pp. 29-30; and *FEER* 14, No. 2 (1953), pp. 41-44.
59. *CNA*, No. 43 (1954), p. 6.

"facilitating a timely understanding of various aspects of the situation, and insuring that the proper coordination would be established between various economic links." It was further stated that the situation of rather great division of power which had existed for the past three years could not meet the circumstances of 1953.[60]

Governmental organizational consolidation was viewed as involving simplification of the political power hierarchy. This involved an increase in the leadership of the center, the province, and the municipality, apparently at the expense of the region. Concurrently with the "Decision on Change in the Structure and the Tasks of the People's Governments of the Administrative Regions," two resolutions were passed, one regulating the provinces' and districts' (ch'ü) organs, and one increasing the number of central organs. The creation of the State Planning Commission at this time was the hallmark of the call for increased centralization and unification in planning.

That this move increased the centralized nature of the state is evident from several viewpoints. By bringing all six regional authorities to the same status as the North China Administrative Committee (the name given to the Ministry of North China Affairs in December 1951),[61] all regions could be administered uniformly.[62] Moreover, the role of the military was diminished in the new Administrative Committees.[63] Along with this development went a steady transfer of high-ranking military men from the regions to General Headquarters in Peking.[64] Thus, if a degree of regional autonomy had been associated with the need to cope with varying military environments in the different regions, events dating from the 1952 decision worked to erode this autonomy.

Chou Fang writes in 1955 that "in 1953, as our country entered

60. HHYP, No. 38 (1952), pp. 9-10.
61. S. B. Thomas, "Structure and Constitutional Basis of the Chinese People's Republic," Annals of the American Academy of Social and Political Science, No. 277 (1951), pp. 46-55. See also footnote 25 above.
62. FEER 14, No. 2 (1953), p. 44; and McColl, "Supra-Provincial Regions," p. 57.
63. McColl, "Supra-Provincial Regions," p. 57; and Gittings, Chinese Army, p. 271; and Thomas, Government and Administration (1955), p. 85.
64. Gittings, Chinese Army, p. 272.

the period of national economic planned construction,[65] we needed progressively to strengthen the center's unity and concentrate leadership; therefore we adopted the direction of gradually eliminating the Great Regions."[66] Although he was speaking from hindsight, there is an important piece of evidence that shows that the central government was in fact in the process of eliminating the regions as early as January 1953. For at that time a resolution was passed at a meeting of the Central People's Government Council calling for elections for local people's congresses, and no mention was made of a regional congress or of a regional level of administration. Rather, congresses were to be elected for only the *hsiang*, *hsien*, province, and municipal levels.[67]

The fifth and final measure concerning the regions—the one which mandated their abolition—was preceded by three months by an article in *Hsin-Hua yüeh-pao* decrying the blind development of organs, with their internal levels "piled up layer on layer" and their vague division of labor. The article pointed out that simplifying organizational structures, decreasing personnel, and merging duplicating structures would strengthen these organs, lessen problems in the bureaucracy, and help the country industrialize.[68] Here is the preparation and the official justification for the imminent change in national administrative structure.

When the "Decision on the Abolition of Regional First-Grade Administrative Machinery and Changes in Provincial and Municipal Structures" was finally promulgated on June 19, 1954, the motives given were quite similar to those offered in November 1952.[69] Thus, the country's embarking on the stage of planned economic construction was cited as the primary factor. This was said to demand further "strengthening of the concentrated and unified leadership of the central government." Abolition of the regional machinery was done to enable the central government:

65. In late 1952, the beginning of the First Five-Year Plan was heralded with the announced introduction of large-scale industrialization. See, for example, *HHYP*, No. 36 (1952), pp. 7-10.

66. Chou Fang, *Wo kuo*, p. 81.

67. Peking, *New China News Agency*, January 14, 1953, quoted in Thomas, *Government and Administration* (1955), p. 131.

68. *HHYP*, No. 53 (1954), pp. 21-22.

69. Translated in *SCMP*, No. 832 (1954), pp. 8-9. See also *FEER* 17, No. 4 (1954), pp. 101-102, and *CNA*, No. 43 (1954).

directly to assume leadership of the provinces and municipalities, for a more concrete understanding of conditions in the lower ranks; to effect a reduction in the different levels of the administrative structure, an increase in work efficiency and the overcoming of bureaucratism; to economize the employment of cadres in order to increase their supply to the factories, mines, and other enterprises; and to strengthen the leadership of the provinces and municipalities.[70]

Thus, the center, provinces, and muncipalities were to be relied upon more heavily than before, and linkages between them built up. Also, administrative cadres were needed in economic construction and could no longer be spared for office work. And, in reference to the regional organs, it was claimed:

These machineries have produced important effects and victoriously fulfilled their missions, in the thorough implementation of central government policies, the enforcement of measures for the people's democratic political machinery construction, the promotion of various social reform movements, the restoration of the national economy, and various tasks in economic construction, cultural construction, and construction in other phases.[71]

Apparently, the leaders in Peking felt that the regional regimes had already accomplished what was expected of them, and were now standing in the way of a strengthened center's direction of the whole country. The regime's completion of one stage of national growth and its achievement of an important degree of central control appears in other events of the same period.

Just four days before the decision was proclaimed, the Draft Constitution of the PRC was also made public. National elections, both for local congresses and for the first National People's Congress, were completed in early 1954 and local congresses held. The election campaign and the process of registering voters had been utilized to carry out the first nationwide census under the new regime. And on September 15, 1954, the National People's Congress was convened, which adopted the new constitution.[72]

Later that year, a new Ministry of Defense was created directly

70. *Ibid.*
71. *Ibid.*
72. Thomas, *Government and Administration* (1955), pp. 136-140.

under the cabinet. This brought the military under the direct supervision of the civil administration. This downgrading of the military and concern with centralized civilian control may also have been related to the abolition of regional rule, which had been associated with instituting military order.[73]

In sum, the abolition of the regions represented a certain degree of concentration of power at the center, and paved the way for a further consolidation. The pace of events—in local reform and rehabilitation, and in increasing central command over this process—evolved through fits and starts, and if national unification was the intended goal from the start, the steps along the way were the result of a process of experimentation.

The Kao-Jao Conspiracy

Before concluding this discussion we should examine one last controversial point. The abolition of the regions came close on the heels of the Fourth Plenum of the Seventh Central Committee of the Party, held in February 1954. At this meeting, Kao Kang and Jao Shu-shih, Chairmen of the Northeast and East Administrative Committees, respectively, were castigated, paving the way for their eventual purge from the Party in March 1955.[74] Some have concluded that the regions were suddenly dismantled because the central leaders feared further autonomy in other regions of the sort for which these men were removed[75]— "treating their own regions and departments as individual capital and independent kingdoms."[76] However, it is important to be aware that in many ways Kao and Jao, especially Kao, represented quite special cases among the leaders in the regions.

First, among the leaders of the six regional areas, only Kao Kang held the top Party position, two top military positions (Military Region Commander and Political Commissar), and top government post in his region. He was also the only regional leader to become a Vice-Chairman of the Central People's Government Council. Also, the distinctive character of the Northeast is relevant: most of the strategic state-owned enterprises

73. A. Doak Barnett, *Communist China* (1965), p. 309.
74. *HHYP*, No. 53 (1954), pp. 9-11.
75. For example, Whitney, *China*, p. 84; McColl, *"Supra Provincial Regions,"* p. 58; *FEER* 17, No. 4 (1954), p. 101; Barnett, *Early Years*, p. 308.
76. *HHYP*, No. 53 (1954), p. 11.

were located in Manchuria. Here too were based the railway and naval facilities under joint administration with the Russians; and here was the logistical base and staging area for the Korean War.[77] For these reasons, generalizations probably should not be abstracted from Kao's case.

Moreover, the core of the charges against the two focused on "unprincipled struggle" to seize Party and state leadership power. Kao in particular was said to have laid claim to leadership of "the Party of the revolutionary bases and the army."[78] Also, it is likely that policy disputes centering on alternative strategies of economic development were involved. For Kao and Jao ruled areas where economic development and industrialization had proceeded furthest. In some interpretations, Kao favored giving high priority to his area, the Northeast, and to the increased industrialization which was the strong point in this area.[79] Those who follow this line of argument claim that Mao, opposed to Kao, preferred a more balanced developmental strategy, giving equal or greater weight to other regions and favoring a greater emphasis on agricultural cooperativization as the road to development. These issues also pertain only to the two purged officials, and not to all regional Chairmen.

Finally, an indication that Kao and Jao alone were the targets in dismantling regions (if regions were indeed abolished to demote individuals) is their "promotion" in November 1952. At that time, Kao was appointed as head of the State Planning Commission, the body charged with direction of the First Five Year Plan. Jao was made a member of the Commission and was also named to head the important Organization Department of the Party Central Committee. These new appointments required that the two men take up residence in Peking, leaving their local power bases behind. It has been suggested that the two may have been brought to the capital as a preliminary move in curtailing their

77. Donald W. Klein and Anne B. Clark, *Biographic Dictionary of Chinese Communism, 1921-1965* (1971), pp. 431-436.

78. For example, see Frederick Teiwes, "A Review Article," *China Quarterly*, No. 41 (1970), pp. 122-135. See also Philip Bridgham, "Factionalism in the Central Committee," in John W. Lewis, ed., *Party Leadership and Revolutionary Power in China* (1970), p. 203-235; Edward E. Rice, *Mao's Way* (1972), pp. 129-132.

79. As, Gittings, *Chinese Army*, pp. 274-279; Schurmann, *Ideology and Organization*, pp. 146, 268-271, and 332-334; and Richard C. Thornton, "The Structure of Communist Politics," *World Politics* 24, No. 4 (1972), pp. 505-509.

regionally based power.[80] And in fact, charges against the two did surface as early as the summer of 1953. Teng Hsiao-p'ing relates that warnings were first given to Kao and Jao at a National Convention on Finance and Economic Work held at that time.[81]

In short, there is much that set Kao and Jao apart from their colleagues in the regions, and no clue that autonomy in all the regions had reached or threatened to reach dangerous proportions. Chapters Three and Four will trace in more specific detail evidence for the gradual nature of the abolition of regional government, in contradistinction to the notion that regions were suddenly removed in connection with discovery of a Kao-Jao conspiracy. They will also show that, at least in the Southwest, the power of the regional-level administration was diminishing and not increasing with time.

The abolition of the regions in 1954 can be interpreted in the same terms used above to account for their creation. Ideologically, the uniformity portion of the "local initiative-uniformity" contradiction, or the centralism aspect of "democratic centralism" became increasingly primary after 1952. The large-scale, planned construction then under way called for strengthening centralization and concentrating leadership. It was pointed out above that such an undertaking has been seen by the Communists, to require fewer levels of administration.[82]

Further, the original conceptions of the regions included the view that strong, militarily oriented organs were to be temporary. Apparently by 1952 and certainly by 1954 it was felt that the amount of power required by a viable regional layer of administration was inconsistent with the overall goals of the regime at that time.

And, in terms of the various rationales for establishing regions and dividing the country, it could be said that the regions had served their purposes and could be discontinued. Thus, local reforms having been carried out, the center was now ready to handle the load which it was not prepared to bear in the war-torn environment of 1949. Significant similar experiences, providing a

80. John W. Lewis, "Revolutionary Struggle and the Second Generation in Communist China," *China Quarterly*, No. 21 (1965), p. 130 (note).
81. Teng Hsiao-p'ing, "Report," p. 204.
82. Chang, "Special Features"; Chou, *Wo kuo*.

common political framework, were now shared by all the regions as the population in each had been pushed through the same mass movements. More personnel had been trained to manage the local levels of government. And the advent of peacetime meant that the military exigencies important in setting up regions were no longer relevant.

Finally, this chapter began with a discussion of the interplay between regionalistic forces generally focused at the provincial level on the one hand, and the administrative measures utilized by central governments throughout history to control these forces, on the other. Seen from a certain perspective, the events in the People's Republic from 1949 to 1954 also fall into this framework.

Thus, the Communist wartime bases, combining political and military functions and operating in a more or less decentralized fashion, formed the prototype and model for the regional governments of the early 1950s. In 1949 the country was divided into regions in order to deal with the same sorts of local disparities and military exigencies that informed the creation of the border area bases.

At the time of takeover, however, a central government bent on concentrating national power at the highest level hoped to utilize these areas to unify the country. This it tried to do by placing a small group of key Communist officials in both central and regional posts, by making ideological pronouncements on the need to combine unity with local initiative, and by defining the rights and duties of the regions within an overall context of central review and supervision.

And the ultimate fate of the regions, though not programed from the start, was in the end consistent with the history of central structuring to control subordinate levels. For whether or not all the regions and their officials had misbehaved as Kao Kang and Jao Shu-shih were charged with doing, their very existence stood as an obstacle to centralized direction and coordination of the national state and the national economy. The chapters that follow will explicate the history, functions, and powers of the Southwest regional administration and show its contribution to the centralization achieved by 1954. First, however, Chapter Two will set the stage by showing the nature of the Southwest society with which this administration would have to deal.

CHAPTER II

Regionalism in Southwest China
under Republican Rule

In the twilight of the Republic, the four provinces that were soon to compose the Southwest Great Administrative Region had a great deal in common. In Szechwan, Sikang, Yunnan, or Kweichow a traveler might have encountered bright poppy fields, human beasts of burden, and minority nationality groups in tribal garb. And each of these sights symbolized a significant phenomenon characteristic of Southwest society.

For example, opium cultivation was dominated by warlords and secret societies who lived off its profits and who ran the politics of the area. The region's treacherous topography— unnavigable rivers and continual precipitous cliffs—meant that it was necessary to rely on human transport. Finally, these peaks were the homelands for a plethora of minority groups who had been pushed out of the valleys over the centuries by immigrating Han.

Despite these resemblances among the Southwest provinces, the area as a whole did not constitute an integrated unit. There was no one center on which all loyalties and activities were focused. In fact, the regionalism that did exist there—the distinctiveness, consciousness, and agitation, backed up by local control of local economic and military resources and decisional autonomy— tended to operate in subprovincial localities. This chapter will describe the types of regionalism and local-level integration that were present in this area, show at what level these phenomena existed, and explain how they operated.

Basically, the first proposition in this chapter is that Integration I—referring to the macro-level situation in which the part, in this case the Southwest as a whole, is linked with the nation—did not exist in the Southwest prior to 1949. Second, neither was Integration II present. That is, on a more micro level, there was little or no unification within this part, no integration of the localities at the level of the Southwest area as a whole. The overall explanation for this situation lay in the fact that compartmentalization into small localities characterized all aspects of life in the Southwest before 1949. As a consequence, no genuine integration existed there at the supraprovincial level.

This chapter will describe that compartmentalization, and will indicate the absence of these two types of integration by examining five aspects of the Southwest situation prior to the Communist takeover. First, it will show how the geography of the area influenced its development before 1949. Next, it will sketch out the historical developments here during the Republican era, particularly for the 1930s and 1940s, emphasizing those dimensions of history that bear a relation to Integration I. This will be an attempt to determine to what extent the area as a whole was related to the central government and, by implication, to the rest of the country.

Then, the shape of local life within the region will be investigated in terms of economics, culture, and politics. This section will be concerned with discovering what the nature of regionalism was *within* the Southwest, and at what level homogenous regions could be said to exist here. It will be geared at testing whether or not Integration II was present at the supraprovincial level of the greater Southwest.

Geography

A central fact about the geography of the Southwest provinces before 1949 was their isolation from the rest of the Mainland—a seclusion imposed by mountain ranges that ringed the region and rivers often too swift to navigate. This isolation set the conditions for noninterference by outsiders in the 1920s and early 1930s in this area; but it also caused Chiang Kai-shek and his government to eye it with interest when the coastal and central provinces were under attack.

Geography also shaped intraprovincial politics and trade within the area and with other parts of China. Finally, it conditioned the cultural nature of the Southwest, a homeland for a myriad of minorities. For the Southwest, as a land of rugged mountains and hills with intermontane basins,[1] is characterized more than is the rest of China by segregated concentrations of settlement. This has made local autonomy at the lowest levels of society both more common and more easily maintained than elsewhere.[2]

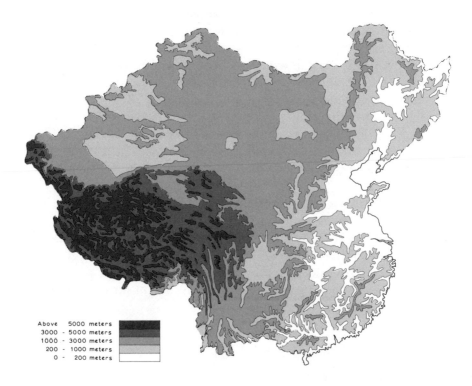

Above   5000 meters
3000 - 5000 meters
1000 - 3000 meters
200 - 1000 meters
0 -   200 meters

Map 2. Topographic map of China.

1. Norton S. Ginsburg, "China's Changing Political Geography," *Geographical Review* 42, No. 1 (1952), p. 108.
   2. *Ibid.*, p. 109.

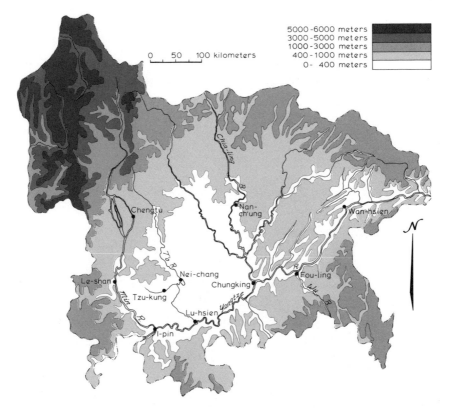

Map 3. Topographic map of Szechwan Province. Note: These are the borders as of 1949-1954.

The topography of the region can be divided into three main sections. The first is the Tsinghai-Tibet Plateau, which extends into west Szechwan and northwest Yunnan. This district is dotted with many mountain peaks and ridges interspersed with deep valleys. The second section includes all of the Yunnan-Kweichow Plateau. This portion is elevated and rugged. The land here is a spur of the great Tibetan Plateau which reaches into Kweichow and Yunnan and is cut by deep valleys and crossed by towering mountains. Scattered throughout are high plains, small in area and separated by mountains.[3] In Kweichow, land even approximately level amounts to only 4 or 5 percent of the total land; and in Yunnan, only 4 percent of the land was considered cultivable in 1946.[4] The basins here, surrounded by mountains, provide the main farming land for the plateau.

3. George B. Cressey, *China's Geographic Foundations* (1934), pp. 369 ff.
4. G. B. Cressey, *Land of the Five Hundred Million* (1955), pp. 225, 228.

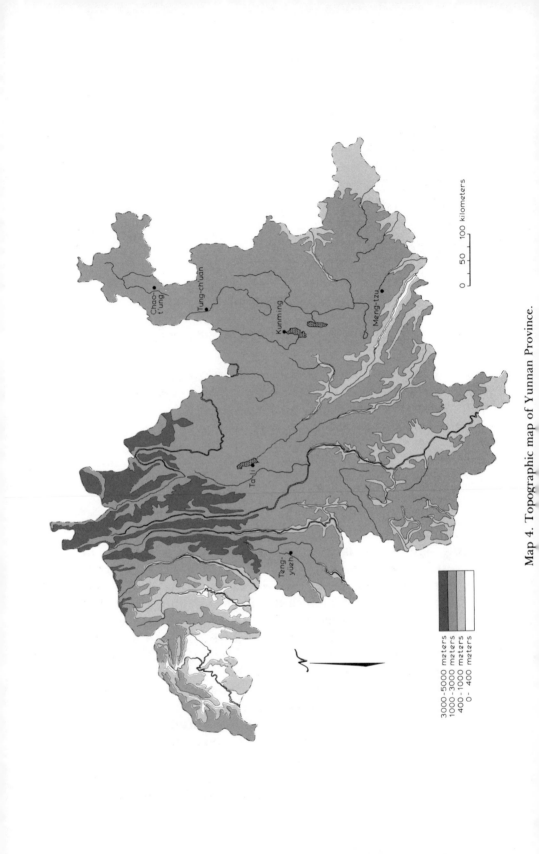

Map 4. Topographic map of Yunnan Province.

Third, to the east of the Tsinghai-Tibetan Plateau and north of the Yunnan-Kweichow Plateau is the Szechwan or Red Basin, which contains the Chengtu Plain. Encircled by mountains, the largely hilly ground here is well served by irrigating waters and consitutes the rich farming territory for which Szechwan is famous.[5] With the exception of the Chengtu Plain, the main subregion of the Szechwan Basin, the entire Southwest is mountainous or hilly.[6] The plain itself is surrounded on all sides by mountains which prohibit easy access. The difficulty of crossing these hills makes the area dependent on the Yangtze and its streams for contact with the outside.

The four rivers that give Szechwan its name, all tributaries of the Yangtze, are these: the Min, which joins the Yangtze at I-pin; the T'o, which enters at Lu-hsien; the Chia-ling, which meets at Chungking; and the Wu, which feeds in from the south at Fouling.[7] Each of these, as well as the short southern tributaries of the Yangtze, are "navigable after a fashion" as far as the limits of the Basin, though river transport here in pre-1949 times required manually forcing small boats up the rapids.[8] Even for powerful river steamers, the gorges were formidable.[9] Almost none of the rivers of Kweichow and Yunnan was navigable in that era, because their steep-sided canyons and frequent rapids formed serious barriers to travel.[10]

These obstacles to transport induced a geographer in the 1930s to say of Szechwan that the province "has probably been more hampered by inadequate transportation than by any other single factor."[11] Before the improvements made by the Nationalists during World War II, conveyance of goods throughout these provinces was slow and inefficient, largely relying on manpower—to move junks over the rapids, to push carts along the narrow stone trails that served as roads, and to carry burdens. Even pack animals and carts were few and far between.[12]

5. "Economic Geography of Southwest China," U.S. *Joint Publications Research Service* [hereafter *JPRS*], No. 15069 (1962), p. 16.
6. Cressey, *China's Geographic Foundations*, pp. 310 ff.
7. Cressey, *Land*, p. 180.
8. Cressey, *China's Geographic Foundations*, p. 312. Alexander Hosie, *Three Years in Western China* (1890), pp. 204-205.
9. Cressey, *Land*, p. 182.
10. Cressey, *China's Geographic Foundations*, pp. 370, 379.
11. *Ibid.*, p. 320.
12. *Ibid.*, pp. 320-321, 378.

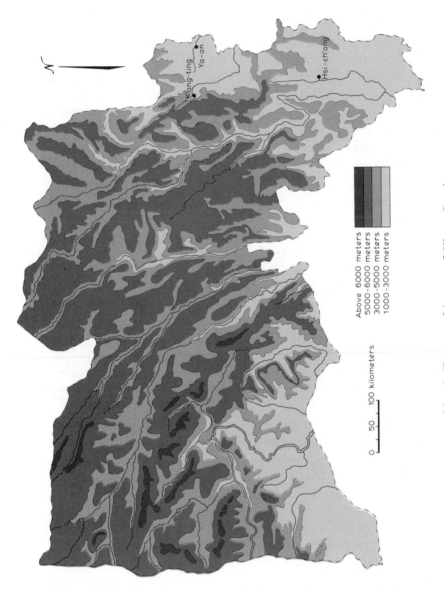

Map 5. Topographic map of Sikang Province.

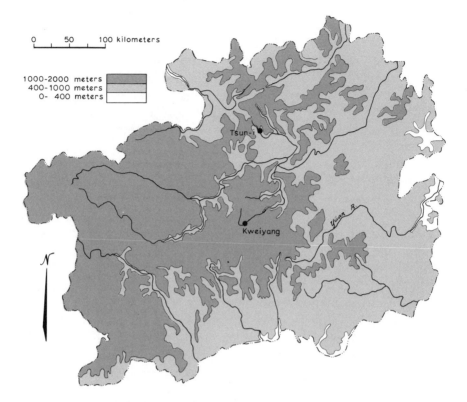

Map 6. Topographic map of Kweichow Province.

In the early 1940s, wartime needs demanded that the central government improve roads and river channels, build airports, and begin work on railways to ensure its control here.[13] According to Communist sources, the mileage of highways nearly doubled in Szechwan during this period, with roads going to Hunan, Yunnan, and Hupeh.[14] In Kweichow, several highways were built during the war, leading to Hunan, Kwangsi, Szechwan, and Yunnan, and some local roads were also constructed. Although these efforts vastly improved the situation there, no railways were attempted.[15]

In Yunnan, up until the war, only the French-financed Tien-Yüeh Railroad reaching into Vietnam served for modern trans-

13. Cressey, *Land,* p. 183; *JPRS* 15069 (1962), p. 63.
14. *JPRS* 15069 (1962), p. 63.
15. *JPRS* 15069 (1962), pp. 337-338.

port, though trails radiated out of Kunming north to the Yangtze through Tung-ch'uan and Chao-t'ung; west to Burma through Ta-li and Teng-Yüeh; north from Ta-li toward Sikang; and south and east, through Meng-tzu, to Indochina and Kwangtung, respectively.[16] Yunnan, like its neighbors, experienced a temporary prosperity during the war, when many roads were built within the province and lines of transport were extended to Szechwan and Kweichow and into Burma. These facilities, however, were neglected after 1945.[17]

Finally, in Sikang, marked by precipitous peaks and swift rivers broken by rapids,[18] transportation also was quite primitive and slow. An observer in the late 1930s stated that the only road construction then completed in the province was a part of the road bed of the Szechwan-Sikang Highway, and that workers were just then being conscripted for the Szechwan-Yunnan West Road.[19] During the war, a road was built from Ya-an to Chengtu, mainly in Szechwan; and several other roads were constructed mostly within Sikang itself—one from Ya-an to K'ang-ting, one into Tsinghai, one from Hsi-ch'ang to Chia-ting (in Szechwan), one from Ya-an to Yun-ching, and one from Hsi-ch'ang to Yunnan. But road maintenance was neglected before 1949 and only two sections of road were occasionally passable for small motor vehicles.[20]

These elements of Southwest geography and the obstructions to transportation which were part and parcel of this geography prior to 1949 produced a situation whereby the Southwest was relatively secluded from the other areas of China. Further, the dissected relief that marked the area obviated internal integration even within provinces and made total control of one province a mammoth undertaking. The next section will show the political correlates of this seclusion and internal dissection.

16. Cressey, *China's Geographic Foundations*, pp. 378-379.

17. *JPRS* 15069 (1962), pp. 502-503.

18. Li I-jen, ed., *Hsi-k'ang tsung-lan* [A General Survey of Sikang] (1947), p. 91.

19. *Ibid.*, p. 269.

20. "An Observer in Sikang," *Office of Naval Intelligence Review* [hereafter *ONI Review*] 4, No. 2 (February 1949), p. 34. The two open lengths of road were sections of the Ya-an–K'ang-ting road and of the Hsi-ch'ang–Chia-ting road, respectively.

*Integration I: Interactions between the Southwest Provinces
and the Central Government, 1911-1949*

Throughout the first half of the twentieth century, each of the provinces in the Southwest was more or less autonomous. In general, there was relatively little cooperation between the provinces of the area. And, as time went on, the leaders in each province strove jealously to safeguard provincial independence from central government encroachments.

Even in late dynastic times these provinces were not linked as a unit administratively known as the Southwest. They were rather joined together in twos: under the Ch'ing dynasty Yunnan and Kweichow, as one *tsung-tu-ch'ü*, shared a viceroy;[21] and, as of 1911, Sikang existed as a special border region (*ch'uan-pien t'e-pieh ch'ü-ü*) on the west of Szechwan. Szechwan itself was a *tsung-tu-ch'ü*. The first step which led to the separate formation of Sikang was the Kuang Hsü emperor's appointment of Chao Er-feng, a high-ranking officer, to govern this border area in 1905.[22] When Sikang became a province in 1939, it was carved out from Szechwan and Tibet.

Despite their separateness, throughout the twentieth century the historical experiences of the provinces in this part of China ran parallel or coincided at several key points in time. In each of the three provinces existing in 1911 (exempting Sikang) the Republican revolution had an active local component. In each case the uprising was followed by the reconstruction of a new provincial government within the traditional framework and the reassertion of traditional social power. And in both Kweichow and Szechwan the Ko Lao Hui, the secret society that flourished at local levels in the Southwest, was instrumental in tying together various cells of revolution throughout the province.[23]

21. In the sixteenth century, *tsung-tu*, alternatively translated as governors-general or viceroys, were appointed to rule over the newly created *tsung-tu-ch'ü*. These officials had supreme control over civil affairs and military forces within the territory under their jurisdiction. In 1911 there were nine governors-general. See H. S. Brunnert and V. C. Hagelstrom, *Present Day Political Organization of China* (n.d.).
22. *ONI Review*, 4, No. 2 (1949), p. 28, and Li I-jen, *Hsi-k'ang*, p. 120.
23. Charles H. Hedtke, "The Genesis of Revolution in Szechuan" (1965); William R. Johnson, "Revolution and Reconstruction in Kweichow and Yunnan" (1965). See also Agnes Smedley, *The Great Road* (1956), p. 91.

Thereafter, a short period of cooperation occurred between the Southwest provinces.[24] When the Yunnan Army rose in late 1915 under Brigadier General Ts'ai O and proclaimed itself the "Protection Army" (Hu Kuo Chün) in revolt against Yüan Shih-k'ai's regime, eight regiments of this army marched from Yunnan into Szechwan to wipe out Yüan's forces there. At the same time the Yunnan Army's second division moved into Kweichow in an attack on Yüan's troops in that province. The assault was joined by revolutionaries from Szechwan. Meanwhile, the Protection Army brought in reinforcements from Yunnan and Kweichow until a total of twenty-six regiments were pitted against Yüan's armies. Thus the Protection Army became the chief arm in the West and Southwest of a national movement to protect the 1912 constitution and to unseat Yüan Shih-k'ai. However, this short-lived interprovincial collaboration did not last beyond the rebellion. Following the defeat of Yüan in this area, civil war ensued between the Yunnan troops in Szechwan trying to control that province and the Szechwan militarists under Generals Hsiung K'o-wu and Liu Ts'un-hou. This war lasted until the Yunnanese were thrown out of Szechwan in mid-1920.[25]

Soon thereafter, the militarists in the various provinces turned their attention to their own provincial affairs.[26] In Yunnan and

24. For relations between the three provinces over the period 1911-1915, see Donald Sinclair Sutton, "The Rise and Decline of the Yunnan Army, 1909-1925" (1970), Chapters 6 and 7. In 1912 Yunnan governor Ts'ai O carried out relief campaigns into Kweichow and Szechwan as a contribution to the revolutionary uprising at Wu-ch'ang. In 1912 Ts'ai O was also made military and civilian chief of Kweichow under pressure from Kweichow's civilian leaders.

25. Smedley, *The Great Road*; Li P'ei-t'ien, "Lung Yün Lu Han en-ch'ou chi" [The Affection and Enmity Between Lung Yün and Lu Han], *Hsin-wen t'ien-ti* [News World] (Hong Kong), Nos. 777-785 (1963), Parts 12 and 13. Over this period (1916-1920) T'ang Chi-yao, the governor of Yunnan, had plans to rule over a confederation of the three provinces of Kweichow, Szechwan, and Yunnan, where he was the most prominent militarist. A modus vivendi existed between leaders of the three provinces up until 1920, based on the fact that most Southwest militarists agreed that they should stand together against the North. However, General Hsiung K'o-wu of Szechwan never agreed to an "alliance" of the three provinces proposed by T'ang, in which Szechwan and Kweichow would have been Yunnan's junior partners. See Sutton, *"Rise and Decline,"* pp. 216-217, 227, 231.

26. By 1920 Yunnan's influence outside its borders was sharply reduced. In Szechwan, General Liu Hsiang replaced Hsiung K'o-wu and Liu Ts'un-hou in 1921 and capitalized on the rising provincialist feeling there. See Sutton, *"Rise and Decline,"* pp. 228, 233-234, 239.

Szechwan the decade succeeding the battles of the Hu Kuo Chün was marked by infighting among provincial warlords.[27] After a coup in Yunnan by four provincial garrison commanders in 1927,[28] Lung Yün acceded to the provincial governorship, a position he held until 1945.[29] In Szechwan during the 1920s, a pattern of decentralized local military control established during the 1911 revolution was consolidated with the creation of the garrison area (fang-ch'ü) system.[30] Under this arrangement, the province was split into civil-military areas, each controlled by one warlord and his loosely organized network of subordinates.[31] Though by 1933 Liu Hsiang had managed to bring the greater part of the province under his command, divided domination of subprovincial areas persisted. In fact, even after the Nationalist government began to move into Szechwan in 1935, the provincial militarists continued to think in terms of the garrison area system.[32]

In Kweichow by 1935, Wang Chia-lieh, like Liu Hsiang in Szechwan, was the dominant militarist among the provincial warlords. He, however, had fewer opponents than Liu Hsiang had, having only two significant rival-subordinates, Hou Tzu-tan and Yu Kuo-ts'ai.[33]

In 1928 Liu Wen-hui, one of the Szechwan militarists, was appointed to the post of Commander-in-Chief of the Szechwan-Sikang Frontier Defense Force. The central government decided to lop a Sikang region off from Szechwan at least partly from a desire to simplify the chaotic state of politics existing in Szechwan at the time. However, the political situation there was never fully separate from politics in Szechwan, for Liu did not give up his

27. In Yunnan after 1920 T'ang Chi-yao was no longer in real control. Rather, power was wielded by locally based generals in the various regions within the province. See Sutton, "Rise and Decline," pp. 238, 242. See also Li P'ei-t'ien, "Lung Yün," Part 25; and Robert A. Kapp, Szechwan and the Chinese Republic (1973), Chapter 1.

28. See John C. S. Hall, "The Yunnan Provincial Faction, 1927-1937" (1974), Chapter 1.

29. Hall, "Faction," Chapters 2 through 8; and Li P'ei-t'ien, "Lung Yün," Parts 18 through 21.

30. Kapp, Szechwan, pp. 34-35.

31. Ibid., pp. 38 ff.

32. Ibid., p. 122.

33. A. Garavente, "The Long March," China Quarterly, No. 27 (1965), p. 114. See also Hall, "Faction," pp. 283-286, 290.

Chengtu residence or his concern with affairs in his native province.[34]

Coupled with this concern for local affairs as opposed to all-Southwest matters during the 1930s, provincial leaders in the Southwest had no interest in having relations with the central government. From the time of the establishment of the Nanking government in 1927 until the Communists' Long March of 1934-1936, provincial rulers throughout the area paid merely lip-service allegiance to that government. At the same time a large measure of military and economic autonomy reigned within each province here.[35] As the Long March proceeded westward, however, the Nationalists began to attempt to penetrate and control the Southwest. This attempt persisted down to 1949. It is this process that was particularly responsible for the shape politics took on by the late 1940s in this area.

The Nationalists were interested in penetrating the Southwest because the area was isolated and could therefore serve as a haven. When the Communists entered the Southwest on their westward trek, Chiang Kai-shek pursued them in the hope of securing the area for his own regime. Later, he viewed this relatively inaccessible area as a retreat for his government during the Japanese invasions of north and east China in the late 1930s and early 1940s, and again hoped to use it as a fortress against the Communists in the civil war of the late 1940s.

In December 1934, a band of Communists under Hsü Hsiang-ch'ien was expanding westward from a northern Szechwan soviet base, and forces under Ho Lung and Hsiao K'o were increasing their activity in southeast Szechwan. Chiang Kai-shek chose this time to set up a Central Staff Corps to plan and direct an anti-Communist campaign in Szechwan, Yunnan, and Kweichow, and to inspect and supervise these provinces' armies in this effort. A Military Training Academy was established in the summer of

34. *ONI Review*, 4, No. 2 (1949), p. 28; A. Doak Barnett, *China on the Eve of Communist Takeover* (1963), p. 217.

35. Garavente, "Long March," p. 114, regarding Kweichow; Record Group 226, Office of Strategic Services (Research and Analysis Branch), housed in the Modern Military Records Division, U.S. National Archives, Washington, D.C. [hereafter OSS], No. 2254, and Barnett, *China on the Eve,* p. 284, and Hall, "Faction," Chapters 4 through 8, regarding Yunnan; Kapp, *Szechwan,* Chapter 4, regarding Szechwan; K. Bloch, "Warlordism," *American Journal of Sociology* 43, No. 5 (1938), p. 700.

1935 to train and indoctrinate officers from these three provinces.[36]

Chiang went on to take further advantage of Liu Hsiang's weakness in the face of Communist incursions. Since Szechwan was then in the midst of an economic crisis, Chiang was able to force Liu to trade a national government presence in his province for Chiang's economic and military support. Thereafter, Chiang began an active attempt to control every aspect of Szechwanese civil, military, and economic life.[37]

In Kweichow, Chiang appointed Hsüeh Yüeh as Pacification Commander in February 1935. When the forces under Wang Chia-lieh were defeated by the Communists, Wang's flight to the south ended his rule as military leader of Kweichow.[38] Also, the commission to set up Sikang as a province was created by the central government at this same time. The appointments of personnel to this commission amounted to a central recognition of the de facto local regime. However, the very move to institutionalize the power relations here through bestowal of central legitimacy was an attempt to force local acceptance of national rule. It was only Yunnan, where Chiang Kai-shek was impressed with Lung Yün's professions of loyalty and with the industrialization program of his regime, and where the government was unified and strategic considerations nominal, that this period did not see central control extended.[39]

The Anti-Japanese War and the removal of the central government headquarters and personnel to Chungking at the end of 1938 provided the opportunity to increase central influence in and management over Southwest affairs. In Szechwan, when Liu Hsiang died in early 1938, the militarists there planned to support P'an Wen-hua, Liu's old subordinate, for the post of governor. Chiang, however, afraid that P'an would become a second Liu Hsiang and impede Chiang's control over Szechwan, opposed this.

Initial resistance sprung up among the Szechwanese generals to Chiang's attempt to install Chang Chün, the director of the Generalissimo's Chungking headquarters. To quiet the opposi-

36. Kapp, *Szechwan*, Chapter 6.
37. *Ibid.*, and Chapter 7.
38. Garavente, *"Long March,"* pp. 112, 117.
39. Hall, "Faction," Chapter 8.

tion, Chiang himself assumed the post of acting governor for a transitional period, and deputed Ho Kuo-kuang to take on the position as his agent. Then, when Chang Chün's relations with the local militarists improved, and as central troops gradually established a foothold in Szechwan's strategic points, Chang was made governor in November 1940, and he continued to hold this position until the end of the war. Thus, from 1938 the new provincial regime was to be little more than a branch, if a recalcitrant one, of the central government.[40]

These incursions were resented and resisted by the military leaders in Szechwan. By May 1943 the Szechwan militarists' increasing opposition to the authority of the center was noted in a U.S. Foreign Service officer's report. These generals were said to be demanding a governor suitable to them, equal treatment for their troops, local control of capital development, and a reduction of the land tax in kind.[41] Over a year later, bitterness against the center persisted, the Szechwanese still feeling that they wanted a greater voice in national affairs.[42] And in February 1945, it was reported that blocks of Szechwan were still controlled by warlords who, though held in check by the national government and its non-Szechwanese armies, were by no means wiped out.[43]

The Nationalists were not deterred, however. After the war, though the government offices were moved out of Szechwan, Chiang was still interested in weakening and removing the power of P'an Wen-hua. He therefore abolished the Pacification Office for the Szechwan-Shensi-Hupeh Border Region which P'an had headed. P'an's command was then changed to the Szechwan-Kweichow-Hunan-Hupeh Region, where the territory was poor and communications difficult.[44]

Teng Hsi-hou had served as Pacification Commissioner of Szechwan and Sikang from March 1938 until the end of the war

40. Liu Chin, *Ch'uan K'ang i-shou ch'ien-hou* [Before and After Szechwan and Sikang Changed Hands] (1956), pp. 32-34; Howard L. Boorman, *Biographic Dictionary of Republican China* (1967), Chang Chün entry; Barnett, *China on the Eve*, p. 107.

41. *Foreign Relations of the United States, Diplomatic Papers: China, 1943* (Washington: U.S. Government Printing Office, 1957) [hereafter *Foreign Relations 1943*], see papers for May 31 and May 18.

42. *Foreign Relations 1944*, see September 13.

43. OSS No. 119156.

44. Liu Chin, *Ch'uan K'ang*, p. 34.

and, with P'an Wen-hua and Sikang's governor, Liu Wen-hui, was considered one of the three pillars of Szechwan-Sikang political and military power. He was made acting governor of Szechwan in 1946 and confirmed in the post in May 1947.[45] According to sources reporting from Szechwan at the time, he was considered by Chiang to be the most trustworthy of the three.[46] His appointment was apparently made as a concession to provincial powerholders, while at the same time being a relatively safe one from the center's point of view.

However, by April 1948 the central government was not getting the taxes it demanded from Szechwan. It was also confronted with student demonstrations, rice riots, and the Provincial Senate's opposition to its policy of military conscription. Therefore, the center appointed a new governor, Wang Ling-chi, who was viewed as more reliable than Teng. Wang's principal jobs were to keep down unrest and to foster a higher degree of provincial obedience to national government commands.[47] He remained in office until the takeover in 1949.

P'an, Teng, and Liu, meanwhile, embittered by central maneuvers against them and hoping to side with the purveyors of perquisites, jointly telegraphed their turnover to the Communists in September 1949 and waited hopefully for the arrival of the People's Liberation Army (PLA).[48]

Liu had reason to be alienated from the central government because of events in his own Sikang. Key sections of the province—those near Ya-an and K'ang-ting—were the private preserve of General Liu and his Twenty-Fourth Army. However, this army was integrated into the National Army as the Twenty-Fourth Division in 1945, following the formal inauguration of the province in 1939. By 1948, Liu and his forces were subordinated to the overall Szechwan-Sikang-Yunnan-Kweichow command of Nationalist General Chu Hsiao-liang in Chungking. In southern Sikang, a delicate balance of power was maintained between the garrison commander, Ho Kuo-kuang (a central government man sent with his own troops by Chu) on the one hand, and Liu's men

45. Barnett, *China on the Eve*, p. 107; OSS No. 7930; Boorman, *Biographic Dictionary*, entry on Teng.
46. *Foreign Relations 1943*, see May 18; OSS No. 57523.
47. Barnett, *China on the Eve*, pp. 107-108.
48. Liu Chin, *Ch'uan K'ang*, pp. 20 ff; *New York Times*, December 15, 1949.

on the other. Ultimate authority was split between them, and the capital, Hsi-ch'ang, was a special region under joint central-provincial military control. Between the two sides relations were minimal and far from cordial. Moreover, the Ministry of National Defense sent about 200 officers to watch over Liu's forces. Although these officers were largely ineffectual, still they represented another form of central incursion into the Southwest.[49]

In Kweichow, one central appointee followed another in the wake of Wang Chia-lieh's defeat in 1935. Wu Ting-ch'ang came in at the end of 1937, chosen in part because he could be trusted. He remained in office nearly eight years. He was responsible for abolishing opium cultivation, the mainstay of provincial militarists in the province, and he eliminated the provincial army as well. His government was described by an American Foreign Service official as "efficient if ruthless." Wu himself was said to have influence in Chungking circles, and Kweichow as a whole was considered thoroughly loyal to the central government under his rule. A harsh and repressive spy system was run under Wu to silence any criticism of Kuomintang (KMT) rule.[50]

However, when the Japanese neared Kweichow at the end of 1944, Yang Sen, a Szechwanese general, was offered the governorship. In return, he agreed that his Szechwanese troops would guarantee the defense of the province against Japanese invasion.[51] The appointment of Yang served to continue Chungking's control over Kweichow, and put in power a man with experience in the anti-Communist campaigns then being waged.[52] His rule lasted only until April 1948, when he was removed to become the mayor of Chungking and director of its KMT Headquarters.

For the final year prior to takeover, Yang was succeeded by a man known as the "Father of the Chinese Military Police," Ku Cheng-lun. Ku, though a Kweichow native, had been active in KMT circles since the Party's Fifth National Congress elected him to its Central Executive Committee in 1935. Also, as director of

49. *ONI* Review, 4, No. 2 (1949); Barnett, *China on the Eve,* p. 221.
50. OSS No. 97062. Wu had been the leader of a major financial and banking group before the war and had headed a department in Chiang Kai-shek's war cabinet in 1937 responsible for moving industrial plants from East China to Chungking. His appointment in Kweichow was also motivated by a hope that he would be able to bring private investment into Kweichow.
51. OSS No. 119156.
52. OSS No. 116180.

the Szechwan-Kweichow-Hunan-Hupeh Border Area Pacification Office, he had been fighting Communists since 1939.[53]

In Yunnan too, the same story of central intrusion and local
indignation was played out. Despite Lung Yün's close cooperation with the central government against Japan, central interference in Yunnan's internal affairs markedly if gradually increased
beginning in about 1939.[54] By early 1943, a U.S. Consul in
Kunming reported, "central government economic hegemony
has been secured, chiefly through national control of currency,
banking, and foreign trade." At that time provincial authorities
still had "almost complete control over political affairs within
Yunnan" and the provincial troops had not yet been assimilated
into the national forces. Nonetheless, the provincial government
was opposing the continuous arrival in Yunnan of central forces,
and local resentment against central Maritime Customs was
making itself felt. Moreover, Yunnan's best provincial government troops, which had left for the war against Japan in 1937 and
1938, were not being permitted to return home. And those
troops still in the province in 1943 were outnumbered at least
four to one by central forces stationed there.[55]

With the center's appointment of General Ch'en Ch'eng as
Commander-in-Chief of the Chinese Expeditionary Force in
Yunnan in March 1943, civil officials in the province began
coming under the central military authorities' control. Ch'en was
a long-time close associate of the Generalissimo's, and he quickly
consolidated provincial power in his hands, as the group army
commanders under him steadily strengthened their control over
local administration in the areas in which they were stationed.[56]

In retaliation and in self-defense against these encroachments,
Governor Lung Yün supported the cause of constitutional government in Yunnan, thereby rallying anti-central-government
sentiment to his own benefit. He encouraged and aided the
Democratic League, which was advocating an end to KMT
dictatorship and calling for compromise with the Communists.

53. Boorman, *Biographic Dictionary*, entry for Ku Cheng-lun. There is a conflict in the sources here: Liu Chin says that P'an Wen-hua was made director of
this area after the war. See Liu Chin, *Ch'uan K'ang*, p. 34.

54. Barnett, *China on the Eve*, p. 284.

55. OSS No. 34044.

56. OSS No. 41213; *Foreign Relations 1943*, see April 14; OSS No. 49278.

Lung also protected the reform movement of liberal students and professors at National Southwest Associated University (Lien Ta).[57]

But Chiang permitted Lung to remain as governor throughout the period of the Resistance War. With its end, Chiang was doubtful that Lung would throw Yunnan behind him should civil war break out again.[58] Therefore he ordered Yunnan's troops under General Lu Han to Vietnam to accept Japan's surrender there in October 1945. He then seized the opportunity to stage a coup, to which Lung Yün, shorn of military support, was compelled to capitulate. Lu Han, Lung's half-brother, was named governor. However, Lu's absence from the province at that time allowed Chiang to appoint a KMT Party man, Li Tsung-Huang, as acting governor.[59]

This maneuver spelled the beginning of intensive KMT control in Yunnan. By July 1946, the province was infiltrated by KMT secret service men. Furthermore, the garrison command of Kunming's troops was turned over to central troops; the office of chief of police was taken over by a member of Tai Li's secret service organization; and the Provincial Ministry of Civil Affairs was headed by a member of the KMT's CC Clique.[60] During the summer of 1946 Democratic League members were harassed in Kunming. Several of the League's ranking members were assassinated, and many believed this to be the work of the KMT secret service.[61]

When the news of these murders spread, Yunnanese troops sent north against their will to fight in the civil war began to defect to the Communists. Chiang Kai-shek responded with repression. Nevertheless, in October 1948 the entire Sixtieth Army of Yunnan turned over at Ch'ang-ch'un and was reorganized into the PLA.[62] Meanwhile, Lu Han took on the position of governor in 1946. He managed to poise himself and Yunnan on the fence, refusing to support the civil war actively and, influ-

57. OSS No. 125981; Chang Wen-shih, *Yün-nan nei-mu* [Behind the Scenes in Yunnan] (1949), p. 2.
58. OSS No. 25741; Chang Wen-shih, *Yün-nan*, pp. 3, 12.
59. OSS Nos. 19378, 125981, 25741; Chang, *Yün-nan*, p. 5; Li P'ei-t'ien, "Lung Yün," Parts 32, 33.
60. *Foreign Relations 1946*, July 26.
61. *Foreign Relations 1946*, July 17; Chang, *Yün-nan*, p. 40.
62. Chang, *Yün-nan*, pp. 43, 52 ff.

enced by the Yunnanese troops' turnover, hoping to leave open his option to negotiate with the winner.

Throughout 1949, Lu attempted to restaff local government posts with his own men, and to strengthen local control over provincial finances. He also permitted criticism of the central government and praise of the Communists. At the same time, Lung Yün, living in Hong Kong, sent telegrams urging the Provincial Council to declare in favor of the Communists.[63] However, under increasingly relentless pressure from national authorities, Lu Han apparently capitulated, allowing the government to send in armies from Kweichow, and adopting a stronger anti-Communist stand. In exchange, he was granted greater freedom in managing the financial, political, and military affairs of Yunnan.[64] But not long thereafter, he, like his troops and his half-brother, was to declare allegiance to the Communists.[65]

This review has shown that the fate of the provinces of the Southwest ran in tandem at several key junctures of twentieth-century Chinese political history. With the victory of Yüan Shih-k'ai, the three then-existing provinces were left to follow their own courses in searching for a leader, both blessed by central noninterference and cursed by the difficulties of extending total control within any one of these isolated and dissected units. The period of near hegemony for any one ruler was relatively brief in each case, coming to an end with the Long March and the War of Resistance. For at each of these crises Chiang Kai-shek and his government rushed more and more central troops into the area and tightened the vise of central civil control by pushing out provincial strong men and appointing loyal KMT personnel in their places.

What was the effect of this series of political events on the top leadership of these provinces? In the first place, it alienated these men from the KMT and its power-grabbing strategies. Thus embittered, many of these leaders—P'an Wen-hua, Teng Hsi-hou, Liu Wen-hui, Lung Yün, and Lu Han—went over to the

63. Barnett, *China on the Eve*, pp. 286 ff; Chang, *Yün-nan*, p. 78.
64. Barnett, *China on the Eve*, p. 290; *New York Times*, September 10, 1949; September 11, 1949; October 2, 1949.
65. *Far Eastern Economic Review* 9, No. 5 (1950), p. 136; *New York Times*, December 10, 1949; December 11, 1949.

Communists in late 1949. But at the same time these militarists were busy making deals to try to preserve as much of their power as possible and attempting to hold open their options, so that they might share in the victors' spoils without relinquishing their own bargaining chips. Thus, because of this experience in provincial independence followed by central invasion, and because these men developed methods of dealing with this experience, they were to pose a problem for Communist control of the Southwest.

In light of central inability to control the Southwest effectively, as well as the recalcitrance of local leaders there in the face of central penetration, we can conclude that Integration I was absent there before 1949. None of the individual provinces was a contributing part of the national system; and certainly the Southwest as a whole, at the level of the entire area, was not integrated in this respect into the nation. In the years before the Long March, the leaders in these provinces paid little heed to the Nanking government. And after the Long March, from the mid-1930s until 1949, increasing central intrusions met with local resistance and often did not lead to real central control. This control was impeded because of the obstacles raised by embittered and alienated provincial rulers, who were not pleased by threats to their long-term autonomy.

Integration II: Local Economics, Culture, and Politics within the Southwest Area

If Integration II had been present at the level of the Southwest area as a whole, there would have been cooperation and interchange among the whole population of the area in the fields of economics and politics, and there would have been homogenity as to culture. Further, there would have been a directing center here, capable of controlling all the localities within the area in economic and political matters. This section is geared toward determining whether or not such integration existed in this area in the period preceding the Communist takeover.

To illustrate the general fields of economics, politics, and culture, three problem areas that best represent the nature of each field as it appeared in the Southwest before 1949 will be examined. In the field of economics the nature of trade relations will be the focus. For politics, concentration will be upon the local structure of power relations, and especially upon the type of leadership involved in local political groups. Finally, in the realm of culture, the mass of minority tribes in the Southwest will be described, and the social traits of some of these will be highlighted. Activities connected with these three issues—trade, local political groups and leadership, and minorities—were particularly characteristic of the type of integration and malintegration that marked Southwest local life. Thus in examining them the reader should obtain a broad picture and general flavor of affairs in the Southwest provinces. Finally, use of these topics for analysis provides a handy bridge in comparing pre-1949 society in the Southwest with that after takeover. For these three problem areas, because they were especially troublesome here, became the principal concerns of the new regime in dealing with the Southwest after 1949.

Economics: Commercial Affairs

Commerce throughout much of the Southwest was shaped by the geography of the area. It was also interrelated with the political situation in the localities, which will be described in a later section, and which, in turn, was also influenced by geography. Two similarities in commercial affairs marked local places throughout the area. First, the costs and difficulties of transport in much of the region made trade unfeasible for all but the basic necessities;[66] and, second, control of resources and goods was often in the hands of locally based groups or individuals. But, despite these similarities, the area as a whole could not be said to constitute an economic region with a regional market linking up all commerce within the area.

The impact of geography was such that trade in the area was basically bifurcated. Where waterways were accessible, commerce was well served. In the bulk of the area, however, goods were stopped up in isolated enclaves and near self-sufficiency was the rule.

Szechwan, particularly in the area of the Red Basin, is well watered, with good internal communications; and Chungking, at the joining of the Yangtze and Chia-ling rivers, has long been the chief river port for West China and the principal outlet for

66. These same costs and difficulties of transport also encouraged a booming trade in opium. See the end of this section.

Szechwan's trade.[67] In the Basin, large urban centers grew up along the Yangtze and its tributaries, especially at their points of confluence. These included I-pin, Lu-hsien, Fou-ling, and Wan-hsien, all of which served as distribution and gathering points for commercial produce. Lesser centers, also tied to areas of agricultural production and serving the same functions as the above, included Nei-chiang, Le-shan, and Nan-ch'ung.[68] Goods moved along the Yangtze downriver to Hankow and Shanghai, passing first through the provinces of the central interior.

Chungking also has long served as the entrepôt for the trade of Yunnan's and Kweichow's major cities, to which it was traditionally linked by the Yangtze's tributaries; exports from Sikang and Tibet passed through it as well.[69] In the late-nineteenth century, a traveler through the Southwest noted that Kweichow's lack of salt tied it and its trade to Szechwan;[70] and that Yunnan received processed cotton and salt from Szechwan, sending back tea, lead, copper, and tin in return.[71] But areas not accessible to the Yangtze and its tributaries were not tied into this trade.

In Yunnan, the capital city Kunming was the active commercial center. Customers did business in Kunming from all the major cities of the province and from Szechwan and Kweichow, either through a firm which stationed a permanent representative there, through correspondence, or through traveling hawkers. Merchants in Kweichow's capital, Kweiyang, also had outside contacts.[72] However, from the capital in Yunnan the largest quantity of goods traveled to Ta-li, an active trade center on the Burma Road. Relatively few goods went to the mountainous east and other less accessible parts of the province.[73]

That the areas in Szechwan that were served by the Yangtze had a far brisker trade than other parts of the Southwest can be seen in their marketing schedule. These areas held markets at the standard marketing level at least nine times per month.[74] Since

67. Edwin John Dingle, ed., *The New Atlas and Commercial Gazeteer of China*, (n.d.), p. 12.
68. *JPRS* 15069 (1962), p. 74.
69. Dingle, *New Atlas*, pp. 12, 115.
70. Hosie, *Three Years*, p. 207.
71. *Ibid.*, p. 64.
72. Chang Hsiao-mei, *Yün-nan ching-chi* [The Economy of Yunnan] (1942), p. R3; *idem.*, *Kuei-chou ching-chi* [The Economy of Kweichow] (1939), p. K34.
73. *Idem.*, *Yün-nan*, p. R4.
74. J. E. Spencer, "The Szechuan Village Fair," *Economic Geography* 16, No. 1 (1940), p. 52.

the remainder of Szechwan was geographically similar to most of Yunnan, Kweichow, and Sikang, the trading patterns there probably resembled trade in these less commercially active places.

Throughout much of the Southwest commercial relations were characterized by what has been referred to as "truncation around the peripheries" of regional economies.[75] This phrase describes the phenomenon whereby some standard marketing systems are only indirectly connected with an intermediate marketing system and the higher levels of the hierarchy of central places. In such an unintegrated system, the degree of commercialization and economic specialization tends to be lower.[76] Indeed, in the Southwest, where geographical barriers and a low level of transport development cut off many localities from active intercourse and linkage with the great centers of trade, these conditions were common.

In Yunnan, for example, there was virtually no water transportation, for most rivers and streams were not navigable. Badly paved or unpaved roads were the mainstay of transport. These difficulties in interdistrict communications meant that commerce suffered. In most rural communities, nearby markets were very small or practically nonexistent. And even in the larger market centers, temporary markets were held only every six days.[77] In Kweichow too, marketing was on a six-day schedule,[78] and markets offered only bare necessities.[79] In both Yunnan and Kweichow commerce was largely carried on through direct producer-consumer transactions and by traveling peddlers.[80]

In the late 1930s and early 1940s, studies were made of typical villages in inaccessible regions of Yunnan and Kweichow, respectively, and analogous pictures emerge.[81] One study reported on a village fictitiously called Yi-ts'un situated in a river gorge surrounded by high mountains and steep trails in Yunnan. It was not possible for this village to depend heavily on foodstuffs from outside, for transporting rice over the mountains would have

75. G. W. Skinner, "The City in Chinese Society" (1968), p. 4.
76. *Ibid.*, pp. 15, 16.
77. Fei Hsiao-t'ung, *Earthbound China* (1945), pp. 12, 47, 170, 299.
78. G. W. Skinner, "Marketing and Social Structure in Rural China," *Journal of Asian Studies* 24 (1964), No. 1, p. 13.
79. Chang Hsiao-mei, *Kuei-chou*, pp. K33-K34.
80. Fei, *Earthbound China*, p. 47; Chang Hsiao-mei, *Kuei-chou*, p. K1.
81. Fei, *Earthbound China*, pp. 139, 157; Chang Hsiao-mei, *Kuei-chou*, pp. K33-K34.

exhausted the village's entire labor supply. Since the people here were not able to be totally self-sufficient, however, they had to go to market for necessities they could not produce, but often suffered in bargaining because of their difficulties in traveling to market. Thus, they themselves had to produce for market only those articles for which there was great demand (such as paper in this case), and such items often brought the least return. At the same time, local special products and handicrafts did not get the market or bring the profit which they otherwise could have, given the poor facilities for marketing and transport.

The other study described Ting-fan, a *hsien* fifty-five kilometers from Kweiyang and connected to it by a highway. Even in a place so relatively well located, transportation was obstructed, so self-sufficiency was forced to be high. In much of Kweichow, the cost of transporting rice for two days equaled the value of the rice.[82]

Sikang's situation was similar to that in these hilly regions to its southeast. Here the general price level and cost of living were three times what they were in Chengtu. Prices rose with the altitude and the distance, because of a need to rely on human transport.[83] Moreover, in much of the province commerce was still based on barter through the late 1930s, and peddlers were often afraid to use what roads there were because of frequent Lolo raids and bandit attacks.[84]

Thus, the descriptions of trade in these provinces provided by economists and anthropologists of the Republican era mesh well with the notion of "truncation around the peripheries." Under such conditions no genuine regional market system could be said to have existed here.[85] In the ideal-type marketing system, each such local system is focused on a central market place which services that system, and the progressive hierarchy of local places ultimately leads up to a regional central place and market. The internal geographical barriers in the Southwest area and the consequent near self-sufficiency of parts of the hinterland meant there was a lack of commercialization and economic specialization here. Hence, a full-scale regional economy never developed in the Southwest before 1949.

82. Cressey, *China's Geographic Foundations,* p. 380.
83. *ONI Review,* 4, No. 2 (1949), pp. 35-36.
84. Li I-jen, *Hsi-k'ang,* p. 331.
85. Skinner, "Marketing," pp. 3-43.

Further proof that trade in this area was not organized along the lines of a genuine regional economy comes from the fact that each province here had commercial orientations to places outside the Southwest at least as strong as those it had with other parts of the Southwest. Szechwan's trade was oriented at least as much to the eastern ports and cities down the Yangtze as it was to its neighbors to the south and west; and much of Yunnan's commerce was connected to Vietnam through the Tien-Yüeh Railway and to Burma over the Burma Road. Also, a portion of Yunnan's trade went eastward via the West River to Kwangtung, and part of Kweichow's commerce flowed east and northeast over the Yüan River into the Tung-t'ing Lake in Hunan, outletting into the Yangtze west of Hankow.[86]

Moreover, a Chinese economist in the early 1940s reported that before the Resistance War, Yunnan sold 80 percent of its produce within Yunnan itself, only 5 to 6 percent to Szechwan, and 14 to 15 percent to Kweichow. After the war began, the situation changed somewhat, with Yunnan's percentage dropping to less than 70 percent, and Kweichow's and Szechwan's percentages climbing to 16.5 and 22.3, respectively.[87] But on the whole, these facts tend to strengthen the notion that the provinces in the Southwest were not tightly linked into the region for the mainstays of their commerce.

As noted above, regional commerce was thwarted by the topography of the area, and trade throughout the Southwest tended to concentrate in relatively small and inaccessible localities. It was not difficult for local men of means and power to take advantage of this situation and control the trade in these enclaves. In Szechwan this local control operated on two distinct but intermeshed levels before 1949. The first and more encompassing of these was based on military control. It was structured at the highest stratum by the system of garrison areas. Each garrison area housed the administrative-military organization of one of the several militarists who dominated Szechwanese politics, particularly before 1935. Each army commander utilized the resources and revenues of his own area to maintain himself and his troops. And below each commander was an array of lower-level officers in charge of tax collection in the area. Their autonomy in

86. Hosie, *Three Years*, pp. 205-206; Dingle, *New Atlas*, p. 62.
87. Chang Hsiao-mei, *Yün-nan*, pp. R3-R4.

controlling the revenues they gathered split each garrison area into small, financially discrete units. Thus, besides monopolizing access to the salt, tobacco, opium, or other riches particular to their districts, a militarist's subordinates commanded taxation of various sorts. The taxes they handled included those accruing from the numerous likin stations set up to tax the trade within their areas.[88] These military men also dealt in opium and manipulated commodity prices by hoarding food.[89]

On a second, more basic level, the militarist's control of local finances could only be assured through his cooperation with the Ko Lao Hui or Elder Brothers' Society, that mighty secret society whose lodges existed within every unit of local social organization.[90] Thus, collusion with the local militia and gentry leaders, all of whom were members of this society, was the only way in which a militarist could achieve and maintain local control and successfully carry out his tax collecting.

Each society lodge was organized around one standard marketing community, though a given community could house two lodges. Each of these lodges, then, had control of the markets in its community. Control was exercised by ensuring that certain key positions in the marketing system were reserved for society members and that a portion of each commission agent's fees were retained for the local lodge.[91] In certain areas, local coal mines and salt works could not market their goods until they had paid the society large sums on each shipment. Certain key items such as rape seed and rice were bought up and sold by the society in wholesale quantities without any goods being handled. In this way the society could keep a record of transactions and collect taxes in place of the government. Finally, the society controlled many inland communications, operating chains of control points similar to customs houses, where society members could stop merchants and other travelers for contributions.[92]

In Yunnan the geographical situation tied an isolated peasant to a market which required arduous and time-consuming travel

88. Kapp, *Szechwan*, pp. 40-43.
89. OSS No. 115263.
90. Kapp, *Szechwan*, p. 55.
91. Skinner, "Marketing," pp. 37 ff.
92. Liao T'ai-ch'u, "The Ko Lao Hui in Szechuan," *Pacific Affairs* 20, No. 2 (1947), p. 170.

for him to reach. This meant that he was at a disadvantage in bargaining as well as in transportation. While he was charged higher prices for the goods he bought because of the costs of conveyance, he was often forced to sell wholesale at a loss.[93] The financial difficulties of these people were supposedly attended to by credit societies, each of which was run by a big merchant. His power to determine who got money at the end of the term and to set the amount of interest enabled him to control the finances of the locality.[94] Moreover, in Yunnan, where minority tribes constitute about one-third of the population, each tribe had a monopoly on the production and trade in certain types of products and medicines.[95]

In Sikang, where the Tibetan religion dominated all sectors of society, most of the native businessmen were lamas, their capital coming from temples.[96] Among Han merchants, trade was mostly in the hands of Shensi people, who established a main office in K'ang-ting with branch shops scattered in various other cities. These shops hired people who spoke the language of the natives and delegated them to go out to the lower levels to peddle goods.[97] Also, trade was localized in Sikang as it was in Szechwan by the lodges of the Ko Lao Hui, here in conjunction with Liu Wen-hui's Twenty-Fourth Army and the provincial authorities. These individuals monopolized the trade in opium, the most valuable item of trade from Sikang, to the rest of China. It was the job of Liu's army to collect this opium, in which task it required the cooperation of the Lolo and other minority tribes, who in turn produced it to trade for small arms.[98]

Opium in fact was popular throughout the region, both because the soils of the Southwest were conducive to its cultivation, and because it yielded the highest values that could be obtained from a given area of land, making it attractive for taxation.[99]

93. Fei, *Earthbound China,* p. 191.
94. *Ibid.,* p. 209.
95. Inez de Beauclair, *Tribal Cultures of Southwest China* (1970), p. 26.
96. Li I-jen, *Hsi-k'ang,* p. 331.
97. *Ibid.*
98. *ONI Review,* 4, No. 2 (1949), p. 36.
99. Cressey, *China's Geographic Foundations,* p. 316. On the importance of the opium trade to the Southwest provinces, see J. C. S. Hall, "Opium Prohibition and the Chinese Communist Party" (1975); and J. C. S. Hall, "The Opium Trade in Yunnan Province, 1917-1937" (1974), pp. 1-28.

Moreover, where flat land was scarce and the cost of transportation exorbitant, opium, because of its high value in proportion to its bulk, became the leading cash crop in Kweichow, Yunnan, and Sikang.[100] In 1923 it was estimated that the poppy occupied two-thirds of the cultivated land in Yunnan in winter; and that in Kweichow the situation was similar.[101] Both the benefits for taxation and the easy transport enticed local warlords throughout these provinces to reap its profits and to neglect the production of foodstuffs.[102]

In the Southwest before liberation, because there was no energetic governmental program or investment to improve the transport and communications network which geography made imperative here, trade was often stopped up and stuck at the far reaches of the system; and local power groups cultivated the soils, concentrated the resources and manipulated the finances of pockets of territory. So, given the level of development here before 1949, geography and politics interacted, such that there was minimal integration within the Southwest area as a whole commercially.

Culture: Minorities

A multitude of minorities inhabit the Southwest. Their scattered existence throughout the provinces carves the land here into many discrete cultural enclaves. The presence in large numbers of a few key minority peoples—the Miao, the Yi or Lolo, the Pu-yi or Chung—does set the Southwest as a whole apart from other areas in China.[103] However, the central feature of minority habitation in the Southwest is the piecemeal quality these peoples lend to the landscape. For here the mountainous topography which slices up the area has created natural homelands for a plethora of tribes, some of which, never conquered, lived in what amounted to independent states before 1949.[104] And each separate tribe, with its individual political and social

100. Dingle, *New Atlas*, p. 182.
101. Cressey, *China's Geographic Foundations*, p. 375.
102. *JPRS* 15069 (1962), p. 502.
103. *China News Analysis* [hereafter *CNA*], No. 232 (1958), p. 2.
104. De Beauclair, *Tribal Cultures*, p. 18; Li I-jen, *Hsi-k'ang*, p. 91; Cressey, *China's Geographic Foundations*, p. 371.

history, presented its particular set of problems to the liberators in 1949.

As of 1957, national minorities in the Southwest were reported by the government to number over 12 percent of the more than one hundred million persons who populated the Southwest.[105] De Beauclair, in a book on Southwestern tribal cultures, cites Eberhard as having divided the Southwest minority groups into seven large families of tribes. Among these tribes the most numerous are those of the Tai family, which includes the Chung, and whose members live in Yunnan, Kweichow, Hunan, Kwangsi, and Kwàngtung; those of the Tibetan-Burmese family, which includes the Lolo, found in Yunnan, Sikang, Szechwan, and Kweichow; and those of the Miao family of Hunan, Szechwan, Kweichow, Kwangsi, and Yunnan.[106] In Szechwan, according to the 1953 census, minorities totaled two million, or 3 percent of the population; in Kweichow, four million, or 25 percent; and in Yunnan, nearly six million, or more than one-third.[107] In 1948 a rough estimate of Sikang's population claimed that two-thirds of the province's 3.5 million inhabitants were members of non-Han groups.[108] Though the proportions of minorities vary within each province, the problems they posed to integration were common throughout the Southwest.

The approaches taken by late-dynastic and KMT rule toward the minorities, along with the social, political, and cultural forms indigenous to the tribes themselves, together influenced the type of political problem each of these tribes posed by 1949. The *t'u-ssu* (native chief) system of administering the tribes through appointing their own chiefs to rule them was begun by the Yüan dynasty, but grew to full flower under the Ming and early Ch'ing. Through this system, native chieftains throughout Yunnan, Kweichow, Szechwan, Sikang, and Kwangsi were given nobility and seals. Under loose supervision by provincial authorities, they were eventually enjoined only to pay taxes and supply soldiers. The principal tribes so ruled were the Miao of Kweichow, the Tai tribes in Yunnan, and the Lolo of the Yunnan-Szechwan-Sikang border areas.

105. *JPRS* 15069 (1962), pp. 19-20.
106. De Beauclair, *Tribal Cultures*, pp. 24-25.
107. *JPRS* 15069 (1962), pp. 66, 339, 503.
108. *ONI Review*, 4, No. 2 (1949), p. 32.

By the end of the Ch'ing, the system was gradually abolished and territories formerly governed by it were put under Han officials. Though the KMT government formally terminated the system by 1931, the *t'u-ssu* of the Tibetan and Lolo tribes never lost their power among their own peoples, and incited them to resist Han rule. They were the instigators of local disturbances which persisted at least up until and maybe beyond the Communist takeover, harassing magistrates, kidnapping Chinese, and pillaging villages.[109]

The power of the Lolo *t'u-ssu* was linked to the strong political and social organization at the apex of which he stood. Lolo society was divided into three classes, over which the Black Lolos acted as ruling class. Although originally the *t'u-ssu* were drawn from a small, hereditary pool of aristocratic Blacks, as their heirs dried up, power passed to *t'u-mu,* once subordinates or close relatives of the *t'u-ssu.* The Blacks, as both landlords and political elite, possessed absolute authority of life, death, and property over their subordinates.

Dealings between the Black on the one hand, and their White Lolo subjects and Han household slaves on the other, were governed by obligations and responsibilities on both sides, such that the Whites never rebelled against their masters. Whereas the Blacks relied on the total support of these other classes who were their subordinate clan members, the Whites also depended on their superiors for protection. The clan was the most extensive form of social organization, and any injury to one's clan members had to be answered by a feud with the clan of his attacker. An age-old tradition of feuds among Lolo clans not only instilled a martial spirit in this people, but increased the entire group's solidarity against the invading Han.[110]

The Miao, known to be fiercely independent,[111] for the most part lacked the closely knit, political-social structure the Lolo enjoyed. Rather, they were grouped into loose tribal formations

109. De Beauclair, pp. 12-13; Li I-jen, *Hsi-k'ang,* p. 119 ff; George Moseley, "The Frontier Regions in China's Recent International Politics," in Jack Gray, ed., *Modern China's Search for a Political Form* (1969), pp. 302, 309; *Current Background* [hereafter *CB*], No. 150 (1952), p. 12.

110. *CB,* No. 150 (1952), p. 5; Lin Yueh-hua, *The Lolo of Liang Shan* (1961), Chapters 7 and 8.

111. *CNA,* No. 232 (1958), p. 5; Hugo Adolf Bernatzik, *AKHA and MIAO* (1970), p. 625; de Beauclair, *Tribal Cultures,* pp. 112-113.

among which there existed animosity and mutual contempt.[112] Even the Flowery Miao of northwest Kweichow and the Ch'uan Miao of southwest Szechwan, who were thought to exist in clans and had hereditary chiefs, only bestowed religious and not political authority on their headmen.[113] However, despite their resistance to control, the lack of solidarity among the Miao made them open to tactics designed to split them. Thus, when Miao peoples revolted in 1854 in Kweichow against a government decree, the Ch'ing government used some Miao tribes to defeat other Miao.[114]

Among the Chung, a Tai people of southwest Kweichow, there was more class differentiation than among the Miao. Members of the Chung upper classes openly cooperated with the Han to protect their own rule; and the Han officials, in turn, utilized Chung landlords to control and exploit the Chung lower classes. Many of these upper-class Chung actively participated in KMT rule, responding to KMT orders to Chung *hsiang* or *pao* chiefs to conscript men and raise money. Those who could afford to offer gifts to the officials escaped these exactions, while the poorer classes had to succumb to them or seek another powerful Chung to support them. Such dissensions served to increase the power of the minority upper classes over their territories.[115]

Along the Yunnan-Burma frontier and in southwest Yunnan, the Chinese Shan states and an independent Tai state, respectively, dominated the political life in each area. The *t'u-ssu* system bolstered the position of the Shan rulers; and the Tai had taxation powers over those in their territories.[116]

The history of independence and the social structure of each of these major tribal groups thwarted integration among peoples living in the Southwest. Also, most of the minorities here were knocked into timidity by the treatment they had received from the Han,[117] and, except for the Black Lolo, these tribes all acknowledged the superiority of the Chinese.[118] However, they all

---

112. De Beauclair, *Tribal Cultures*, p. 27.
113. *Ibid.*, pp. 131-132; Bernatzik, *AKHA*, p. 62.
114. *CB*, No. 150 (1952), p. 5; Hosie, *Three Years*, p. 228.
115. *CB*, No. 150 (1952), pp. 10-11.
116. De Beauclair, *Tribal Cultures*, p. 23.
117. Hosie, *Three Years*, p. 226.
118. De Beauclair, *Tribal Cultures*, p. 29.

shared a hatred for the Han,[119] which made Han-minority cooperation largely impossible before 1949. The tribes that were
greatest in number posed additional political problems for the
Communists. In the case of the Lolo, a tight group solidarity had
to be split to dismantle their rulers, and thereby disrupt their
organized hostile behavior toward the Han. For until their society
was dismantled, they posed a threat to social order, with their lack
of respect for Han government, frequent raids on Chinese
villages, and occupation of "Independent Lololand" in Ta Liang
Shan at the joint borders of Szechwan, Sikang, and Yunnan,
where no Chinese dared to enter.[120]

The Miao, while lacking this solidarity, had to be won over, for
their characteristic pattern after years of retreating in the face of
Han advance was to withdraw to a farther territory when they felt
encroachments upon their freedom. Furthermore, the bitterness
existing between various Miao tribes, like the disunity among the
classes of the Chung, had made them easy prey to the manipula-
tions of the KMT. Those who had cooperated with the KMT
were seen as counter-revolutionary elements by the Communists.

Finally, wherever independent political states existed their
autonomous powers had to be broken down before they could be
amalgamated into a Chinese nation. In each case a form of localism obstructed integration within the Southwest as a whole. Thus
the genuine regions culturally were the individual homelands of
the dozens of tribes that occupied local areas.

Politics: Local Leadership and Groups

Political control in the Southwest provinces by the 1940s was
the complicated, patchwork outcome and counterpart of the
various influences outlined above. The variegated nature of
society here was reflected in discrete spatial blocks of authority
where the spheres of warlord, secret society chief, t'u-ssu, local
gentry, tribal headman, and lama overlapped and interlocked.
And overlaid on this network of bailiwicks was the KMT's steadily
increasing attempt to penetrate the local levels during these
years, which was more successful in some areas than in others.

In Sikang, the varieties of local rule were perhaps most numerous. On the extreme eastern rim, the area around Ya-an and

119. Cressey, *China's Geographic Foundations*, p. 371.
120. Hosie, *Three Years*, pp. 64, 107, 179; Lin, *Lolo*, pp. 1, 11, 17.

K'ang-ting constituted the domain of General Liu Wen-hui and his Twenty-Fourth Division. To his south, control of Hsi-ch'ang was shared between Liu's forces and central troops.[121] In the area under Liu's command, secret society lodges of the Ko Lao Hui and Lolo *t'u-ssu* dominated the lower levels of politics and social organizations, and in certain cases they cooperated.[122] The juncture of these two social groups can be explained more than anything else by the omnipresence of the Ko Lao Hui, with which nearly all the civil and military authorities of Liu's coterie also had connections.[123] Moreover, the elaborate structure of *t'u-ssu* rule[124] did not prevent penetration by certain secret society leaders. At least one of these leaders commanded a large number of Lolos, and during the final days of the civil war was reportedly willing to lead them against Liu Wen-hui for KMT General Hu Tsung-nan.[125]

As one advanced westward into the more mountainous land on the Tibetan Plateau, most of the population was Tibetan. Here Chinese political forms mainly existed in name only. Under these forms the Tibetans were governed by their own chiefs: feudal lords and lamas. This largely nomadic people was organized into loose groups and grasslands, and the important permanent settlements were lamaseries, through which the Buddhist priesthood dominated every form of life. Despite Chinese garrison posts at each *hsien* city and in every *hsiang*, local Tibetan self-defense units persisted.[126] Beyond the Yangtze, which split the province into two equal parts, no Chinese influence existed whatsoever. Here the lama, the local prince, and the envoy from Lhasa held sway.[127]

The pattern of local control in Yunnan in the 1940s was affected, as in Sikang, by the fact that minority tribesmen occupied the greater part of the territory, and many of them were under the rule of native headmen. Although the provincial government had long been the domain of one governor, as in Sikang, Lung Yün's authority by 1944 was not so absolute as Liu

121. *ONI Review,* 4, No. 2 (1949), p. 30.
122. Liu Chin, *Ch'uan K'ang,* p. 148.
123. *ONI Review,* 4, No. 2 (1949), p. 36.
124. See Li I-jen, *Hsi-k'ang,* pp. 121 ff, for a description of this structure. Basically, *hsiao t'u-ssu* (small native chiefs) served under the *t'u-ssu,* and each of the chiefs belonged to one of four big divisions.
125. Liu Chin, *Ch'uan K'ang,* p. 148.
126. *ONI Review,* 4, No. 2 (1949), pp. 31-32; Li I-jen, *Hsi-k'ang,* pp. 457, 459.
127. *ONI Review,* 4, No. 2 (1949), p. 32.

Wen-hui's, and factions existed within the top levels of provincial administration.[128]

Complicating local politics in early 1943, Chiang Kai-shek appointed Ch'en Ch'eng as Commander-in-Chief of the Chinese Expeditionary Force in Yunnan. From that time, the central government steadily penetrated *hsien* politics, displacing native magistrates and causing bitterness against the center which reached down into the lower levels of society.[129] Dissatisfaction against the national government was reflected in the 1944 Yunnan People's Political Council, which petitioned the government and passed eight resolutions criticizing it.[130]

And despite the inability of the Yunnanese to stem the tide of central intrusion, in this province more than in any other in the Southwest known anti-government forces swelled to significant proportions by 1949. These included local Communist regulars, of whom there were about 20,000, Communist irregulars, and supporters of the deposed Lung Yün, often led by local gentry and bandits. These various groups did not work together, however, and only managed to control large cities for short periods,[131] adding to the confusion in local politics.

In Szechwan, basically separate and autonomous lodges of the Ko Lao Hui existed at all levels of social organization.[132] Although each *hsiang, chen,* and village organized itself into individual lodges, and though social status, family position, and one's profession divided members into different lodges,[133] a spirit of mutual help and a communications network between lodges made the society a potentially awesome force in Szechwan.[134] Membership linked militarist, gentryman, landlord, merchant, and local government official on the one hand, with lower-class transport workers, peasants, and bandit elements on the other. At

128. OSS No. 108699.

129. OSS Nos. 41213, 49278, 34044.

130. OSS No. 78406.

131. Barnett, *China on the Eve*, p. 293.

132. Skinner, "Marketing," p. 41.

133. Sung Chung-k'an, *Ssu-ch'uan ko-lao-hui kai-shan chih shang-chüeh* [Consideration of the Reform of Szechwan's Ko Lao Hui] (1940), pp. 3, 4; Wei-ta Fa-shih (pseudonym), *Chung-kuo pang-hui* [Chinese Secret Societies] (1949), p. 115; Liao, "Ko Lao Hui," p. 163.

134. Sung, *Ssu-ch'uan ko-lao-hui*, p. 6; Wei-ta, *Pang-hui*, p. 115; Liu Chin, *Ch'uan K'ang*, p. 132; Liao, "Ko Lao Hui," p. 162.

all levels of politics, the leadership of the society, largely composed of men of property and means, exercised control over the political affairs in their own particular locales.[135] *Hsien* and *ch'ü* officials had to rely on gentry secret society members to enforce compliance with government orders.[136]

Moreover, the local society lodge acted as an extra-legal government itself, punishing offenders, protecting criminals, mediating disputes, and providing mutual defense and social security.[137] One observer has reported that the average villager knew only that he had a certain secret society leader (*ta yeh*), and did not know that any other government existed.[138] Leadership of local peasant uprisings throughout the 1940s—against KMT press-ganging for the army and for road building, and against KMT tax levies in kind—was generally attributed to the society.[139] The strength of these local Ko Lao Hui cells or lodges apparently partially stymied the central government's intervention into local affairs during the Anti-Japanese War. Chang Chün, the KMT-connected governor whom Chiang Kai-shek installed in Szechwan in 1940, had very little control outside Chengtu, and even within the city itself, half the population was reportedly tied to the society.[140] Also, the central government's policy of compromising with local authorities fostered more localism during the war. Bullies, ruffians, ex-officials, warlords, and secret society leaders were appointed members of the provincial council. The council's duty to elect the People's Political Council enhanced the power of these elements.[141]

Politically, the strong local organizations in the Southwest before 1949—whether Ko Lao Hui, warlord cliques, *t'u-ssu*-led clans, or other minority tribes—had two features that posed

135. OSS No. 34815; Barnett, *China on the Eve*, pp. 127, 129; Skinner, "Marketing," p. 41.

136. Sung, *Ssu-ch'uan ko-lao-hui*, p. 11; Liao, "Ko Lao Hui," p. 170; Frederic Wakeman, "The Secret Societies of Kwangtung, 1800-1856," in Jean Chesneaux, ed., *Popular Movements and Secret Societies in China, 1840-1950* (1972), p. 33; OSS No. 34815.

137. Barnett, *China on the Eve*, p. 129; Sung, *Ssu-ch'uan ko-lao-hui*, p. 6.

138. Sung, *Ssu-ch'uan ko-lao-hui*, p. 11.

139. *Foreign Relations 1943*, September 29; OSS No. 2254, pp. vii, 38, 53-54.

140. OSS No. 2254, pp. 37-38.

141. Liao, "Ko Lao Hui," p. 169; OSS No. 115263.

immediate dilemmas for the Communists. First, the Ko Lao Hui and the warlords had been embittered by the policies of the KMT. They had clashed over control of opium and brothels with the KMT-operated Blueshirts;[142] and they were alienated by Chiang Kai-shek's men's high-handedness during the Anti-Japanese War. This may have helped to defeat the KMT in this area, and several of the warlords who reportedly prepared the ground for the takeover were said to be Ko Lao Hui members.[143] However, by the same token, these groups were unwilling to brook any rival, and were thus no more amenable to interference by the Communists.[144] Similarly, minorities who hated the Han when Han people ruled through the KMT would be no less well disposed to Han Communists, at least initially.

Second, the strength of the various organizations in the Southwest meant that the peasants here were accustomed to joining together for mutual aid and defense. These habits of cooperation may have facilitated integration. On the other hand, however, these groups were locally based, often united disparate social classes, were tightly organized under powerful leaders, and in some cases even formed autonomous quasi-political systems. Associations so bound could not be easily dislodged, as Lieberthal has shown for Tientsin.[145]

The fractured state of politics within each province was doubtless connected to the complexity of the topography and the attendant difficulties of extending control beyond discrete enclaves. Control of local resources by local powerholders was encouraged by the fact that products and resources were stopped up in land pockets by transport problems. And the intricacies of the human environment here also contributed to the complexity of linking larger areas, given the level of transport development and the lack of an energetic and far-reaching policy of integration by the government. In sum, Integration II—entailing connections between subprovincial localities within a supraprovincial area—was absent, whether one looks at politics, economics, or culture.

142. Han Su-yin, *Birdless Summer* (1968), pp. 85-87.
143. *New York Times*, December 8, 1949; Liu Chin, *Ch'uan K'ang*, describes the behind-the-scenes machinations which led to takeover in Szechwan and Sikang, according to his own understanding; OSS No. 2254, pp. 53-54.
144. OSS No. 2254, p. 38.
145. Kenneth Lieberthal, "The Suppression of Secret Societies in Post-Liberation Tientsin," *China Quarterly*, No. 54 (1973), pp. 242-266.

This chapter has shown that no region existed at the supraprovincial level of the Southwest area before 1949. Commercial and political affairs were not organized even at the province level throughout the Southwest; and the cultural distinctiveness of the area lay only in the fact that many different minorities were scattered across the land here. Further, there was no one center the control of which could have assured domination of the remainder of the area.

Thus, to the extent that integration was present in the Southwest of this period at all, it was valid only for quite local areas, most likely at the level of the *hsien*. In this same vein, if regionalism—distinctiveness, consciousness, and local control—existed in the Southwest, it also pertained to these relatively small districts. This chapter has also demonstrated that, owing to the lack of political or social organization at a supraprovincial yet subnational level in the Southwest, there was no unit or device for integrating these localities, either one to the other (Integration II) or all at once to the nation (Integration I). Later chapters will analyze how the Communists handled this situation in their nation-building venture.

From another angle, however, the region was a logical unit. It had a syndrome of traits that distinguished it from all other parts of China. By the middle of the twentieth century, a largely common geography and an abundant smattering of minority groupings had given a common cast to the trade relations and political affairs of this area. And for this reason, though creating a genuinely integrated Southwest region was a mammoth undertaking for the Communists, they were able to deal with this set of provinces as a group precisely because of the similar problems there. The following discussion presents an examination of how the CCP went about molding this area so that it would become integrated along the lines of the two types of integration described above.

CHAPTER III

Integration I: Gradual Loss of the
Special Character of the Southwest and
Its Integration into the Nation

The Southwest was not an internally integrated region, as we have seen, and lacked vital sinews of cooperation in political and economic affairs. Still, it stood apart from the rest of the country in several important respects in the period surrounding takeover. In this chapter, the special problems the Southwest as a whole posed in late 1949 and 1950 will be presented. Then the military campaign that liberated the Southwest will be described; and the superimposition on the area of a set of regional military, administrative, and Party organs will be discussed. This campaign, along with these organs, combined to mold one region out of the individual provinces of the Southwest.

This chapter will also examine the gradual integration of this area into the nation. Basically, this was a process in which a backward region was dragged along on a path delineated from afar. The discussion will illustrate this process by examining the interplay between centrally designed tasks and programs on the one hand, and the changing situation in the Southwest from 1949 to 1954 on the other. It will show how this process—Integration I—consisted of two parts. In the first, the regional organs attempted to institutionalize local differences peculiar to the area under their control in line with central programs and policies; in the second, as the Southwest lost its special identity in the eyes of the leadership, work in the area was coordinated with work in the rest of the country. Thus a phase focusing on a geographical organization of work preceded a second phase in which work was functionally structured.

The Special Nature of the Southwest, 1949-1950

Certain features of Southwest society were particularly outstanding in the eyes of the Communists in late 1949 and early 1950. These were the aspects that posed the greatest difficulties in the course of takeover and in instituting Communist programs just after takeover.

The most protruding problems were caused by the people the Communists termed "counter-revolutionary." Throughout the Southwest provinces, this class was made up of similar types of groups. For example, since the Southwest was the last place to be liberated, hordes of Nationalist (KMT) troops chose this final battleground as the place in which to surrender. Also, this area had served as the site of the final stand of the Nationalist government, and many old KMT officials, either unable or unwilling to flee, were left stationed here. The secret societies, with their upper-class ties, posed yet another problem. Secret agents had supposedly been left behind by the fleeing KMT. And, finally, a group of KMT soldiers who had escaped across the border to Burma made frequent forays back into Yunnan province in attempts to topple the new regime.

According to the Communists, more than a million ex-KMT personnel were left in the Southwest after takeover. Among these were about 900,000 turncoat troops, soldiers who had voluntarily surrendered, and prisoners-of-war; about 400,000 government employees and teaching staff; and 100,000 state-operated enterprises' employees.[1]

The Communists claim that various groups were in league: secret agents, bandits, tyrants, reactionary parties, and reactionary religious sects (referring to secret societies). Together, these groups arranged about fifteen "guerrilla bases" in the Southwest. Also by these accounts, approximately 80,000 "spies" were left behind by the KMT armies, having been instructed by the KMT to contact local powerholders; and about one million bandit

---

1. *Hsin-Hua yüeh-pao* [New China Monthly] (Peking) [hereafter *HHYP*], No. 6 (1950), pp. 1350-1352.

guerrillas were organized. The Communists maintain that while a part of these groups were engaged in open warfare, others concealed themselves within factories, mines, government organs, schools, mass groups, democratic parties, and in various trade workshops in order to carry out destruction.[2] Local power-holders, in particular landlords, delayed paying taxes and, the Communists assert, conspired to disrupt the tax collection.[3]

Finally, the Communist victory caused the flight of approximately 15,000 Nationalist troops into Burma. These troops, under a General Li Mi, formed an anti-Communist force that maintained itself on the mountainous Yunnan frontier. From this base, the force frequently made small-scale, hit-and-run intrusions into Yunnan, from the time of takeover until at least mid-1952. The Chinese charged, and the United States did not openly deny, that flights from Taiwan aided by the United States brought supplies to the group.[4]

Westerners living in Szechwan and Yunnan corroborate this account, insofar as they agree on the widespread presence of resistance activity. Skinner, for example, living in Chengtu, noted initial distrust of the invading military and their political workers from provinces to the north. He saw that this was coupled with apprehension, which eventually turned to hostility, toward the Communist program.[5]

However, these sources trace the resistance to specific behavior of the liberating armies.[6] Mainly, there was opposition to a recollection of the 1949 grain tax that was undertaken by the Communists to maintain their occupying troops and the hundreds of

2. *Hsin-Hua jih-pao* [New China Daily] (Chungking) [hereafter *HHJP*], November 21, 1951, p. 2.

3. *HHYP*, No. 11 (1950), pp. 1063-1065; *HHJP*, October 25, 1950.

4. George V. H. Moseley, *The Consolidation of the South China Frontier* (1973), p. 34. See also *New York Times*, April 26, 1951; June 15, 1951; July 28, 1951; August 3, 1951; August 5, 1951; December 28, 1951; May 25, 1952; June 14, 1952; July 12, 1952.

5. G. W. Skinner, "Aftermath of Communist Liberation in the Chengtu Plain," *Pacific Affairs* 24, No. 1 (1951), pp. 61-76.

6. The following is based on: Skinner, "Aftermath"; W. G. Sewell, *I Stayed in China* (1966), pp. 73 ff; L. Earl Willmott, "Tentative Manuscript for Diary of a Revolution," (unpublished manuscript), quoted by permission of the author; "The Situation in Kunming," *Far Eastern Economic Review* [hereafter *FEER*] 9, No. 5 (1950), pp. 135-136.

thousands of turncoats.[7] Also, the new government's policy of eliminating silver specie and demanding that it be exchanged for *jen-min-pi* (the new Communist currency) was unpopular among the people. Apparently, mass lack of confidence in the new regime caused problems for this policy, and a wave of inflation followed as people tried to hoard silver.

Finally, an anti-Communist source attributes the resistance to three issues: the grain tax, monetary difficulties, and a third issue—an order to hand over the guns that individuals held for their own protection and on which rural village leaders partially depended for their local positions of power.[8] This source describes the solidification of revolt around the secret societies. It claims that although rebellion was organized by old KMT personnel, some democratic parties, and some local gentry, all these groups were led by local secret society chiefs.[9]

According to all these sources, the resistance groups cut transport lines to stop the flow of supplies. They refused to pay the grain levy and engaged in armed rebellion. Apparently, their uprising was only quelled as the rank-and-file secret society members were won over and their leaders arrested and killed.[10]

Related to the bandit problem were troubles in trade. The originally difficult situation in commerce was aggravated as communications lines were cut. Attendant shortages caused prices to fluctuate so that inflation became rampant. Also, there were larger than usual discrepancies between the prices of given items in different localities.[11] Local products were more unmarketable than ordinarily, and industry and trade stagnated. Speculating merchants were quick to take advantage of the crippled market.

Moreover, additional problems plagued finance in the South-

---

7. In February and March 1950, a grain tax was levied on each farmer. According to Skinner, the total amount levied at this time, at least in the Chengtu Plain, was about 25 percent larger than that which the KMT had already collected on the same crop the autumn before. See Skinner, "Aftermath," p. 64.

8. *Ibid.*, p. 126.

9. Liu Chin, *Ch'uan K'ang i-shou ch'ien-hou* [Before and After Szechwan and Sikang Changed Hands] (1956), p. 152.

10. *Ibid.*, pp. 144-153.

11. Huang Fu-chung, "Hsi-nan ch'eng-hsiang kuan-hsi ti hsien mien-mao" [The New Look in Urban-Rural Relations in the Southwest], *Ching-chi chou-pao* [Economic Weekly] (Shanghai) 12, No. 18 (1951), pp. 16-17.

west. Since an insufficient amount of taxes was collected, there was an imbalance between income and expenditure. The resultant huge deficit meant that the Southwest had to be heavily dependent on subsidies from the central government.[12] Industry had been damaged by the recent civil war and from plunder by escaping KMT troops. Also, many of the enterprises in the Southwest had been converted to serving the war effort when the KMT government was stationed in the Southwest during World War II, and had never been readapted to peacetime production. Capital and raw materials were scarce, and the numbers of the unemployed were many.[13] In the villages too, agriculture, handicrafts, and sideline work were depressed; a summer drought marked the first post-liberation harvest; and water conservancy works were in disrepair.[14]

In transportation, the 244 kilometers of extant rail lines were negligible in proportion to the size of the area, figured at 1,300,000 square kilometers.[15] And whereas the average density of rail lines (in kilometers of line per 1,000 square kilometers of land) was two for Mainland China as a whole and as high as twelve in the Northeast, for the Southwest it was less than .2.[16] Similarly, the density of highways here was four, while the national average was six, and the number for East China as high as fifteen. The density of both railroads and highways in the Southwest ranked last among the six Great Administrative Regions.[17]

Besides problems with counter-revolutionaries, commerce, finance, and communications, new difficulties were associated with the national minorities in this period. Counter-revolutionary guerrillas in Yunnan based themselves in hill areas where the minority tribes resided, and were probably protected by these tribes. In fact, one analyst claims that in Yunnan it was the minorities who were most resistant to Communist rule.[18]

12. *HHYP*, No. 12 (1950), p. 1232.
13. *HHYP*, No. 6 (1950), pp. 1350-1352.
14. *HHYP*, No. 11 (1950), p. 996.
15. Norton Ginsburg, "China's Administrative Boundaries," *FEER* 10, No. 4 (1951), p. 106.
16. See Wu Yuan-li, *The Spatial Economy of Communist China* (1967), pp. 13, 115, 118, 135, 137.
17. *Ibid.*, p. 118.
18. Moseley, *Consolidation*, pp. 35-37.

Thus the local political autonomy and separatism, disjointed trade, and cultural disparities that were hallmarks of the Southwest during the Republican era continued to set the Southwest apart, and complicated takeover for the Communists here. The first step in reforming this area according to Communist prescriptions was to bring the provinces here together through military and administrative measures, so that the underlying similarities throughout the area could be tackled systematically.

Military Takeover and the
Imposition of Regional-Level Organs

Takeover

The military campaign that liberated the provinces here constituted the conclusion of the Chinese civil war, and linked these provinces into the final of six Great Administrative Regions in China.[19] This campaign began in October 1949 and was planned to be a two-pronged one. It was carried out almost simultaneously by forces of the First Field Army under General Ho Lung moving down from the Northwest on the one hand, and by troops of the Second Field Army of General Liu Po-ch'eng coming westward from recently liberated East and Central-South China, on the other.

First, the main force of Liu's army advanced westward after the liberation of Canton and concentrated in west Hunan province. At the same time, another part of the same army, under the cover of Lin Piao's Fourth Field Army, pretended to be aiming only at attacking warlords in Kwangsi, but, after the defeat of the troops there, moved on to conquer Kweichow and south and east Szechwan. Thus, the Second Army was split: its troops gathering in Hunan were advancing quietly to avoid undue attention; and its forces under Lin Piao appeared to be still concerned with the Southeast. But ultimately they were heading toward the same destination.

19. The following is based on: *HHYP*, No. 4 (1950), p. 882; Li Ta, "Chieh-fang ta hsi-nan chih chan" [The Campaign to Liberate the Great Southwest], in *Hsing-huo liao-yüan* [Sparks Light up the Prairie] (1958), 10:475-485; William W. Whitson, *The Chinese Communist High Command* (1973), pp. 187-189; *HHYP*, No. 7 (1950), p. 22.

Meanwhile, Ho Lung's Eighteenth Army had been detached from the First Field Army stationed in the Northwest. Since early September, Ho's army had been feinting in southern Shansi (on Szechwan's northern border) to distract KMT General Hu Tsung-nan and lead him to believe that the main attack on the Southwest would be launched from the north.

After the various armies of the Second Field Army joined forces and liberated most of Kweichow, they proceeded northward to subdue Szechwan. Once the east and south of that province had fallen, Chungking was taken on November 30. Ho Lung then began to edge slowly southward toward Chengtu, in the wake of the turncoating of KMT Generals Teng Hsi-hou and P'an Wen-hua of Szechwan, and of governors Lu Han and Liu Wen-hui of Yunnan and Sikang provinces, respectively, on December 9. Soon afterward, many KMT regiments trying to escape to Sikang successively surrendered. The People's Liberation Army (PLA) continued to take over remaining pockets in north Szechwan and Kweichow throughout December; Chengtu was captured on December 27.

With their shift in allegiance to the Communist side, the governors of Yunnan and Sikang proclaimed the peaceful Communist liberation of their provinces. However, the PLA did not take over the administration of these areas until early March, since units of the Second Field Army still had to carry out mop-up campaigns, first in Yunnan and then in Sikang. Continuous defections of local Nationalist troops contributed to victory in each area.

Thus, though the conquest of the Southwest was organized to be carried out in a piecemeal fashion, the moves of the various PLA armies were well coordinated throughout the area. The conquering forces—Ho's Eighteenth Army and Liu's Second Field Army—remained to cooperate as garrisons and governors for this block of Southwest provinces.

The Imposition of Regional-Level Organs

In each of the six Great Administrative Regions created in the wake of takeover, regional-level military, administrative, and Party organs were set up. The very institution of this apparatus meant that, for purposes of control, governance, and development, the provinces within each such area were to be handled more or less uniformly. It also meant that programs and policies would be applied on a regional basis during the period when this apparatus existed; and that provisional laws pertinent to each area of jurisdiction could be promulgated at the regional level according to particular regional problems.[20]

The administrative organ received the most press coverage of the three regional organs. In the Southwest, General Liu Po-ch'eng was appointed Chairman of the new region's Military Administrative Committee in the fourth meeting of the Central People's Government Council in December 1949.[21] While this Committee was to serve as the governing organ in the area, it was not instituted until July 27, 1950, when its First Plenum was held.[22] Its members were not formally appointed until the fifty-fifth meeting of the Government Administrative Council in November 1950.[23]

By the end of 1950, the Committee was listed as housing four coordinating committees: a Finance-Economic Committee, a Culture-Education Committee, a Committee for Nationalities Affairs, and a People's Supervisory Commission. The Finance-Economic Committee was to direct and coordinate the work of the Departments of Finance, Trade, Industry, Communications, Labor, Agriculture-Forestry, and Water Conservancy, and also the Bureau of Cooperative Affairs. The Culture-Education Committee supervised the Departments of Public Health and Culture and Education, and the Bureau of News and Publications. Temporarily the Departments of Civil Affairs, Public Security, and Justice were without a coordinating committee.[24] By the end of the next year, however, two new committees were added to the apparatus: a Political-Legal Committee to direct the Civil Affairs, Public Security, and Justice Departments; and a Land Reform

20. On this last point, see the "Organic Law of the New Regional Government Councils," translated in *Current Background* [hereafter *CB*], No. 170 (1952), pp. 19-22, Article 3.

21. *Jen-min jih-pao* [People's Daily] (Peking) [hereafter *JMJP*], December 5, 1949.

22. *CB*, No. 27 (1950), p. 6.

23. *Survey of China Mainland Press* [hereafter *SCMP*], No. 13 (1950), p. 12.

24. See *Jen-min shou-ts'e* [People's Handbook] [hereafter *JMST*] 1951 (1951), pp. 卯, 34-38. See also *CB*, No. 170 (1952), pp. 20-21.

Committee.[25] Subsequent chapters will look at the work of some of these bodies and try to determine their respective roles in running the region. (See Figure 1.)

Besides the Military Administrative Committee, two other regional-level structures shared in the management of each region. First was the Regional Party Bureau, a branch of the Central Committee of the Chinese Communist Party (CCP). Second was the Military Region, set up immediately after take-over and controlled by the troops that had participated in the takeover.

There will be more occasion to comment on the work of the Party and its changing functions over time in Chapter Four. Briefly, its principal roles were to coordinate the numerous Party branches being created within every organ—administrative, military, educational, industrial, rural—in the Southwest area; to mobilize mass movements; and to insure the constancy and effectiveness of political propaganda work on all policies. As we shall see later on, the Party's initial duties all lay within the ideological realm, but as the number of Party members grew with time, the scope of its work increased accordingly.

The troops under the Military Region were involved in many kinds of work on a local basis, including the following: taking over cities; exterminating bandits; helping the minorities in construction, production, and health work; reforming KMT turncoat troops; supporting the war against Korea; training cadres; propagandizing and organizing the masses; helping in building local political organs; public security; road construction; agricultural production; land reclamation; water conservancy; and national defense work.[26] The military also organized the masses into local militia organs.[27]

However, there were various tasks that belonged to the top regional military command, by virtue of which the Military

25. See *JMST*, 1952, pp. 184-185. Also, new bureaus were apparently added as work needs demanded. Thus, there are references to a Food Grains Bureau, placed under the Finance-Economic Committee on October 29, 1951; a Geological Bureau; a Light Industries Bureau; a Tax Affairs Management Bureau; and a Building Construction Bureau, to name a few.
26. *HHJP*, October 20, 1950; December 19, 1951; October 1, 1952; February 13, 1953; and *SCMP*, No. 775 (1954), pp. xi-xiii; No. 400 (1952), pp. 20-21; No. 376 (1952), p. 20; No. 400 (1952), p. 22; No. 766 (1954), pp. 29-30.
27. *SCMP*, No. 596 (1953), pp. 30-31; No. 793 (1954), pp. ix-xi; and *HHJP*, February 13, 1953.

The Political-Legal Committee and the Land Reform Committee were created sometime in 1952, although the departments under the Political-Legal Committee were in existence from 1950. After 1952, when the Military Administrative Committee was changed in name to Administrative Committee, all the departments were changed into bureaus, some of which were taken over directly by competent departments of the central government (See Chapter Four). Also, references are made in the press to other departments, apparently created sometime after 1952. These include the Food Grains Department and the Geology Department. See also footnote 25.

Key

Committee = *wei-yüan-hui*
Department = *pu*
Bureau = *chü*

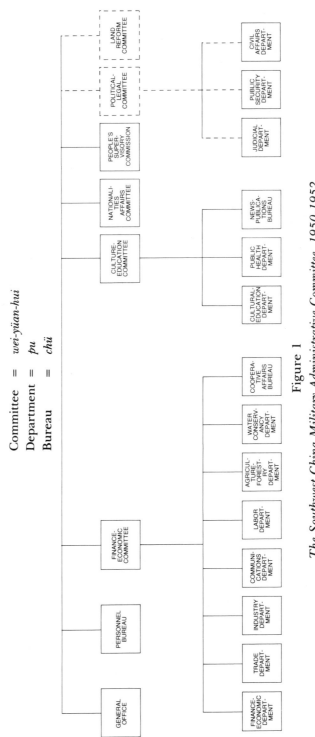

Figure 1

The Southwest China Military Administrative Committee, 1950-1952

Region served as a separate regional government, with jurisdiction over military affairs. First, the Southwest Military Region had a military court which had the power to decide on criminal punishment for important counter-revolutionaries. It was empowered to execute the top ringleaders among these elements who had been arrested in the region.[28]

Second, the Military Region had a large role in planning and implementing the campaign to liberate Tibet.[29] Third, it was responsible for organizing the construction and labor supply for the Chengtu-Chungking Railway, begun in June 1950.[30] Fourth, the Military Region had a part in impelling the land reform movement. Its units transferred cadres to compose land reform work groups, under the direction of the Military Region's Political Department.[31] These four areas of work—criminal punishment, military and labor conscription, and social reform—were of major significance, and in coordinating them, the Military Region made its presence felt as a unified high-level military command for the Southwest.

To summarize the argument to this point, the Southwest which confronted the invading PLA armies in late 1949 and early 1950 was essentially different from the rest of the country because of the configuration of local-level autonomy that had been present here during Republican years. The Communist advance, moreover, had aroused the most recalcitrant groups to militancy; and adverse reaction to the CCP's new programs initially aggravated the already problematic situation in transport and commerce. However, with military conquest and the creation of all-regional

28. *HHJP*, October 19, 1951; December 3, 1951. On p. 188, Liu Chin, *Ch'uan K'ang*, also mentions a Southwest Military Administrative Committee Special Military Tribunal which interrogated high-level KMT commanders and politicians and sentenced them to hard labor.

29. *HHJP*, November 2, 1950, and November 12, 1950. See also Chang Kuo-hua, "Hsi-tsang hui-tao le tsu-kuo ti huai-pao" [Tibet Returns to the Fatherland's Embrace], in *Hsing-huo liao yüan* [Sparks Light Up the Prairie] (1958), 10:525-543.

30. *HHJP*, November 26, 1950. Work on this railroad—including surveying, design, and roadbed construction—was begun as early as 1903, and sporadic attempts were made to complete the construction under the KMT. According to the Communists, however, these efforts were quite preliminary. See *HHJP*, December 6, 1951, p. 2.

31. *HHJP*, October 30, 1951.

organs, the disparate and rebellious localities were at least united for purposes of control and rule. The next section will consider the steps taken to pacify the area and integrate it into the nation.

Center-Region Interaction and
Gradual Integration into the Nation

This section will examine the process of integrating the Southwest provinces, once they had been constituted as an Administrative Region, into the nation. It will contain three themes. The first is that the Southwest, liberated last and replete with difficulties from the Communists' point of view, was perceived as a backward region, which had to be coaxed along. In fact, at times it was not even possible to wait for sufficient conditions before pushing onward in the Southwest when a new policy was declared nationally.

The other two themes relate to the process of integration, which had two phases. The second theme is that in the initial phase of integration, the function of the regional organs was to apply nationally set programs and centrally formulated policies to the area. This in turn would synchronize administration within the Southwest, in the ultimate interests of creating a unified nation. The third theme is that in the second phase there was a gradual integration of the area into the nation, as the local leaders' focus of attention progressively shifted from purely local problems to those being dealt with across the country.

The overall process can best be understood by assuming a tension between the central government's need to unify the country and the Southwest's need to deal with its own special problems. This tension appeared in the interplay between centrally designated tasks on the one hand, and the accomplishments and problems in work in the Southwest, on the other. As time went on, however, there was an increasing mesh between what was happening in the Southwest at a given point in time and what was happening nationally. The interpretation that follows relies entirely on the official press accounts of the period.

In July 1950, when the Southwest Military Administrative Committee held its First Plenum, the Third Plenum of the Seventh Central Committee of the CCP had recently convened. If the work tasks set out at the two conferences are compared, a striking contrast emerges. At the Southwest plenum, the first concerns were to consolidate the national defense line in the Southwest, to continue to wipe out bandits, to carry out the rent reduction movement (the precursor to land reform), and to restore and develop the economy.[32]

At the national Party conference, however, the first priority was to carry forward the land reform.[33] Next followed an order to consolidate unified control in finance and economic work, a task that presupposed that economic recovery work was well under way in localities other than the Southwest. A third instruction, to begin to demobilize the PLA, was in sharp conflict with the Southwest's concern with national defense and bandits. Other Southwest tasks, such as overcoming local natural disasters, prohibiting opium, and doing work among the minorities, had no national analogues.

Moreover, the description of work in the Southwest was phrased in terms intimately tied up with the special character of Southwest society. Thus, Chairman Liu Po-ch'eng spoke of the "obvious political nature" of the bandit activity in the Southwest, and of the "very deep conservative feudal power on which it relies" when he called for bandit suppression. Addressing the question of the rent reduction movement, he noted that "in the Southwest . . . land is very concentrated," that "warlords, bureaucrats, local ruffians, and oppressive gentry have robbed others and concentrated land by hook or crook." As to economic construction, the Southwest was to stress transport rehabilitation and construction. Other work too, such as liberating Tibet and reorganizing the turncoat troops, related specifically to the distinctiveness of post-liberation conditions in the Southwest.

A last example of Southwest specialness was its cadre problem. Chairman Liu pointed out to the plenum the weakness of the cadre force presently governing the area. He explained that, of the approximately 180,000 local work cadres, those from the old liberated areas and the army along with underground Party cadres in the area numbered only 30,000, or about one-sixth of the total number of cadres. While this small fraction was to form the backbone of the working force, about one-half of the total

32. *HHYP*, No. 11 (1950), pp. 996-999.
33. *CB*, No. 1 (1950), pp. 3-5.

cadres were leftover old KMT personnel. The rest were newly and hastily trained youths and students. As of July 27, 1950, small numbers of active elements among the workers and peasants were just beginning to be recruited as cadres.

Thus, the initial focus of attention of the Southwest leadership just after takeover was the special nature of the Southwest and the distinctive character of the difficulties there. Later, this was to change as the Southwest progressively became a part of the nation.

During the years when the Southwest Military Administrative Committee existed (1950-1952), the Southwest leadership constantly stressed that the tasks outlined by the center were heavy. Accomplishments, if steady and increasing with time, were often greatly tempered by weaknesses in work. Throughout 1950, a whole spate of social reform tasks, assigned by the central level, were the focus of the Military Administrative Committee's efforts. First, peasants had to be organized and mobilized into peasant associations and militia organs in order to dissociate them from the control of the feudal secret societies and to fashion a support base for Communist policies in the countryside. Industrial management was to undergo democratic reform and private industrialists taught to contribute to national construction. Employed workers had to be unionized and relief was needed for the unemployed.

Intellectuals and teachers were to undergo cultural reform in order to remold their bourgeois thought. Work with members of the minority nationalities needed to be strengthened and everyone had to learn patriotism and love for the fatherland. Cadres had to be trained and their work style required rectification. The local all-circles' representative conferences had to be convened, to engage the masses in a form of democratic participation in the daily affairs of their lives. Finally, Tibet was still to be liberated, and this campaign would be in part the responsibility of the PLA forces stationed in the Southwest.[34]

In the face of this awesome list of centrally imposed tasks, achievements in work in the Southwest during 1950 were notable. In dealing with the bandits, an initial policy of leniency[35] was soon

34. *HHYP*, No. 11 (1950), p. 996.
35. Liu Chin, *Ch'uan K'ang*, p. 92; Sewell, *I Stayed*, p. 86.

switched to one of military extermination.[36] By July 1950, Chairman Liu reported that, except in the frontier districts and the mountains, bandit and secret-agent activity had received a fatal blow.[37] Then, less than three months later on National Day, it was claimed that the chief bandit bands were fundamentally liquidated and social order established. Four hundred thousand bandits reportedly had been annihilated.[38]

This achievement laid the groundwork for various other phases of work and lent an air of euphoria to the general outlook in the Southwest. The recollection of the 1949 grain levy was basically fulfilled.[39] Industrial and commercial activities were set in motion in May 1950, spurred on by the start of work on the Chengtu-Chungking Railway in that month. Urban-rural trade increased as highways became safer for trade. State-operated commercial organs invested in local products, regulated shipping, and promoted the sale of native goods.[40]

A foundation was created for mobilization of the peasantry in the course of grain collection and bandit suppression. Peasant associations were set up in the majority of *hsien* (counties) and *ch'ü* (districts), ready to take on their role as leaders in the rent reduction movement due to begin in late autumn. Cadres were being trained, schools set up, and minorities were getting aid of all forms.[41]

However, the hardships facing the new administration were still outstanding and almost seemed to counterbalance the successes. Thus, while prices were stabilized, a large deficit existed.[42] Although industry had undergone some regulation, the cadres in the Southwest basically lacked experience in this field.[43] And, more important, whereas there had been some success in counter-revolutionary work, feudal power was still said to be in control

36. *HHJP*, November 21, 1951.
37. *HHYP*, No. 11 (1950), p. 996.
38. *CB*, No. 20 (1950), pp. 21-22.
39. See footnote 7 above.
40. *HHYP*, No. 11 (1950), p. 1064.
41. *Ibid.*; see also Chang Chi-ch'ün, "Kuan-yü hsi-nan ch'ü chien-tsu wen-t'i ti pao" [Report on Questions in Rent Reduction in the Southwest], in *Cheng-fu kung-tso pao-kao hui-pien* [Compilation of Government Work Reports] (1951), pp. 1005-1010.
42. *HHYP*, No. 11 (1950), p. 996. See also *HHYP*, No. 12 (1950), p. 1232.
43. *HHYP*, No. 12 (1950), p. 1232.

of the countryside, bandit and secret-agent activity was still rampant in some areas, and the masses had yet to be fully organized and indoctrinated with the Communist ideology.[44]

In spite of this mixed situation in the Southwest, the imposition of centrally planned programs had to go on. Thus, by November 1950, the waves of the "anti-despot, reduce-rent, return-deposits movement" began successively to hit various areas in the Southwest.[45] By February 1951, the movement had been launched throughout the region, and in May was concluded everywhere except in Yunnan.[46] Next, in selected localities of north and south Szechwan, key point land reform was begun. This set in motion a series of four stages, whereby areas with fewer complications and lesser concentrations of minority settlements carried out the land reform first, while the work in areas with relatively more problems was delayed to later stages.[47]

Another centrally outlined plan was the invasion of Tibet. By the spring of 1950, Ho Lung had already begun to plan the invasion. The actual attack was carried out by Chang Kuo-hua's Eighteenth Corps of the Second Field Army, plus elements of Ho's Eighteenth Army. These forces were joined by troops of the First Field Army coming south from Tsinghai in the Northwest. By October the invasion had begun; and in May 1951, an agreement was signed for the "peaceful liberation" of Tibet. Within another six months Communist military control was firmly established there,[48] under the aegis of a military administrative committee and a military area headquarters set up in Tibet by the May agreement.[49]

The support functions for the invasion of Tibet had been the responsibility of the Southwest Military Administrative Committee. These included the reconstruction of roads and the erection of bridges for the march, as well as the provision of supplies and manpower.[50] Thereafter, however, Tibet was not administered as part of the jurisdiction of the Southwest Military Administrative

44. *Ibid.*
45. Chang Chi-ch'ün, "Chien-tsu wen-t'i," p. 1005.
46. *SCMP*, No. 105 (1951), pp. 34-35.
47. *SCMP*, No. 343 (1952), pp. 32-33.
48. Whitson, *High Command,* pp. 192-193; Chang Kuo-hua, "Hsi-tsang."
49. *CB,* No. 76 (1951).
50. Robert B. Rigg, *Red China's Fighting Hordes* (1951), pp. 305-308.

Committee, and was once described as an autonomous region on a level corresponding to the other Great Administrative Regions.[51]

Yet another task imposed on the Southwest during this period involved the consolidation of commercial affairs within the Southwest. A Southwest Trade Work Conference was held in January 1951 to promote the exchange of the minority regions' local products.[52] State-operated trade companies had organized small mobile teams to buy up native products in the various localities throughout the area. These companies were instructed at the conference to promote sales, organize supply and marketing cooperatives, set up trading stations, promote buying and selling on commission, and encourage private merchants to go to the minority districts to do business.

At the end of that same month, the Second Southwest Military Administrative Committee Plenum was held. By this time, the work tasks enumerated to the participants had a more universalistic tone than those specified at the First Southwest Plenum six months earlier: to develop the nationally planned "Resist-America-Aid-Korea Movement"; to speed up the land reform; to continue to stabilize prices and develop industry, trade, and agriculture; to strengthen cultural and educational work; and to consolidate the democratic united front. By this time, the call to suppress counter-revolutionaries had moved down from being the number-two priority it had been at the First Plenum to being number five.[53]

However, even at this point the Southwest situation alone could not have accounted for the imposition of the new tasks, for the problems in work were still outstanding. Although the Southwest Military Administrative Committee was promoting national programs, the region still retained its basically backward character. Again, however, its apparent achievements were impressive: success was claimed in annihilating bandits, communications were said to be restored, goods exchange was occurring smoothly. Big bandit chiefs had been suppressed, and initial success had been made in banning reactionary sects. Peasant associations had been regulated and more than ten million peasants were now

51. *SCMP*, No. 737 (1954), pp. 28-31.
52. *HHYP*, No. 17 (1951), pp. 1114-1116; pp. 1116-1118; pp. 1119-1120.
53. *HHJP*, January 31, 1951.

members; over one million peasants had joined the militia ranks. The public grain tax collection had been completed and prices were stable; and there had been progress in culture and education, in the rectification of cadres, and in minority work.

On the negative side, though, some landlords were still conspiring to destroy these accomplishments; bandits and secret agents continued to carry out covert sabotage; and mass mobilization was incomplete. Moreover, since financial power in the Southwest was limited, there were still many economic problems that would be hard to solve for a time. And in the management of factories and mines and in the schools a lack of experience obstructed work. From this it appears that the Southwest leadership was compelled to push forward despite shortcomings, and to continue to widen the focus of the local population's attention to encompass nationally set goals even before all the particular problems of the Southwest were solved.

By November 1951 when the Military Administrative Committee's Third Plenum was held, the most important tasks for the future were announced to be the "patriotic campaign to increase production and practice strict economy" and the campaign for ideological reform.[54] These were also the work items stressed at the Third Session of the First National Committee of the Chinese People's Political Consultative Conference held in late October.[55] And they were the same tasks set at other regional meetings throughout the country held at the same time.[56] At the meeting, it was claimed that the Southwest was now "catching up with," even if still basically behind, the rest of the country.[57]

Though once again one gets the impression that achievements were offset by problems, the stated balance appears by now to be weighted in the direction of the successes. Thus, Tibet had been liberated, the campaign to Resist America had been developed everywhere, and two phases had been completed in the land reform movement in the Southwest. The counter-revolutionary

54. *CB*, No. 146 (1951), pp. 23-24.
55. *CB*, No. 130 (1951), pp. 2-3, and *CB*, No. 134 (1951), pp. 2-16.
56. Regarding the Northwest Military Administrative Committee, see *SCMP*, No. 228 (1951), pp. 10-12; on the East China Military Administrative Committee, see *SCMP*, No. 220 (1951), pp. 14-15; on the Central-South Military Administrative Committee, see *SCMP*, No. 222 (1951), pp. 18-19.
57. *HHJP*, November 21, 1951, p. 1.

suppression movement had gone through a high tide, presumably at the instigation of the harsh "Statute on Punishment for Counter-Revolutionary Activity," passed nationally by the Government Administrative Council in February 1951.[58] Also, social order was achieved, and the people's political power consolidated. Prices were stable, industry and agriculture were recovering and beginning to develop; and both public and private industry had begun democratic reform. Trade in local products was planned and organized, transport facilities were greatly expanded, and the Chengtu-Chungking Railway was bringing life to stagnant industries, stimulating trade, and providing employment. A beginning had been made in the thought reform of intellectuals and in reorganizing the schools; and more than 150 minority political power organs had been set up.

Probably because of these accomplishments, regional weaknesses were no longer discussed in terms of the Southwest's specialness, as they had been at the First Plenum, and the problems that persisted were not emphasized so strongly. Thus, it was reported that mass mobilization was uneven, goods were in short supply, and progress in democratic reform and ideological reform was still incomplete. Then, some bandits were still stationed on the border and in mountain areas, and secret agents had apparently infiltrated various organs and enterprises and were subverting normal work operations. And poor peasants and hired laborers were having problems in production after land reform, since there was a shortage of draft animals and fertilizer.[59]

The interesting point here, however, is that by this time the Southwest government was organizing its problems and its tasks in the jargon of the current national vocabulary. The focus of its leadership had "caught up with" the rest of the country. As its work shifted away from simply attacking the particular obstructions that the Southwest area itself posed to the Communist program, it was taking on tasks proposed at the national level. The era of concern with problems immediately connected with liberation was passing.

58. "Statute on Punishment for Counter-Revolutionary Activity, 1951," in Albert P. Blaustein, ed., *Fundamental Legal Documents of Communist China* (1962), pp. 215-221.
59. *HHJP*, November 16, 1951.

Following the Third Southwest Plenum, in 1952 the area was occupied with two sets of mass movements, one urban and one rural. Both these movements were also being promoted nationally during that year. In retrospect, they can be viewed as helping to lay the groundwork for the imminent program of large-scale national economic and cultural construction announced in the autumn of 1952.

The urban component, the *san-fan* and *wu-fan* (three-anti and five-anti) movements, grew out of the campaign of late 1951 to increase production, economize, and fight against corruption and waste. These new campaigns attacked various forms of malpractice, first within the Party and state organs, and second, within the bourgeois class. In the course of the *wu-fan* movement much of private industry was brought under government control and its capital transferred to the state. In the countryside, the mutual-aid and cooperative movement was spurred on by an editorial on January 1, 1952, in *Jen-min jih-pao*. The article held that agriculture carried out on an organized basis could make a more efficient contribution to national construction.

After some successes had been registered in these movements, on October 1, 1952, it was announced in Peking that the restoration of China's economy was completed.[60] Also on National Day, Kao Kang, Chairman of the Northeast region Military Administrative Committee and head of the State Planning Commission, spoke on the need for planning in greeting the new period of economic construction.[61]

In the midst of this national mood stressing the conclusion of economic recovery work and the anticipation of development, the Fourth Southwest Military Administrative Committee Plenum was held in mid-December. The fact that the eve of the First Five Year Plan had arrived was made clear in the work report.[62] Emphasis was laid on the Southwest's duty to contribute to a national effort. Moreover, the tasks set out at the plenum were national ones, no longer taking the Southwest's special nature into account.

And yet the leadership was still aware, even then, that the

60. Richard L. Walker, *China Under Communism* (1955), p. 103. See also *New China's Economic Achievements, 1949-1952* (1952).
61. *HHYP*, No. 36 (1952), pp. 7-10.
62. *HHJP*, December 13, 1952, pp. 1-2.

Southwest was not yet fully up to par. In discussing the industrial situation in the Southwest, which, from the national perspective, was what mattered most at that point in time, Vice-Chairman Ho Lung told the Southwest Factory-Mine Work Conference held just before the plenum: "From the national viewpoint, compared with the other progressive regions, we are very far behind."[63] And Vice-Chairman Liu Wen-hui, in his opening address to the plenum, listed a series of accomplishments in the Southwest over the past year and concluded, "all these achievements have made the Southwest take on a new social aspect, and have given it *the possibility of joining the other districts* in the country to meet the upcoming national planned economic and cultural construction."[64] (Emphasis added.)

There is no way to know whether the Southwest was actually fully ready, by national standards, to participate in the country-wide construction effort by late 1952. More likely, the bulk of the nation was well enough prepared, and the Southwest could not be left out. On the one hand, beginning in September 1952, a chain of articles began to appear in the Southwest press crediting various undertakings with having made great achievements or having been successfully concluded. And certainly the stated accomplishments did counterbalance the weaknesses. But, on the other hand, there was an open admission that the Southwest was behind in industrial development, the most crucial aspect of work nationally at this time.

The many achievements covered numerous areas of work. In democratic political power construction, it was announced that as of August 1952 various levels of all-circles' representatives conferences had been held. At the province level, at least one meeting had now been held everywhere; in the areas other than Kweichow, Sikang, and East Szechwan, two meetings had been held. In the cities, five or six convenings had occurred; in *hsien*, four or five.[65]

In financial work, the factories, mines, and transport enterprises were all recovering and developing. Most of the important industrial products had surpassed pre-liberation peaks in output. The success of the *san-fan* and *wu-fan* movements had led to

63. *HHJP*, December 7, 1952.
64. *HHJP*, December 11, 1952.
65. *HHJP*, September 27, 1952.

stable commodity prices, lowered production costs, and improvements in quality. And encouragement of urban-rural exchange had solved the problems of market stagnation.[66]

Minority governments had been established on a wide scale, and measures had been taken to raise all aspects of the people's livelihood in these regions. Three academies had been set up for training minority cadres, and more than one hundred short-term training schools had been created. As a result, more than 25,000 minority cadres had been trained.[67]

In military work, the Southwest Military Region had basically concluded its twofold duty as a struggle force and a work brigade. Its fighters had killed one million "bandits," and had set up people's militia forces throughout the Southwest.[68] In rural work, the Southwest had "had a rather complete experience."[69] In higher education, regulation of the school system had set a foundation for introducing the specialized education necessary for national construction.[70]

Land reform, having gone through its third and fourth phases during the course of the year, was completed for 91.85 percent of the population. Twenty percent of the peasant households in the region had already been organized to take part in various kinds of mutual aid in labor. It was time now to consolidate temporary, seasonal mutual-aid teams and, where possible, to form regular, permanent teams; and at key points, to raise the strong teams to the level of agricultural producers' cooperatives.[71]

In the cities, industrial and mining enterprises were basically done with democratic reform; and seventeen universities had initially finished thought reform. The judicial reform movement that had swept across the entire country had been successful in the Southwest, and the majority of *hsien* now had health stations.[72]

In January 1953, the Southwest was said to have completed the restoration of its agriculture;[73] by February its communications

66. *HHJP*, September 29, 1952, p. 1.
67. *HHJP*, September 29, 1952, p. 2.
68. *HHJP*, October 1, 1952.
69. *HHJP*, December 7, 1952.
70. *HHJP*, December 11, 1952.
71. *HHJP*, December 13, 1952, pp. 1-2.
72. *Ibid.*
73. *SCMP*, No. 498 (1953), p. 24.

facilities were totally rehabilitated. Also by February peoples' representative conferences or peasant conferences had been convened in most of the *hsiang* (townships) throughout the area; 126 nationality autonomous areas and more than 380 nationality democratic coalition governments existed.[74].

However, in spite of this multi-faceted success, the Southwest was not really ready for large-scale industrial construction in the same sense that most of the country was. This was revealed in an article that appeared in the national *Jen-min jih-pao* in early 1953.[75] The article exposed the weaknesses and general state of disorganization in basic construction work in the Southwest. The hallmarks of the problem were "blindness" and "decentralization." Blindness referred to a lack of investigation, research, preparation, and specialized organization in work. Decentralization was manifested in haphazard use of manpower and materials and consequent waste. For several years, the article revealed, not even 70 percent of the Southwest's basic construction tasks had been fulfilled. This situation amounted to a particularly glaring deficiency at this point in time, when industrial development was the primary national goal.

Nevertheless, in the eyes of the central leadership bent on economic development planning, the Southwest henceforth had little individual identity separate from other parts of the country. From February 28, 1953 (when its Military Administrative Committee, like those in the other Great Regions, was demoted to Administrative Committee status),[76] until the time when regional government was abolished altogether in mid-1954,[77] the Southwest provinces were coordinated principally for purposes of implementing the national economic construction plan. The problems in the Southwest that had formerly been matters of concern were consequently slighted for the time.

In this vein, the Hong Kong *Ta-kung pao* published a series of

74. *SCMP*, No. 516 (1953), pp. 25-26.
75. *JMJP*, January 12, 1953.
76. The national regulation for Military Administrative Committees to be converted to Administrative Committees was promulgated on November 15, 1952. In the Southwest, changeover occurred in February. See *HHJP*, March 1, 1953.
77. Although the decree for abolition of regions came on June 19, 1954, the Southwest Administrative Committee was not dissolved until August. See *HHJP*, August 26, 1954.

articles characterizing each of China's six regions solely in terms of its outstanding economic traits. The Southwest was billed as "the area where communications are being developed and natural resources are being investigated."[78] The article pointed out that, in order to exploit the rich underground resources in the Southwest and provide the conditions for establishing an industrial base there, the state was making relatively sizable investments in the Southwest both in large-scale communications construction and in prospecting and surveying natural resources. Gradually, the view of the Southwest had shifted. No longer was it seen as an area with a particular character posing unique problems. Rather, now it was but a cog in the wheel of economic development for the First Five Year Plan.

The December 1952 Military Administrative Committee Plenum was the last plenum held at the regional government level in the Southwest. After the demise of the Military Administrative Committee, all-region administrative conferences were simply called "enlarged meetings." These were apparently abbreviated and single-focused gatherings whose only purpose was to transmit important central directives. Thus, the functions of regional administration in the Southwest were gradually being pared away.

The first such "enlarged meeting" was convened in late October 1953. On October 1, 1953, *Jen-min jih-pao* began to propagate the new general line of the state, which Mao later explained would entail the socialist transformation of agriculture, handicrafts, and private industry and commerce. Thereafter, from October 31 to November 2, the Southwest Administrative Committee held an enlarged meeting solely to pass on information about the content of the general line, and to provide a forum for influential officeholders to rally to its support.[79]

Then, at the Fourth Plenum of the Seventh Central Committee of the Party, held February 6 to 10, 1954, a resolution was passed on "strengthening the Party's solidarity." At the same time, an attack was launched against "splittism" and sectarianism within the Party and against pride and conceit among certain high-level

78. *Ta-kung pao*, February 9, 1954, translated in *CB*, No. 281 (1954), pp. 17-19.
79. *SCMP*, No. 686 (1953), pp. 30-31.

cadres.[80] Following this conference, the Southwest Regional Party Bureau held an enlarged session in mid-March to hear and discuss reports on the plenum's resolution.[81] Thereafter, the Southwest regional or first-grade level organs arranged study of the plenum's documents.[82] Finally, in late August 1954, an enlarged meeting of the Southwest Administrative Committee was convened to discuss how to implement the Central People's Government's decision on abolishing the regional organs and handing over work.[83] Thus, none of these Administrative Committee meetings showed the breadth of concern or the powers of organizing action that the Military Administrative Committee meetings had exhibited.

Reviewing the events in the Southwest from takeover up to the abolition of regional government, it is clear that the special problems in the Southwest provinces were gradually dealt with by the regional organs' promotion of national programs and policies throughout the area. Also, as these problems were tackled, the Southwest was progressively seen as having "caught up with" the rest of the country, and the regional leadership began to perceive national problems as local problems at the same point in time as the other regions were handling these same problems. However, this section has also stressed that a tension existed between central policy and the Southwest situation. Thus, even though this tension lessened with time as the Southwest did some catching up, the Southwest was essentially never quite ready in time for the next big push.

This chapter began with a view of the Southwest as an area divided into small localities along several dimensions and cut off from the rest of the country. The problems of malintegration that existed here before 1949 were intensified at takeover. However, the takeover campaign itself, followed by the institution of a set of all-regional organs, served initially to bring the provinces in the area together into one administrative whole.

The subsequent process of unification described here illustrates the concept of Integration I. For this concept pertains to

80. *HHYP,* No. 53 (1954), pp. 9-11.
81. *SCMP,* No. 787 (1954), pp. 7-8.
82. *SCMP,* No. 789 (1954), pp. 15-16.
83. *HHJP,* August 26, 1954.

the process by which the part—the Southwest area—is brought in to be a contributing member of the nation, responsive to and cooperative with other segments of the country and the central government. The main actors in this process in this case were the regional-level administrations, the Military Administrative Committee and then the Administrative Committee; their tools were the mass movement, the campaign, and the central policy.

The history described here has demonstrated that this process of Integration I involved two phases. First, under the Military Administrative Committee, geographical integration—the pulling together and unifying of component localities within the geographical part according to their special problems—preceded functional integration under the Administrative Committee— that means of coordination whereby work sectors are organized nationally from the center downward according to their function while local differences are ignored. The First Five-Year Plan, based on functional principles of organization, could not begin until the first three years of geographical integration had been completed. In the next chapter we shall see how these changes were effected administratively.

CHAPTER IV

Integration I: Changes in Administration as the Southwest Great Administrative Region Became Integrated into the Nation

The last chapter showed how the focus of the regional leadership's concern shifted as Integration I proceeded. It also noted how the Southwest gradually lost its special nature in the eyes of the central leadership as local problems were tackled and how, with new central economic goals, the new problems to be faced in the Southwest became ones generalized beyond the immediate Southwest context. This chapter will concentrate on the changes in administration that were involved as the Southwest area was integrated into the nation.

Chapter Three described Integration I as a two-step process, whereby a geographically based unification within the area paved the way for a later stage in which the area became a contributing part of the nation. Here this process will be discussed in more structural terms. The first section will focus on the role of the Military Administrative Committee from 1949 to 1952, emphasizing the methods and devices its leadership used to integrate the area administratively.

The next section, dealing with the second step in Integration I, will present evidence to show that the administrative system in the Southwest changed after 1952 as the regional government lost the initiative it had had in the earlier period. Various types of data offer insight into the mechanisms by which Integration I took place. These data illustrate by what means the basically geographical integration centered on the Southwest Great Administrative Region under the Military Administrative Committee (from 1949 to 1952) was shifted to a more functional type of integration under the Administrative Committee (from 1952 to 1954).

Geographical Integration: Administration under the Military Administrative Committee, 1949-1952

As explained in Chapter One, the Military Administrative Committee was initially designed to have a dual nature. It was to be the highest administrative authority in the localities (at the level just below the central government), and also the representative organ of the Government Administrative Council in directing the workings of the local governments.[1] This twofold role meant that the Military Administrative Committee acted with some initiative in certain matters, but also had a key part to play in serving as a go-between in the center's dealings with the provinces and levels below. Later, when Administrative Committees became the governing regional organs in November 1952, they lost the first of these functions, and were to be simply middlemen.[2] This section will describe the work of the Military Administrative Committee in terms of its two aspects.

The Highest Administrative Authority in the Localities

As the highest administrative authority in the localities, the Military Administrative Committee could issue directives or take certain other actions on its own initiative pertinent purely to the Southwest situation. Most often these directives and actions dealt with regulation of the economy in the Southwest. Analysis of this work helps to clarify the process of geographical integration, the first step in Integration I.

Directives published in the Southwest press will be the data base for this analysis. Those directives that made no mention of central instructions, of forwarding a central policy, or of being based on the spirit of a central report or meeting will be considered to have been promulgated on the Military Adminis-

1. *Current Background* [hereafter *CB*], No. 170 (1952), Article 3, p. 19.
2. *CB*, No. 245 (1953), pp. 10-11.

trative Committee's own initiative. According to these criteria, the normal and publicly discussed range of activity of the Military Administrative Committee was relatively large just after takeover, but became more limited as time went on.[3]

In 1950, just after takeover, the Military Administrative Committee had a wider range of responsibilities than it did later, basically for two reasons. First, certain measures had to be decided upon locally because, as shown in Chapter Three, the Southwest at this time was still afflicted by its own particular problems. For example, at that time the Military Administrative Committee ordered the banning of opium[4] and the repair of dikes.[5]

Second, certain areas of work could not be regulated on a national basis by the central government until the regional organs had organized these aspects of work locally. For example, the Southwest Military Administrative Committee Tax Management Bureau handled the unification of tax collection regionally before the Southwest was ready to respond to national guidelines.[6] Similarly, before liberation, more than one hundred kinds of instruments for measuring grain existed throughout the Southwest. In June 1950 the Food Grains Bureau of the Military Administrative Committee set a standard for scales, in order to unify trade transactions within the Southwest.[7] Thus, in the first year after takeover, the Military Administrative Committee had a crucial coordinating function to perform.

By 1951, however, Military Administrative Committee directives tended to become narrowed down to the following limited areas of work: intraregional trade,[8] production,[9] grain collection

3. The implicit assumption here is that one can learn about an administrative organ's responsibilities and powers by studying the range of its decision-making authority. Naturally, this ignores for the time being initiatives that can be taken during the implementation process. This is the subject of Chapter Seven.

4. *Hsin-Hua jih-pao* [New China Daily] (Chungking) [hereafter *HHJP*], November 13, 1950.

5. *HHJP*, November 24, 1950.

6. *HHJP*, December 30, 1950.

7. *HHJP*, October 18, 1950.

8. See, for example, *HHJP*, October 12, 1950, on state-operated companies; November 6, 1950, on sulphur-nitrate; September 12, 1951, on cotton yarn; October 18, 1951, on ox skins; and October 19, 1952, on the price of salt.

9. See *HHJP*, October 7, 1950, on controlling moths; October 21, 1951, on winter production; November 30, 1951, on oranges; September 23, 1952, on sowing; and December 17, 1952, on exterminating moths.

and granary upkeep,[10] and protection against the effects of un-
favorable weather conditions.[11] Apparently the Military Administrative Committee's role had become more circumscribed as
internal integration within the Southwest proceeded. Once the
early regulations and mass movements more or less standardized
the Southwest provinces' frame of reference, Military Administrative Committee directives came to emphasize more mundane
operations in economic work.

As time went on, and as the orders passed down by the Military
Administrative Committee tended more and more to concentrate
on economic matters, the committees or departments that most
often issued published directives were these: the Finance-Economic Committee or its subordinate Finance Department; and
the Departments of Trade and of Agriculture-Forestry, both of
which were under the Finance-Economic Committee. Moreover,
the number of orders related to economic affairs represented a
steadily increasing proportion of the total number of orders
issued in given periods over time.[12] In fact, insofar as regional-
level-initiated directives indicated a measure of control, this
control more and more belonged mainly to those organs under
the Military Administrative Committee concerned with finance
and economics. For, to judge from the directives, these were the
organs most involved in all-regional or regional-level affairs.

Through issuing these directives, the Military Administrative
Committee took charge of the active regulation of economic

10. See *HHJP*, October 22, 1950, on granary preparation; November 10,
1950, on paying attention to grain quality; September 20, 1952, on autumn
collection; and December 20, 1952, on strengthening grain protection work.
11. See *HHJP*, October 6, 1950, on preventing grain mold caused by rain;
October 17, 1950, on preparing for natural disasters; November 26, 1951, on
crop protection; and December 14, 1951, on protection against drought.
12. I have collected all the Military Administrative Committee directives
published in the Southwest press over a three-month period in the autumn of
1950, a three-month period in the autumn of 1951, and a four-month period in
the autumn of 1952. In 1950, there were forty-one such directives, of which
twenty-three, or just over one-half, concerned economic matters. In 1951, I
found a total of twenty Military Administrative Committee orders, of which
fourteen involved trade, production, and transport. Then, in 1952, I located
thirty-two Military Administrative Committee directives. Here twenty-three, or
nearly three-quarters, were published under the name of a department connected with the Finance-Economic Committee. Of the other offices under the
Military Administrative Committee, the Culture-Education Committee, the
Civil Affairs Department, and the Supervisory Commission issued regulations
occasionally; the Nationalities Affairs Committee and the Departments of Public
Security and Justice very rarely published any instructions.

affairs within the Southwest area. During the period when the Military Administrative Committee was in existence (from 1949 to 1952), this economic work covered the following: managing the trade, distribution, and prices of various materials; controlling the production process; designing the regional budget within the scope of the national budget; and unifying measurements, accounting units, wages, and taxation procedures within the Southwest area.

Particularly in late 1951, a series of articles appeared in the press on the management of certain goods, such as cotton, ox skins, and scrap tin.[13] These articles stressed the need to adjust supply so as to meet demand, to furnish production departments and the military with supplies, and to stabilize the market price. Purchasing units had to prove their need for the goods they demanded, obtain local and regional governmental approval, and buy from designated markets or state-operated companies. Local administrative organs were ordered to make a thorough examination of this type of work and report to higher levels on policy implementation. Trading in these items outside the Southwest region was strictly controlled.

Besides regulating the distribution of goods, the Military Administrative Committee monitored production in both agriculture and industry. Aside from the overall instructions that always came out of the large work conferences,[14] the Military Administrative Committee also sent down notices on particular problems at given points in time. An example of this in agriculture was an order to take care of winter wet fields.[15] In industry, bureaus under the Department of Industry called for raising the quality of products.[16] An attempt was made in each case to ensure that production was efficient and that production conditions were optimal throughout the entire region.

Organs under the Military Administrative Committee were also responsible for organizing the regional budget. An article in the autumn of 1950 explained how the Finance Department, the responsible organ, went about formulating the regional budget.

---

13. For example, *HHJP*, October 12, 1951, on cotton; October 18, 1951, on ox skins; November 19, 1951, on scrap tin.

14. As, *HHJP*, December 5, 1952.

15. *HHJP*, October 21, 1951.

16. For example, *HHJP*, December 1, 1951, on coal tar.

It carried out this task after collecting reports from the lower levels in an all-regional meeting. Before the meeting, the various localities first did key point investigation to calculate the past year's expenses, and then combined that with the following year's prospective situation to make an estimate of the next year's expenses.[17] According to the organizational principles of the several layers of government, each level could then set up a tentative budget within the scope of the national budget, subject to approval at the next higher level.[18] Presumably differences and compromises were finally worked out at meetings like this one, which was described as "twenty days of excited discussion."[19]

Finally, especially in 1950 and to some degree in 1951, the Military Administrative Committee played an important part in unifying economic accounting units, wages, and taxation procedures. In 1950, the Southwest Industry Department issued an instruction on unifying the accounting system, its categories, and forms within the region.[20] At the same time, the Southwest Trade Department was adjusting the seasonal discrepancies in exchange prices between industrial and agricultural products in the area;[21] it was also standardizing the types, prices, and amounts of goods which could be collected in kind for tax purposes in districts where crops other than grain were grown.[22] A year later, the Southwest Finance-Economic Committee set a wage scale to apply to all state-operated factories in the area.[23] Unification of these matters was doubtless a vital factor in organizing the Southwest area to act as an economic unit. And the area, so organized, could later be handled as one section of the larger nation in terms of its provinces' similarities for economic construction purposes.

If one looks at the types of matters on which the Military Administrative Committee publicly issued directives, at the types of organs that were most active in promulgating orders, and at the nature of economic work in the Southwest under the Military

17. *HHJP*, October 18, 1950, p. 2.
18. *CB*, No. 170 (1952), Article 3, p. 20; *Hsin-Hua yüeh-pao* [New China Monthly] (Peking) [hereafter *HHYP*], No. 4 (1950), pp. 866-870, on the region's and localities' powers in budgeting, respectively.
19. *HHJP*, October 18, 1950, p. 2.
20. *HHJP*, October 21, 1950.
21. *HHJP*, November 2, 1950, p. 2.
22. *HHJP*, November 2, 1950, p. 3.
23. *HHJP*, November 2, 1951.

Administrative Committee, it is possible to come to some tentative judgments about the Military Administrative Committee's role. Apparently, one of its major functions was the regulation and organization of financial and economic affairs in the Southwest. And in this area of work one of its major goals was to integrate the Southwest provinces during the period that ended in late 1952. After this time, the Southwest was supposedly ready to participate in the large-scale economic construction program being inaugurated nationally.

The Representative Organ of the Government Administrative Council

Aside from being the highest administrative authority below the central government, the Military Administrative Committee was also meant to act as a go-between, serving as the representative organ of the Government Administrative Council in the Southwest area. In this role, it was the duty of the Military Administrative Committee to transmit central directives, programs, and policies to the lower levels of government and to report back on their implementation. Since the typical central directive was passed downward by the Military Administrative Committee with almost no modification to fit the peculiarities of the Southwest, adaptation to locale was generally left to the implementing units below.[24] Thus, in matters where the Committee received central orders, its work was focused neither on decision-making, which was the prerogative of the center, nor on execution, which was the sphere of the levels below the region. Rather, its business was geared to connecting work in the localities with the tasks outlined at the center.

The Military Administrative Committee's role in this liaison work took several forms. It received, filed, and passed on reports to the central government pertaining to the lower levels' execution of central directives. Also, when central directives authorized the provinces to devise special measures in applying a policy, the

24. Numerous directives appearing in the press all bear this hallmark. For example, *HHJP*, November 2, 1950, on clearing up judicial cases; October 31, 1951, on marriage law implementation; December 24, 1951, on people's tribunals; September 22, 1952, on factory injuries; December 19, 1952, on tree felling.

province was required to notify the Military Administrative Committee as to the methods it utilized.[25]

Along these same lines, it was the job of the Military Administrative Committee and its organs to spot check the Southwest area and pinpoint problems and deviations in the implementation of central work tasks.[26] Where errors were found, the Military Administrative Committee was charged with diagnosing the problem and specifying remedies.[27] Where behavior was commendable, the regional organ was authorized to award prizes, based upon centrally set standards.[28]

The regional level was also a crucial link in any mass movement or campaign, because it was to activate the successive levels below it to create committees to promote the movement, and was to outline the procedures they were to follow.[29] Finally, in almost every Military Administrative Committee administrative meeting, decisions were passed on appointments and dismissals of lower-level personnel, of which most had to be ratified either by the Government Administrative Council or by the Central People's Government Council.[30] In all these types of work, the Military Administrative Committee was the filter responsible for ensuring the conversion of central policy into suitable local behavior.

The Military Administrative Committee used three main methods in communicating central policy downward and monitoring its execution by the localities. Interestingly, each method can be viewed as a device for molding the units under its jurisdiction into one larger, integrated unit. These methods were convening

25. *HHJP*, December 17, 1951, on utilizing stored wood; October 20, 1952, p. 1, on employing specialist technical skilled personnel; October 17, 1951, on tree felling; December 6, 1951, stating that all construction projects must be approved by the Southwest Finance-Economic Committee.

26. *HHJP*, October 9, 1950, on tax evasion; November 13, 1951, on finance; December 17, 1951, on industry department's investigations; September 23, 1952, on tax exemption.

27. *HHJP*, September 22, 1952, and October 5, 1952, on safety reporting in industry; December 6, 1951, on prices; December 15, 1951, on corruption.

28. *HHJP*, December 17, 1951; October 10, 1952.

29. *HHJP*, October 14, 1950, on opium abolition; October 7, 1950, on clothes contributions; November 2, 1950, on clearing up cases; December 16, 1951, on economizing; September 7, 1952, on loans; and September 22, 1952, on labor employment and registration.

30. *CB*, No. 170 (1952), Article 3.

work conferences, both departmental and all regional; selecting key points and publicizing model experiences; and creating inspection teams to check on implementation of work by the lower levels.

Work conferences, held at the regional level, whether they were Military Administrative Committee plenums that included all members of the Military Administrative Committee, or functional work conferences attended by representatives of all groups involved in a given functional system, followed similar formats.[31] They generally opened by transmitting a new policy of the central government or of a functional department at the central level; or by stating that the meeting followed the spirit of a particular central conference or directive.

Next, a summary of work in the region focused the content of the conference on the specific situation in the Southwest. Spokesmen were chosen whose support could serve as rallying points for segments of the population who might be unreceptive to the new policy.[32] Deviations in past work were highlighted and the new direction in work spelled out. The measures to be taken in work were stated in uniform and generalized terms to apply to all provinces, all *hsien,* or all *hsiang,* respectively; adaptation to real circumstances was left to the lower levels. Once the conference ended, participants returned to their units and worked out a local agenda to suit their own areas. Still, on the whole the conferences created an amalgam from the various participant geographical or functional units attending and made them aware of their common concerns. In this way, geographical integration was furthered in the Southwest in the light of national norms.

Choosing key points and models also promoted regional unification. When a new policy was to be tested, the regional government had the duty of selecting key points for this experimentation. For example, when a new system was to be introduced for regulating urban finance, the regional Finance-Economic

31. For information on Military Administrative Committee plenums, see Chapter Three. Some functional work conferences are: Culture-Education's Third Plenum, *HHJP,* December 31, 1951; the Third Trade Work Conference, *HHYP,* No. 17 (1951), pp. 1114-1116; Public Roads and Transport Convention, *HHJP,* October 30, 1952; Agriculture-Forestry Conference, *HHJP,* December 5, 1952.

32. Ex-warlord Liu Wen-hui opened the Fourth Military Administrative Committee Plenum, for example. See *HHJP,* December 11, 1952.

Committee chose eight key cities that would first adjust and calculate their expenses in order to provide the committee with
research materials.[33] Also, after rent reduction was completed in
some *hsien* in East and West Szechwan, key point land reform was
begun there.[34] And in the cooperativization movement, permanent mutual-aid teams and agricultural producers' cooperatives
were developed at key points where possible.[35] These key points
gave the less advanced districts methods and goals for their own
development.

Selection of models and propagation of their experience was
another technique similar to the use of key points, since through
use of this device the successes of individuals or small groups
were widely publicized for imitation. These models included
peasants who had harvested bumper crops,[36] national minority
representatives,[37] and trade workers who had helped to lower
shipment costs for trade items.[38] The models themselves had
been created in the course of competitive work situations; and,
after being fêted or given prizes, the workers were urged to pass
on their own experiences to the masses. While encouraging increased output was one motive for praising these individuals,
inviting the popularization of uniform experience was another.
In the case of both key points and models, then, other units and
individuals were expected to accept the experience of the key
point and attempt to reproduce it, or to compete and strive to
attain the norm reached by the model. An aim of both strategies
was to achieve standardized work practices throughout the
region.

The third, and probably most interesting technique used by the
Military Administrative Committee to monitor the localities was
the inspection team. Teams were created through shuffling and
recombining functional or geographic groups, thereby upsetting
routine ways of carrying out business. They were made up of
members of various regional-level functional committees who
were sent down into the provinces to examine different kinds of

33. *HHJP*, October 14, 1950.
34. *Survey of China Mainland Press* [hereafter *SCMP*], No. 62 (1951), p. 30.
35. *HHJP*, December 18, 1952.
36. *HHJP*, March 13, 1953.
37. *HHJP*, October 30, 1950.
38. *HHJP*, November 15, 1951.

affairs; or of several provinces' cadres from one functional system brought together and reassigned. Thus in composing inspection teams, cadres were detached from their usual surroundings and asked to concentrate either on a new functional task, a new geographical area, or both.

For example, to investigate implementation of the marriage law, the Southwest division of the Supreme People's Court brought together cadres drawn from the regional Departments of Civil Affairs, Justice, and Public Security, the procuratory and supervisory organs, the women's work committee and the youth league. Using these individuals the Court created three groups to go to the lower levels to check up.[39] In clearing up counter-revolutionary cases, the Judicial Department redistributed various provinces' judicial cadres to do the work.[40]

Another technique involved combining cadres from different levels of administration. Thus, to deliver propaganda on grain collection to a certain *pao* in South Szechwan, a work group was formed of members of the Military Administrative Committee's Finance Department, the South Szechwan finance hall, and the *ch'ü* government for this *pao*.[41] In another case, the Military Administrative Committee Food Grains Bureau detached and transferred cadres to organize five check-up teams. Of these, four teams were sent one each to each of Szechwan's four administrative offices (East, West, South, North), and one was sent to Kweichow. These cadres then joined local food-grains department cadres to guarantee completion of the grain collection.[42] Finally, in the land reform movement, a more unusual method was employed: work corps personnel came from Peking and Tientsin for the specific purpose of uniting with cadres from the Southwest to take part in the movement.[43] These various schemes to mix and shift cadres were meant to have a unifying effect on the units below the regional level. The impact on the populations inspected is not hard to imagine. They were made aware of their belonging to a system beyond their own locality, and were subjected by strangers to norms that were more universalistic than

39. *HHJP*, November 23, 1951, p. 2.
40. *HHJP*, November 24, 1951, p. 2.
41. *HHJP*, October 8, 1950, p. 3.
42. *HHJP*, October 18, 1950, p. 3.
43. *SCMP*, No. 128 (1951), p. 18; *HHJP*, November 7, 1951, p. 1.

those that were being enforced in their own districts ordinarily by local cadres.

To summarize, in its middleman role, the Military Administrative Committee made thoroughgoing efforts to ensure that central policies were in fact carried out below. And in doing so, the regional-level organs and their cadres acted to reshape and to integrate the lower-level units in the Southwest in accord with national policies, in preparation for integrating this area as a whole into the nation.

Chapter Three posited that during Integration I in the Southwest, a period of geographical integration—internal unification within the Southwest on the basis of the local situation—took place in the period 1949-1952, when the Military Administrative Committee was in existence. This section has shown that the Military Administrative Committee was responsible for this process in a number of ways. As the highest administrative authority in the localities, it had some control over organizing matters, mainly economic, on its own initiative. In the process, it acted to standardize certain aspects of financial and economic work in the Southwest. And as the Government Administrative Council's representative organ, the Military Administrative Committee communicated policy downward through all-regional conferences, and made use of several organizational devices to ensure uniformity of response. The next section will consider how this geographical integration was altered after 1952, and how a more functionally oriented form of integration took its place under the Administrative Committee.

Functional Integration: Administration under the Administrative Committee, 1952-1954

With the change in title of the Military Administrative Committee to the Administrative Committee after 1952, several important shifts began to occur, both in the nature of the regional government organ's work and in its relation to other organs in its environment. Thus, the Administrative Committee had less initiative relative to central government organs and to the regional Party than the Military Administrative Committee had had. Also, the role of the provinces was increasing during 1953 and 1954, compared with their role under the Military Administrative Committee. In some cases, provincial government was taking on work which the Military Administrative Committee had done before. Moreover, greater regulation of affairs by specialized central government units and by the regional Party meant that the geographical or territorial principle of integration that had obtained under the Military Administrative Committee was giving way to a more functional organization of work.

Loss of Initiative by the Regional Administration Relative to the Central Government

Two types of evidence suggest that regional administration under the Administrative Committee lost initiative to the center. First, there were changes in the type and number of regionally initiated directives appearing in the press after late 1952. Second, the role of the region in economic affairs shifted in late 1952. Interestingly, the Administrative Committee was stripped of the Military Administrative Committee's role as the highest administrative authority in the localities. And in discussing this aspect of the Military Administrative Committee's role above, it was shown that this role had just these two components: the independent issuance of directives, and the regulation of economic affairs.

Chapter Three indicated that the focus of work at the regional level in the Southwest gradually expanded to take in more national and fewer purely local concerns in the years after takeover. However, Administrative Committee directives after 1952 tended to be little more than slogans promoting national policies, rather than instances of the regional organ actually taking the initiative. For example, the Southwest Administrative Committee Trade Bureau sent out an order to "grasp the prosperous season to promote sales."[44] And the Administrative Committee itself called on lower levels to "develop the 1953 agricultural emulation campaign to increase production."[45]

As regional work tended more and more to be cast in a national mold in 1953 and 1954, central government organs became concerned with types of work that earlier would have fallen to the Military Administrative Committee to handle. For

44. *HHJP*, January 25, 1953.
45. *HHJP*, March 1, 1953.

example, orders to unify statistical work now came from the center.[46] Earlier, the Military Administrative Committee had been involved in unifying accounting forms and tables.[47] Another example concerned directives about the weather. Where the Military Administrative Committee had initiated pronouncements on taking precautions because of bad weather conditions,[48] now the Government Administrative Council ordered improvements in weather predicting.[49]

A third example is an Administrative Committee directive on spring farming in March 1953.[50] This order was made in response to the Chinese Communist Party (CCP) Central Committee's directive on the subject promulgated in March.[51] Earlier the Military Administrative Committee regulated spring farming independently.[52] The point here is that while the Administrative Committee's role in independently issuing instructions was narrowing, the scope of the center's pronouncements was widening. Also, while the typical regional order now contained a national slogan, the central organs were becoming more involved in substantive local matters.

Finally, fewer and fewer directives of any sort issued by the Administrative Committee appeared in the Southwest press as time went on.[53] This decline was yet another sign that the organs at the Great Administrative Region level were being phased out; and thus that their role in coordinating the Southwest as a separate area was diminishing.

Besides this decline in the number of directives the Administrative Committee issued, its role in economic affairs was less

46. As, *HHJP,* July 29, 1953, and January 13, 1954.
47. *HHJP,* October 21, 1950.
48. See footnote 10 above.
49. *HHJP,* April 17, 1954.
50. *HHJP,* March 26, 1953.
51. *SCMP,* No. 541 (1953), p. 32.
52. See footnote 8 above, and *HHJP,* October 21, 1951, for example.
53. To reach this conclusion, I compared five time periods: the two three-month periods in the autumns of 1950 and 1951, respectively, and the four-month period in the autumn of 1952 mentioned in footnote 12 above; a three-month period in 1953 and two months in 1954. In 1950, an average of 13.67 directives was issued by the Military Administrative Committee per month; in 1951, 6.67 directives appeared each month; and in 1952, there was an average of eight per month. In 1953 and 1954, however, there were averages of only 3.33 and four Administrative Committee orders published a month, respectively.

independent than the Military Administrative Committee's had been. The Military Administrative Committee's role in regulating economic matters had been to monitor the trade, distribution, and prices of local goods, to optimize conditions in local production, to formulate the regional budget, and to standardize measures, units, wages, and taxes in the Southwest. After the Military Administrative Committee's demise, national construction goals dictated economic work in the area.

Accordingly, regional economic work after late 1952 involved coordination of labor and production in the Southwest. By the autumn of 1952, a number of articles began appearing in the press indicating that employment, training, and the utilization of specialized talent were among the focal points for efforts at regional unification economically. Overall planning was to be based on the present and future needs of the whole area's organs, groups, schools, enterprises, factories, and mines, and was to be combined with the concrete situations of various kinds of unemployed personnel.[54] The Southwest Personnel Department, following an editorial in *Jen-min jih-pao,* issued notices to all regional-level organs in the Southwest to register all skilled personnel, with an aim of putting them into the most crucial areas of economic construction.[55]

By December 1952, 2,000 administrative workers in the Southwest had been transferred to construction jobs, and another 3,000 were scheduled for transfer.[56] In the same month, the Southwest Geological Bureau held a conference to allocate personnel to work sites and to make plans for training prospectors.[57] Other offices, such as the Department of Industry and the Bureau of Building Construction, sponsored training classes on a regionwide basis.[58] At the same time, a spate of conferences was held in various industries to mobilize construction efforts from the regional level downwards.[59]

Thereafter, projects in transport and geology, the main thrust

54. *HHJP,* September 7, 1952; September 20, 1952.
55. *HHJP,* October 20, 1952.
56. *SCMP,* No. 469 (1952), p. 17.
57. *SCMP,* No. 485 (1953), pp. 14-15.
58. *HHJP,* November 20, 1952; May 21, 1953.
59. *HHJP,* October 19, 1952, for building construction; November 17, 1952, for the machinery industry; December 16, 1952, for light industry and weaving; December 25, 1952, for the electronics industry and geology.

of construction in the Southwest,[60] were coordinated regionally. In April 1953 it was reported that the amount of drilling in the Southwest for 1953 would be seven times as great as in 1952; and that funds for building new highways and repairing old ones would be three times what was spent in 1952, as a highway network crisscrossing the area was being built up.[61] By the summer of 1953, the Southwest Geological Bureau had sent nine geological teams to explore in various parts of the region, and the Southwest Petroleum Office had dispatched eight geological teams and six surveying teams.[62]

In 1954, efforts at construction on a regional basis continued. In January the Southwest Bureau of Building Construction readjusted its subordinate organs to meet the needs of national construction, and began on-the-job training for cadres.[63] In February 1954 it was announced that a reorganization of education, which had begun in the Southwest in the autumn of 1952, was to be continued to make the schools in the area serve the needs of construction.[64]

Concern with transport and geology also kept apace in 1954. As in 1953, more than 30 percent of capital investment in the Southwest was earmarked for the construction and surveying of lines of communication.[65] The Southwest greatly strengthened key point geological prospecting compared with 1953, and it increased the capital investment in prospecting by four-and-one-half times over 1953.[66] Where the Military Administrative Committee had taken some initiative in independently organizing economic and financial undertakings in the Southwest, the Southwest Administrative Committee merely served as one sector in a unified national construction effort directed from above.[67]

60. *Ta-kung pao*, February 9, 1954, translated in *CB*, No. 281 (1954), pp. 17-19.

61.*SCMP*, No. 560 (1953), pp. 22-23.

62. *SCMP*, No. 615 (1953), pp. 12-13.

63. *HHJP*, January 27, 1954.

64. *SCMP*, No. 746 (1954), pp. 14-15.

65. *SCMP*, No. 749 (1954), p. 25; and No. 615 (1953), pp. 12-13.

66. *HHJP*, April 27, 1954.

67. Also, the Finance-Economic Committee, active on its own before 1952, became involved after 1952 largely in checking up on fulfillment of the national plan. For example, see *HHJP*, March 12, 1953, on the Finance Committee's check-up of factories' and mines' implementation of the national plan; and *HHJP*, March 26, 1953, on that same committee's investigation of basic construction work.

The Southwest Administrative Committee was converted into such a sector as the central government took on greater control over economic affairs in the regions after 1952. The decision to reduce the Military Administrative Committees to Administrative Committees stated that the departments originally under the Military Administrative Committee were to be reorganized under the Administrative Committee into bureaus and offices.[68]

Such bureaus and offices were of two kinds. First, some became bureaus of the administrative region. These were led by the Administrative Committee and guided by its coordinating committees, as under the Military Administrative Committee. The Bureaus of Civil Affairs and Public Health fell into this category. Since the relationship of these organs to the Administrative Committee was essentially the same as their relationship to the Military Administrative Committee had been, there was no leverage for greater central penetration in these realms than there had been previously.

Bureaus of the second kind were to be subordinated directly to various relevant organs of the Central People's Government. They were to be under the jurisdiction of these organs of the central government as special enterprise control bureaus and offices. At the same time, they were also to be subjected to the supervision and guidance of the Administrative Committee and its committees, just as they had been subjected to the Military Administrative Committee in the past. This category included the Commercial Enterprises Control Bureau,[69] the Food Grains Bureau,[70] the Bureau of Finance,[71] and the Geological Bureau.[72]

From this, it is apparent that the bureaus left for the regional level to manage were involved in work unrelated to economic construction and financial affairs; and that the bureaus subordinated to central organs were directly concerned with economic matters. On this basis, it can be concluded that with the demise of the Military Administrative Committee, the region's role in

68. *CB*, No. 245 (1953), pp. 10-11; also in *SCMP*, No. 494 (1953), pp. 36-38. See Chapter One.
69. *Ibid.*; also *HHJP*, May 8, 1953.
70. *SCMP*, No. 558 (1953), p. 45.
71. *SCMP*, No. 677 (1953), supplement, pp. xxi-xxiii.
72. *HHJP*, March 21, 1953.

economic activity was meant to decline. And as it declined, central organs took over direction of the work once supervised on a regional or geographical basis.

So, based both on the change in the nature and number of Administrative Committee directives as compared with Military Administrative Committee orders, and on the shift in the economic role of the regional organ after 1952, it can be inferred that the new Administrative Committee had less initiative relative to the central government than did the Military Administrative Committee. With the growth in functional integration, as various types of work became directed in terms of functional sectors on a national basis, the central government took on greater control of local work (Proposition 4.1). Apparently, the Administrative Committee, a weakened organ, constituted a transitional step in the abolition of regional government.

Loss of Administrative Committee Initiative Relative to the Regional Party

As discussed in Chapter Three, the work of the regional Party during 1949 to 1952 lay mainly in the ideological sphere, while from 1952 to 1954 the scope of the regional Party's work increased. This section will highlight changes in the Party's work after 1952, particularly as these changes meant that the Party gradually encroached on the work of the government organ, the Administrative Committee. These modifications in the Party's role can best be understood by looking first at the Party's functions before 1952, and then comparing these functions with Party work thereafter.

Before 1952, the Party's duties clustered in these areas: mobilizing mass movements, propaganda, work in the schools, thought remolding and study, and intra-Party discipline and Party building. In the realm of mobilization, for example, the Party Bureau in the Southwest was largely responsible for conducting the "patriotic campaign to increase production and practice strict economy" in late 1951. The Party Secretariat set out the plan for the movement,[73] and the Party units in regional-level organs established a committee to run the campaign. Under the committee,

---

73. *HHJP*, November 22, 1951; November 28, 1951.

various organs everywhere set up small investigation groups. Every three days the groups reported to the committee which, in turn, reported to the Party Bureau headquarters once every two weeks.[74] Simultaneously, the Party was mobilizing work personnel to develop the *san-fan* (three-anti) movement, to oppose bureaucracy, corruption, and waste.[75] In this era of large-scale social reform, when one mass movement followed upon the next, the Party was well occupied directing these movements.

Another task assigned the regional Party was to promote propaganda on new policies as they were promulgated. For instance, the Regional Party Bureau in the Southwest was involved in encouraging construction workers to oppose the labor contract system.[76] Following the instructions of the Central Committee's Propaganda Department, construction workers' propaganda teams were formed under the leadership of the Party cell in various industries. It was the job of these teams to propagandize and organize workers to form a labor union in order to overthrow the KMT-era system of labor bosses.

In reforming the school system, in August 1951 the Southwest Party Bureau issued instructions to forbid irregular enrollment and transfer of students; to terminate the "confusion" in the schools over participation in social activities; and to rectify violations of the Party's policy toward intellectuals.[77] After issuance of this order, the Bureau called a symposium geared to finding ways to improve education. In early 1952, the Party Bureau transferred a group of cadres to help teachers do study aimed at ideological remolding, and it also organized cadres proficient in political theory to give reports to teachers on ideological remolding.[78] Later that year, the Bureau's Propaganda Department promoted on-the-job political theory study and called a specialists' meeting on this theme.[79]

Intra-Party affairs and Party building constituted the final category of affairs on which the regional Party apparatus focused in the early years. For instance, in late 1950 the Party committees in

74. *HHJP*, December 16, 1951; December 20, 1951.
75. *HHJP*, December 20, 1951; December 24, 1951.
76. *HHJP*, December 16, 1951, p. 3.
77. *SCMP*, No. 155 (1951), pp. 14-16.
78. *SCMP*, No. 253 (1952), p. 17.
79. *HHJP*, September 8, 1952; September 23, 1952.

the Military Administrative Committee's organs called a Party representatives' meeting to criticize deviations and to strengthen education, discipline, and life in the Party.[80] In early 1952, the same group of committees held a discipline review conference, in which the organs' personnel were urged to maintain Party discipline in the *san-fan* movement and to take disciplinary action against Party members who resisted inspection.[81] Later that year, the Organization Department of the Bureau, calling Party building the Party's central task, issued a notice to strengthen this work. The Department organized specialists to go to the lower levels to inspect Party-building work, and to discover and rectify any problems found.[82]

Thus, in all aspects of its work—directing mass movements, organizing propaganda, sponsoring educational reform, promoting thought remolding, ensuring intra-Party discipline, and encouraging Party building—the Party in the region was the watchdog in the ideological realm before 1952. After late 1952, however, there were indications that the regional Party's role may have been increasing, that the Party had a new relation to government organs, and that the Party was involved in activities it had not been involved in previously.

First, in the past, the work instructions that had been issued by the Military Administrative Committee had invariably called for the cooperation of Party and government units at the various subordinate levels in enforcing directives. After 1952, signs appeared that the Party was taking on an exclusive role in certain types of work or at least a superior position relative to the governmental units. Second, the regional Party organs began holding work conferences on affairs outside the ideological realm, concerned with the more mundane matters of production. Such conferences had formerly been called only by the Military Administrative Committee. Third, the Party began to issue directives on how to solve daily problems in work, another concern which had formerly been the preserve of the Military Administrative Committee alone.

These points can all be illustrated by concrete examples. First, a press item in March 1953 showed that the Party was taking an

80. *HHJP,* November 4, 1950.
81. *SCMP,* No. 248 (1952), p. 16.
82. *HHJP,* October 18, 1952.

exclusive or superior role in certain types of work. It was reported at that time that the Southwest Finance-Economic Committee (under the Administrative Committee) had sent out check-up teams to basic construction sites. The results, the article claimed, were reported to the Regional Party Bureau, which was told to unify Party organs at work sites.[83] Again, in July 1953, the Southwest Party Bureau was said to have directed the Administrative Committee Finance-Economic Committee, in conjunction with several other regional-level organs, to inspect conditions relating to waste of timber.[84] At about the same time the Administrative Committee specified measures for control over the unified distribution of the labor force in building-construction work in the region, and pointed out that the Party committee of every locality should strengthen its leadership for this work.[85] These developments were significant departures from past practice, both because the regional Party had not formerly given directions to administrative units, and also because the Party alone had not been told to take charge of local work in such matters as construction and the disposal of labor.

The second point relates to the Party's holding of work conferences on production. Beginning in late November 1952, the Party became involved in sponsoring such conferences, thereby setting the direction for certain types of economic work. These conferences included industry and mining conferences in November 1952 and May 1953;[86] rural work conferences in December 1952 and July 1953;[87] and a mountain area production conference in January 1954.[88] Previously, conferences of this type were convened only by appropriate departments of the Military Administrative Committee. Third, the regional Party started to initiate directives on daily work. These included one on fighting drought and preserving sprouts,[89] worded much like those which had earlier come only from the Military Administrative Committee.[90]

83. *HHJP*, March 26, 1953.
84. *SCMP*, No. 634 (1953), pp. 10-11.
85. *SCMP*, No. 677 (1953), pp. xxxi-xxxiii.
86. *HHJP*, December 7, 1952; *SCMP*, No. 584 (1953), pp. 27-28.
87. *HHJP*, December 18, 1952; *SCMP*, No. 626 (1953), pp. 21-22.
88. *SCMP*, No. 722 (1954), p. 29.
89. *SCMP*, No. 611 (1953), pp. 17-18.
90. See footnotes 8 and 10 above.

All this suggests that as the Party began to expand in numbers over time,[91] it gradually took on more generalized functions, and began to obtain control and supervisory duties over larger segments of work. The Party was probably seen by leaders in Peking as a nationwide organization whose members were all schooled in a common body of doctrine. With the growth of this nationally unified organization, capable of enforcing ideological norms, there was less need for the coordination of work along mainly geographical lines which the Military Administrative Committee had represented (Proposition 4.2).

Loss of Administrative Committee Initiative
Relative to the Provinces

There is less evidence that the role of the provinces was expanding relative to the regional organs after 1952. However, in light of the fact that the provinces were soon to be operating without the regional middlemen, it is logical to expect that their powers would be growing after 1952. In this vein, two directives on tax reduction and tax exemption in cases of disaster can be compared.

The first, issued in September 1952, pertained to the entire Southwest region. The provincial governments, based on their respective disaster situations (referring to any kind of natural conditions that led to a bad harvest), were permitted to draw up their own regulations (with Military Administrative Committee approval) only in the extreme case that continuous disaster had existed for more than two years. Even then, the overall standards were drawn up by the Military Administrative Committee. Further, the provinces were limited to setting exemptions and reductions for only 60 percent of the whole levy in their territories.[92] In the second directive, issued in July 1953, provincial governments themselves were to formulate measures for tax reduction and exemption.[93]

A second example concerns the cooperative movement.

91. An article in *Union Research Service* 2 (1956), p. 287 states that in the latter part of 1952, Party organs at all levels in Yunnan began to expand. Presumably, this same phenomenon was taking place in other provinces as well at this time. See also *SCMP*, No. 830 (1954), pp. 15-16.

92. *HHJP*, September 23, 1952.

93. *SCMP*, No. 619 (1953), p. 17.

In January 1954, mutual-aid and cooperative conferences were held in Szechwan and Sikang provinces, and an agricultural producers' cooperative work conference was convened in Kweichow province.[94] No mention was made of a regional-level conference on collectivization. Earlier, in December 1952, the movement was dealt with regionally at the rural work conference held by the Regional Party Bureau, and the direction of the movement was set for the entire region.[95] Both examples indicate a transferral of work from regional to provincial organs over time.

Having participated in the social reform movements of the early 1950s, the provincial-level administrations were probably considered sufficiently reliable to set local standards for national policies without these policies being first filtered through the personnel at the level of the region. Also, presumably more Party personnel staffed the provincial governments as time went on and as more cadres were trained. Again, the broad geographical coordination of several provinces maintained under the Military Administrative Committee was breaking down during the period of the Administrative Committee, and making way for a new type of national integration based on functional principles of organization (Proposition 4.3).

To conclude, the Military Administrative Committee was a stronger organ relative to the other organizations in its environment—the center, the Regional Party Bureau, and the provinces—than the Administrative Committee that followed it. Apparently, the process of dismantling the regional administrations was a planned and gradual transferral of work from one set of organs to another, rather than a sudden maneuver in mid-1954.

The Shift from Geographical to Functional Integration

Under the Military Administrative Committee, the Southwest area itself and the problems the area posed for the Communists created the conditions governing work. And, while the focus was upon these special problems in the years just after takeover, a geographical principle dictated the organization of work.

94. *SCMP*, No. 733 (1954), pp. 33-34.
95. *HHJP*, December 18, 1952.

However, once the Southwest was internally integrated, so that work tasks and procedures were standardized throughout the area and the same mass movements had been carried out everywhere in the area according to national prescriptions, integration of the whole area into the nation could proceed according to a more functional principle. Evidence that this was happening has been presented above. This same data can be used to clarify the mechanisms by which this second-stage, functional type of integration occurred.

Apparently, this process of functional integration was a matter of the center, the regional Party, and the provinces increasingly taking over control from the regional administrative organ after 1952. Thus, in order to alter the structure of work on a national basis, specific central organs were given powers over subordinate regional economic units according to the criteria of functional work tasks. Similarly, the growth of the Party as an all-national institution, with its specialized and standardized mode of operations and code of ideology, permitted a decline in the role of separate, territorially based administrations. Finally, by 1952 the provinces, having carried out national mass movements and having been strengthened by an increase of Party personnel, were considered able to take over the direction of work on a more or less uniform basis without having to rely on the supervision of regional overseers.

In short, the process of Integration I—the administrative unification of the various territorial segments of the country into a national whole—proceeded largely through a transfer of work from geographically oriented bodies to organs with a more functional focus. The next chapter will show what role the regional leadership played in this process.

CHAPTER V

Linkages: Personnel and
Military Control Units

The last two chapters have dealt with the process we have called Integration I. Before we discuss Integration II, in Chapters Six and Seven, this chapter will describe the linkage mechanisms that were essential to the building of national integration. In the Introduction, integration was defined as a matter of bridging gaps between competing centers of political loyalty, both horizontally and vertically. This chapter is concerned with showing how personnel appointments and the creation of units for military control were instrumental in bridging these gaps.

The assignment of particular groups of individuals to leadership positions at the regional level, as well as the division of the Southwest into new military units, can be viewed as integrative devices in several senses. In personnel assignments, leaders of different backgrounds were appointed to work together. Thus, native Southwesterners were joined with Communist outsiders, thereby bringing representatives of the local centers of Southwest society and politics together with members of the nationwide Party system. This combination of individuals can be seen as a means of connecting the two related processes of Integration I and II. For whereas Integration I was essentially a matter of uniting the Southwest area with the whole nation, this process could only occur as Integration II progressed—that is, as the people in small localities were linked up with a larger Southwest region. And it was a function of the regional leadership to bring about this linkage.

New units for military control were created in the Southwest by assigning separate corps and armies of the invading Field Armies to occupy and govern different sections of the provinces in the

Southwest. At the apex of the military hierarchy, ruling the entire area and coordinating these subordinate troops, stood the officers of the Southwest Military Region. This arrangement amounted to a superimposition of the organizational structure of the liberating armies onto the territory of the Southwest provinces. Here, too, was a union of locality and a national-level organ, the People's Liberation Army (PLA). And in this case also, this technique facilitated the administrative integration taking place through the two interrelated processes of Integration I and II.

This chapter is divided into two general sections: one on personnel and one on the military deployment of the units used for control. Both sections will be concerned with the devices used to connect the localities with the national political system.

Personnel

The position of the regional-level leadership in the Southwest can best be understood by considering these men as middlemen between the lower levels of Southwest society and administration on the one hand, and the central government on the other. In fact, the officials chosen to head the governments in the Great Administrative Regions were all top Communist officials, serving as "thoroughly reliable unifying links in a chain reaching from the central government to the various regional units and thence to the lower levels."[1]

In considering the implications of this intermediary position, it will be useful to review some of the literature in the field of administrative theory as well as some concepts from political anthropology. After presenting this material, this section will analyze three groups in the Southwest leadership in terms of these theories and concepts. Finally, these findings will be used in comparing leadership at the regional level with the leadership in the provinces in the Southwest.

The Power Position of the Regional Leadership

What was the relative power of the personnel at the regional level during the period of this study? For simplicity, in attempt-

1. S. B. Thomas, *Government and Administration in Communist China* (1955), p. 86.

ing to answer this question the focus will be on three levels: the center, the region, and the base. Here "the base" will apply broadly to all levels below the region. This discussion will concentrate only on the position of the region relative to the center and of the region relative to the base.

In understanding this relative position, it will be helpful to use a notion of "dependency" to elucidate the pertinent power relations. It has been observed that "an organization has power relative to an element of its [task] environment to the extent that the organization has the capacity to satisfy the needs of that element [for resources or performances] and to the extent that the organization monopolizes that capacity."[2] The objective here is to determine the various dependencies of the three levels one to the other in terms of the resources and performances that each had to offer, in order to understand their respective power.

Resources as a whole were not monopolized by any one of these levels. Rather, if five sorts of resources are identified, it can be shown that certain sorts of resources were concentrated at different levels. These five sorts of resources can be termed financial, military, symbolic, cognitive, and associational.

Using these five categories, each of the two upper levels (the center and the region) had superior financial and military resources (and the right to distribute them) relative to its own lower level (region and base, respectively); and each had symbolic command deriving from its control of these resources and from its being the source of authoritative pronouncements to the levels below it. The central government also possessed symbolic resources by virtue of the fact that it was the repository of supreme Party and military power. These three resources belonging to the upper levels—the financial, military, and symbolic resources—will be referred to as the first set of resources.

The base, however, had two sorts of resources that were essential to the upper levels. First, it had resources based on its familiarity with and knowledge of affairs, both sociological and geographical, in its own domain. These will be called "cognitive" resources here. Second, it stood as a unit with a history, with habits, customs, and traditions, and with developed organizational patterns of behavior, all of which conferred upon it "asso-

2. James D. Thompson, *Organizations in Action* (1967), Chapter 3.

ciational" resources. These two resources, then—the cognitive and the associational—are the second set of resources.

The central government was strongest in the first set of resources. The regional government, as the mediator between center and base, appeared to the base to be the representative of the center. Thus, it took on a share of the center's attributes. In the second set, it was the base, as the homeland of traditional China, which was best endowed. And the center had to assume that the region had access to the cognitive and associational resources of the base. Here then, there was a situation of mutual dependency. For although the region and base required central subsidy,[3] were subservient to central military power, and acknowledged the symbolic supremacy of the center, the central leaders were largely ignorant of the lower levels' situation, especially in the Southwest. And where the center had to rely on the regional leaders to communicate about and penetrate the base, the base had to rely on the region to intervene in its behalf.

Thus, both the center and the base were dependent upon each other for different kinds of resources. Moreover, where each relied on the region to intercede in its interests before the other, the region was impotent to satisfy either without the cooperation of the other. In terms of resources, then, the region had no real independent powers.

As to performance, the realm of the two upper levels involved making policy at the top and passing down and checking on implementation at the middle, respectively. At the two lower levels (region and base) crucial performance was based on consent: consent to enforce policies and consent to yield upward the grain and taxes demanded of them. At the regional level, this involved consent to transmit policy downward without distortion; at the base, the consent was an agreement to carry out the specific operational aspects of a policy.

Thus, the center was dependent upon the region's performance. Was the official on the regional level likely to satisfy the center's needs for this performance? In analyzing this, it is helpful to consider the likely determinants of the regional-level official's performance. One of Anthony Downs' theories is rele-

3. *Hsin-Hua yüeh-pao* [New China Monthly] (Peking) [hereafter *HHYP*], No. 11 (1950), p. 1064; *Current Background* [hereafter *CB*], No. 20 (1950), p. 21.

vant in assessing how the regional leader in the Southwest was apt to carry out his job of passing policy downward.

Downs lists four basic causes of conflict that may influence the divergence of an official's goals from his or her organization's goals. These causes of conflict may contribute to the official's distortion of policies as he or she forwards them to lower levels. These are: self-interest, different modes of perceiving reality, differential information, and uncertainty.[4]

The hypothetical regional official's behavior can be analyzed according to these factors. Such an official's concept of his self-interest in the early years of the regime would have been connected with his self-identity. All top regional officials were members of the Central Committee of the Chinese Communist Party (CCP) and of the Central People's Government Council. Also, as an officer of the PLA armies that took over the Southwest, as almost all officials at the regional level were at that time, his identity would have been bound up with the PLA. Because of these identifications with centrally directed bodies, he would not have viewed it to be in his self-interest to distort the orders coming from Peking. Also, his modes of perceiving reality would have been influenced by the Chinese Communist Party creed and by the discipline instilled in a revolutionary army which had lately engaged in civil war.

Of course, the regional official worked with somewhat different information than central leaders had. The information about his area of jurisdiction which he received at the regional level would be more precise than that which leaders in Peking had access to. But it was sadly deficient for truly grasping the social infrastructure of secret societies, minority tribes, and warlord relations in Southwest China society.[5] Finally, the regional official was faced with a high level of uncertainty in coping with this new reality. But his need for financial subsidy from the center to help deal with this reality contributed to increase the official's desire to be compliant and to lower his tendency to distort policy in the face of uncertainty.

On the whole, then, the performance of the regional official was probably conditioned by and dependent upon his ties to the

4. Anthony Downs, *Inside Bureaucracy* (1967), p. 134.
5. *HHYP*, No. 7 (1950), p. 22; *HHYP*, No. 11 (1950), p. 1063; *Hsin-Hua jih-pao* [New China Daily] (Chungking), October 3, 1951 note this unfamiliarity.

center; he probably depended more on the center for relevant performances than the center depended on him for performances pertinent to central work. In this vein, Vogel, describing the situation in the Central-South Great Administrative Region, claims that officials in the regional capital at Wuhan worked very closely with leaders in Peking and were their deputies in carrying out Peking's policies.[6] There is no reason to suppose that circumstances were different in the Southwest.

To summarize, in terms of resources, the regional administration's financial-military-symbolic assets were borrowed, based on reliance on the center; its access to cognitive-associational assets was limited, for full access would have required closer ties with the base than its officials had and a longer stay in the Southwest than they had made. And in terms of performance, its officials on the whole identified more with the national center than with the area they ruled, so that they were less likely than the typical organizational middleman to subvert central orders for the sake of increasing their own power. Their leverage against their superiors was contingent upon their control of the base; and control of the base was at least partially obstructed by the base's cognitive and associational resources. Thus the region was caught between a central government above it that possessed one set of resources and a base below it that operated on yet another set. Its leaders, in short, were middlemen.

Political Middlemen

Thus, as a whole, the body of leaders at the regional level was wedged in between the central government on the one hand and the levels below the region on the other. The concept of the political middleman, used by some political anthropologists, and alluded to in the Introduction, elucidates the role these leaders played.

The political middleman, we may recall, is a person who, keeping a foot in both camps, bridges a gap in communications between the larger system and a smaller structure "encapsulated" within it. Such a role may be consciously created by a larger structure to meet its own deficiencies.[7] A "fraility in authority" generally attends such positions, because their occupants are

6. Ezra Vogel, *Canton Under Communism* (1969), p. 93.
7. F. G. Bailey, *Stratagems and Spoils* (1969), pp. 167-172.

expected to respond to pressures both from above and from below.[8] This accords with what was said above about the position of the regional official and his lack of power.[9]

Writers on this topic stress the intermediary function of leaders working at the middle levels of administrative hierarchies and the limitations on their influence, especially in situations where two distinct kinds of social relations exist. The roles of the various types of personnel in the Southwest can be understood in light of this notion of the middleman. The term also highlights the linkage function of the regional leadership.

Three Types of Regional Leaders

Having considered in theoretical terms the position of the entire Southwest regional leadership, let us examine three groups within that body of personnel, in order to understand more concretely the effort at building up political linkages in the region and the types of individuals who were used to do this.

The sample here consists of persons who filled one or more of four kinds of posts in the Southwest from 1949 to 1954: (1) chairman or vice-chairman of the Military Administrative Committee or the Administrative Committee; (2) department, bureau, or committee head or deputy head under the Military Administrative Committee or the Administrative Committee; (3) ordinary member of the Military Administrative Committee or the Administrative Committee; and (4) officer in the Southwest Military Region.[10] (The Appendix lists these individuals by name, background, and post.) Since a thorough search of the available data revealed no complete listing of Party officials in the region, this category has been omitted. However, at least the senior secretaries of the regional Party were all included among the other categories, and presumably other Party officials were as well.[11]

8. Max Gluckman, "Inter-Hierarchical Roles," in Marc J. Swartz, ed., *Local-Level Politics* (1968), pp. 71-72.

9. Jerry Hough describes the way this same dilemma affects similarly placed officials in the Soviet system. See Jerry Hough, *Soviet Prefects* (1969), especially Chapters 2 and 12.

10. See Tables 1-3.

11. Ying-mao Kao was also forced to omit Party officials for the same reason. I have adopted his justification for exclusion of these individuals. See Ying-mao Kao, "The Urban Bureaucratic Elite in Communist China: A Case Study of Wuhan, 1949-1965," in A. Doak Barnett, *Chinese Communist Politics in Action*

Moreover, all the individuals in this sample were either Party members, men who had had close and long-term association with the Party, democratic personages, or turncoat Kuomintang-era (KMT) generals; thus, indirectly Party personnel in fact figure heavily in the sample.[12] Altogether a total of 139 individuals filled these four types of posts, but since full background information was not available on all these persons, the conclusions will be based on smaller figures.[13]

(1969), p. 224. For example, 1st Secretary: Teng Hsiao-p'ing, also Political Commissar, Southwest Military Region and Vice-Chairman, Southwest Military Administrative Committee and Administrative Committee. 2nd Secretary: Ho Lung, also Commander, Southwest Military Region and Vice-Chairman, Southwest Military Administrative Committee and Administrative Committee. Other senior secretaries: Liu Po-ch'eng, also Chairman, Southwest Military Administrative Committee and Administrative Committee; Sung Jen-ch'iung, also Assistant Political Commissar, Southwest Military Region and Vice-Chairman, Southwest Administrative Committee; and Chang Chi-ch'ün, also Deputy Political Commissar, Southwest Military Region. See Donald Klein and Anne B. Clark, *Biographic Dictionary of Chinese Communism, 1921-1965* (1971).

12. According to the sources listed in footnote 13 below, the vast majority of the individuals in this sample who were neither democratic personages nor ex-KMT generals were specifically cited as belonging to the Party. In the few cases where this was not so, these men were counted here as Party members anyway because of their long-term close association with the Party. Such association with the Party was inferred here since all these men did at least one of the following: held high government or military positions in the Border Regions; participated in the Long March or had been a soldier in the Red Army during its early days; attended the Red Army University or K'ang Ta, the Party's military academy during the War Against Japan; was a Political Department official or a Political Commissar in the PLA; or was a high military officer in a Field Army before 1949. It is quite probable that any individual who engaged even in only one of the above activities was in fact a Party member even if the sources used here fail to indicate this.

13. The sample was compiled from: *Jen-min shou-tse* [People's Handbook] 1951 [hereafter *JMST*] (1951), pp. 卯 34-37 for Military Administrative Committee members and department heads; *Survey of China Mainland Press* [hereafter *SCMP*], No. 494 (1953), pp. 21-27 for Administrative Committee members; and Liang Po-ming, "Chung-kung chün-ch'ü piao-chieh" [Chinese Communist Military Regions], *Chung-kung wen-t'i* [Problems in Chinese Communism] (Taipei) [hereafter *CKWT*], No. 1 (1954), p. 40, for the Military Region officials. The personnel lists for the Military Administrative Committee and the Administrative Committee were virtually identical. The following sources were consulted: Howard L. Boorman, *Biographical Dictionary of Republican China* (1967); Chung-kung jen-ming lu pien-hsiu wei-yüan-hui [Who's Who in Communist China Compilation Commission], *Chung-kung jen-ming lu* [Who's Who in Communist China] (1967); Huang Chen-hsia, *Chung-kung chün-jen chih* [Mao's Generals] (1968); Donald Klein and Anne B. Clark, *Biographic Dictionary*; William W. Whitson, *The Chinese Communist High Command* (1973).

For analytical purposes, the discussion will rely on Chamberlain's three-fold classification of local leaders in three cities in the post-takeover period. He refers to "outside reds," "local reds," and "local whites."[14] Briefly, the outside red is the Communist cadre working in an area other than that of his birth. The local red, then, is the Communist cadre serving in a province in which he was born (or, in this case, in the region that includes the province in which he was born). Finally, the local white is the non-Communist, also employed in the area (here, region) of his birth. Although there are subtypes within these three categories, this broad classification helps in understanding the manner in which integration was carried out in the Southwest.

Reds: Local and Outside. The overwhelming majority of the Communists in the Southwest Military Administrative Committee or Administrative Committee were officers in the Second and (to a much lesser extent) First Field Armies of the PLA. Besides these men, a smattering of persons with Party connections who were not members of either Field Army were also given posts in the regional regime. However, it was the military men, especially men from these two Field armies, who held the important positions among the Party members. This accords with a finding for Fukien just after takeover that the real power was in the hands of the military,[15] and that all the top posts in Fukien were held by the New Fourth Army.[16]

The Second Field Army was definitely the group that dominated the top-level posts in the Southwest region.[17] This army

14. Heath B. Chamberlain, "Transition and Consolidation in Urban China," in Robert A. Scalapino, ed., *Elites in the People's Republic of China* (1972), p. 256.
15. V. C. Falkenheim, "Provincial Leadership in Fukien, 1949-1966," in Scalapino, *Elites,* p. 231.
16. *Ibid.,* p. 234.
17. Of the 139 individuals who filled at least one of the four types of posts listed above, the backgrounds of seventy have been identified. Of these seventy, twenty-three, or one-third, were members of the Second Field Army. Although a few other men were in that army by the time of takeover, here they are not counted in this group, since the criterion for inclusion is common background before 1949. Thus, men are considered part of this Second Field Army group who either worked in a government organ or fought with the troops in the Chin-Chi-Lu-Yü Border Region during the period 1937-1945; and also were in the Central Plains Field Army from 1947.

TABLE 1
Local White, Local Red, Outside Red, and
Background and Job Category

Job Category	Local White		Local Red		Outsiders		Outsiders Known to be Reds
	K	D	U	FA	W	O	O
MAC-AC Chairman	O	O	O	1	O	O	O
MAC-AC Vice-Chairman	5	O	1	1	2	O	2
MAC-AC Department Head	7	1	1	4	6	7	8
MAC-AC Member	5	5	2	5	12	6	16
Military Region Official	O	O	O	1	6	2	8

Key

Local White: K = ex-KMT general
D = Democratic personage

Local Red: U = Underground worker in the SW pre-1949
FA = Entered SW in 1949 with the Field Armies

Outsiders: W = Entering wedge (from a central interior province—Honan, Hupei, Hunan, Kiangsi)
O = From another province outside the SW

NOTE: This table is limited because, of the 139 individuals whose names are known who occupied one of these five job categories, both the province of origin and the background were found for very few. The figures refer to posts; thus, some individuals holding more than one post were counted more than once.

TABLE 2

Background Pools and Job Category

Job Category	Ex-KMT	White	First Field Army	Second Field Army	Other[a]
MAC-AC Chairman or Vice-Chairman	5	O	1	3	1 (N-U)
MAC-AC Department Head	7	2	4	8	6 (3 N)+ (3 N-U)
MAC-AC Member	6	4	3	11	9 (3 U)+ (5 O)+ (1 N)
Military Region Official	O	O	2	6	1 (N)

MAC-AC Chairman and Vice-Chairman	N = 10
MAC-AC Department Head	N = 27 identified (of 69)
MAC-AC Member	N = 33 identified (of 58)
Military Region Official	N = 9 identified (of 10)

NOTE: Figured in terms of posts, as in Table 1. Again, some individuals counted more than once.

[a]The "other" category includes all those Communists who belonged neither to the First or Second Field Army according to the sources used here. The key for this column is as follows:

N signifies "other" who worked in the *North* liberated areas.

U signifies "other" who worked only in the *underground* movement in the Southwest.

O signifies "other" who was detached from an *other* Field Army System to the Second in 1949.

N-U signifies "other" who worked both in the *North* and in the Southwest *underground*.

originated with the founding of the Oyüwan soviet, formed in 1927 at the juncture of Hupei, Honan, and Anhwei provinces.[18] The majority of the men who led the 1949 Second Field Army in the civil war were here in the Ta-pieh Shan to organize the Fourth Front Army under Chang Kuo-t'ao from 1927 through the early 1930s. After defeats, the members of the soviet repaired to Szechwan in 1932, and, by the autumn of 1935, 90 percent of the future Second Field Army leadership was assembled there under Chang Kuo-t'ao.

When the Communist armies were reorganized in 1937 as the Eighth Route Army, its 129th Division under Liu Po-ch'eng showed continuity from its Fourth Army origins. By late 1940 this division had come to control the Chin-Chi-Lu-Yü (Shansi-Hopei-Shantung-Honan) Military Border Region, under Liu Po-ch'eng as its commander and Teng Hsiao-p'ing as its Political Commissar. All the leaders who later served under Liu Po-ch'eng in the Second Field Army came together in this region to plan and execute the 100 Regiments Campaign in late 1940. It was not until this time that the entire body of the future Field Army's command was operating together.

By 1945 this same group of men was formally designated the Chin-Chi-Lu-Yü Field Army. In late summer of 1947, when they withdrew to the south under enemy attack, they expanded a base in the Ta-pieh Shan. At that time they took on the title of the Central Plains Field Army, which they held until early 1949, when the Communists set up the system of numbered Field Armies.

A second set of leaders was associated with a group that had been under Ho Lung's command at one time or another.[19] The common route that this group followed began with participation in Ho's 120th Division after 1937, and included membership in the Shensi-Kansu-Ninghsia-Shansi-Suiyüan Military Headquarters in 1945, also headed by Ho.

18. The following is drawn from Whitson, *High Command*, Chapter 3.
19. Nine men fall into this category, although three of them were transferred to the Second Field Army in 1949 and went east with that army to Nanking, when the Second Field Army took over that city before proceeding to the Southwest. However, since personnel are being classified here by background and not by troop membership at the time of takeover, these three men will be considered as members of the old First Field Army group.

This particular group was detached from the First Field Army and assigned to the North China Field Army, under which it was designated the First Army in 1948. It fought under Nieh Jung-chen until late 1949. Then, in early 1949, it received the desig-nation of Eighteenth Army and was incorporated into the Second Field Army under that title in late 1949. In November 1949, it moved to north Szechwan to support Ho Lung, at that time the assistant commander of the First Field Army, in his occupation of Szechwan.[20] Here this group will be referred to as the First Field Army group, although it was no longer a part of that army by 1949.

Besides those Party members who belonged either to the First or Second Field Army, another fifteen Communists held posi-tions in the Southwest regime. These men had varied back-grounds. (See "Other" category in Table 2.) Six of them had had some experience in underground work in the Southwest; the others had mostly done government work in the liberated areas in North China before 1949. Nine of them were natives of provinces in the Southwest (local reds). On the whole, these men tended to be assigned to less outstanding positions than were the officers of the First and Second Field Armies.

Some have viewed the personnel situation in the Southwest in terms of a balance of power between the two Field Army groups. Whitson supports the balance of power theory; and Liu Chin, an anti-Communist writing from Hong Kong, agrees. Both base their interpretation largely on the fact that the situation in the Southwest differed so markedly from that in most other regions. In most other regions only one Field Army was stationed, and the principal political and military posts were dominated by officers of that one army. In the Southwest, on the other hand, Liu Po-ch'eng of the Second Field Army was made Chairman of the Military Administrative Committee and the Administrative Com-mittee, and his Political Commissar in the Second Field Army, Teng Hsiao-p'ing, was First Secretary of the Regional Party Bureau. But Ho Lung, head of the First Field Army group, was named Commander of the Southwest Military Region.[21]

Whitson terms it "surprising" that Ho Lung was made Com-

20. Whitson, *High Command*, p. 124, n. 27.

21. Liu Chin, *Ch'uan K'ang i-shou ch'ien-hou* [Before and After Szechwan and Sikang Changed Hands] (1956), p. 63.

mander of the region. He suggests that this was possibly done because "Mao and his advisers were reluctant to hand over so much power to Liu," who was quite popular both in Szechwan and among his own troops.[22]

Liu Chin paints a vivid picture of this popularity Liu Po-ch'eng enjoyed in his native province.[23] He describes the network of relations that Liu had built up when he fought in Szechwan's civil wars during the years after the 1911 revolution. Many of his old friends were local KMT generals, Liu Chin relates, who planned to depend on Liu for spoils and leniency when they heard that he was coming to conquer the Southwest. In this same vein, a pamphlet on Liu published in Taiwan claims that Liu's former political and social relations with the people in Szechwan and his friendship with the warlords there made him valuable during the Long March when the Red Army had to pass through Szechwan.[24]

Ho Lung, on the other hand, was feared throughout Szechwan by the military and the common people alike, as a fierce local bandit from neighboring Hunan, according to Liu Chin.[25] He too, however, was not without experience in the area. In the early 1930s, he had harassed the province from its southeast sector with Hsiao K'o and a batch of Communists. Also, Ho had established a new Communist base in the Hunan-Hupeh-Szechwan-Kweichow border area at that time.

Thus, according to this analysis, while Liu Po-ch'eng's familiarity with the Southwest and his reputation there made him useful in liberating the region, Ho Lung's distance from the people there, coupled with some knowledge of the area, made him a likely counterweight to Liu.[26] While it is interesting to speculate that such factors may have had some impact on personnel assignments, there is no way to validate this kind of theory. Moreover, this interpretation may have been influenced by the political stance of the Hong Kong and Taiwan sources noted above.

These same sources tell of poor treatment being accorded the local underground workers. Here again, this cannot necessarily

22. Whitson, *High Command*, p. 191.
23. Liu Chin, *Ch'uan K'ang*, pp. 52-58.
24. [Republic of China] Office of Military History, *Liu Po-ch'eng* (1971), p. 16.
25. Liu Chin, *Ch'uan K'ang*, p. 55.
26. Liu Chin suggests this point, in *Ch'uan K'ang*, p. 64.

TABLE 3
Provincial Origin and Job Category

Job Category	Szechwan	Yunnan	Kweichow	Sikang	SW Total (Locals)	Outsiders
MAC-AC Chairman or Vice-Chairman	5	2	0	1	8	2 Both from Hunan
MAC-AC Department Head	13	2	2	1	18	13 3 from Hupei 2 each from Hunan and Shantung 1 each from Kiangsi, Anhwei, Kiangsu, Shensi, Shansi, and Hopei
MAC-AC Member	13	8	7	6	34	18 4 each from Kiangsi, Hupei, and Hunan 2 each from Shensi and Hopei 1 each from Shantung and Kwangtung
Military Region Official	1	0	0	0	1	8 5 from Hunan 1 each from Shensi, Kiangsu, and Hupei

MAC-AC Chairman and Vice Chairman   N = 10
MAC-AC Department Head   N = 31 identified (of 69)
MAC-AC Member   N = 52 identified (of 58)
Military Region Official   N = 9 identified (of 10)

NOTE: Calculated in terms of posts, with some individuals counted more than once.

be accepted at face value, for Liu Chin does not tell us how he acquired his information.[27] Moreover, these analyses do not provide insights into the linkage patterns set up between the broad categories of insiders and outsiders, whites and reds.

For the purposes of this discussion, the division among Communists that was important is that between local and outside reds.[28] Each of these two broad groups had a different function to perform in the Southwest administration. Those Communists who had been born in the Southwest tended to concentrate in ordinary membership and department head posts.[29] These were the jobs that must have depended upon knowledge of Southwest society and may have required contacts with the local population. Thus these individuals tended to play the role of political middlemen, interrelating community needs to national demands.[30]

The outside reds, however, dominated the Military Region.[31] Chamberlain, citing his own findings along with those of Vogel and Oksenberg, stresses the importance of outsiders among the "wielders of the instruments of coercion" at the local (subcentral) level.[32]

Another interesting point about the outsiders in the Southwest is the predominance of men from the central interior provinces of Honan, Hupei, Hunan, and Kiangsi.[33] (See Tables 1 and 3.) As Chamberlain put it, those born in the central interior provinces, through their common origins and long experience in the Party, acted as a core bloc within the Communist leadership and brought an element of cohesion to this elite. In this way, they "served as an 'entering wedge' for the Peking leadership, an

27. *Ibid.*, pp. 113-114.
28. There were fifty posts in the sample that were definitely filled by Party members. (See Table 1.) (There is some slight overlap where one man might have held two posts, but for the sake of simplicity, the analysis will be made in terms of posts.) Of these fifty posts, then, sixteen were filled by native Southwesterners, and thirty-four were filled by outsiders. Only four of the Southwest natives were underground workers, among those that could be traced. Thus, despite reservations about the Liu Chin interpretation, very few underground workers in fact appeared in the posts in the sample.
29. Twelve of the sixteen held such posts.
30. Marc J. Swartz, in Swartz, *Local-Level Politics,* p. 199.
31. Eight of the nine Military Region officials whose provincial origin is known (of a total of ten Military Region officials) came from outside the region.
32. Chamberlain, "Transition and Consolidation," pp. 288-289.
33. In the Southwest, twenty-two of the thirty-seven outsider cadres identified in one of the four types of posts were natives of these four provinces.

instrument by which the latter might forge linkages between the center and the [region]."[34]

Thus, the outsiders acted as agents of the central, or national, level in Southwest politics. At the same time, the local reds, drawn from all four provinces in the Southwest, blended native origin with Party careers, and represented the meeting of Southwest society with the Communist values being promoted nationally.

As time went on, top officials born in the Southwest (local reds) were slowly weeded out. By mid-1952, Liu Po-ch'eng and Teng Hsiao-p'ing, the two senior officials in the Southwest Military Administrative Committee, had left the region to work full-time elsewhere. Both were native Szechwanese. Although Liu Po-ch'eng had been named Chairman of the Southwest Military Administrative Committee at its inception, and was reappointed as Chairman of the Administrative Committee in 1953, he attended only the first of the four plenums of the Southwest Military Administrative Committee, the one held in July 1950. As early as 1951, he was named president of the PLA Military Academy in Nanking, and thereafter devoted much of his time to that work, rarely coming to the Southwest.

Teng Hsiao-p'ing, as Vice-Chairman of both the Military Administrative Committee and the Administrative Committee, initially took over Liu's duties. He presided over the Second and Third Military Administrative Committee Plenums, in January and November 1951, respectively. But he, too, was destined to depart; after August of 1952 he spent most of his time in Peking, as the assistant premier of the Government Administrative Council.

Leaders on a level just below that of Liu and Teng were given greater responsibility after their seniors departed.[35] These men were not natives of the Southwest. Thus, Ho Lung, a Hunanese and head of the First Field Army faction, had been the Second Secretary of the Regional Party Bureau under Teng. With Teng's removal, Ho succeeded to the post of First Secretary. Moreover, it was he, as the senior cadre in the Southwest at the time, who ran

34. Chamberlain, "Transition and Consolidation," p. 263.
35. The following is based on Klein and Clark, *Biographic Dictionary*.

the Fourth Military Administrative Committee Plenum, in December 1952. Along with Ho, Sung Jen-ch'iung and Chang Chi-ch'ün, both Hunanese, also were promoted up one notch in the Party hierarchy at this time, and took on greater responsibilities than they had had before. Both of these men were from the Second Field Army.

Some have interpreted these changes in relation to the balance of power theory mentioned above.[36] Their interpretation is that the departure of Liu and Teng and the promotion of Ho meant an increase in the power of the First Field Army in the Southwest. However, according to the line of analysis presented here, the key aspect of this shift lay in the exit of leading native Southwest officials (local reds) and the rise of outsiders. This development can be compared with the gradual departure of Yeh Chien-ying, then a top official in the Central-South Region, from his native Kwangtung after 1952. According to Vogel, Yeh had been in sympathy with the localist cause in Kwangtung, and his absence from that province after 1952 coincided in time with an attack on localism in Cantonese politics.[37] It is interesting to note that this withdrawal of local and important reds occurred in both regions at about the same point in time as the Military Administrative Committee's conversion to the Administrative Committee, when regional powers were diminished. Quite possibly this removal of powerful local officials from the regional administrations was one way of cutting down the importance of regional government and of localism generally.

In conclusion, the division into local and outside reds is the important one in understanding central, regional, and local linkages in the Southwest in the early 1950s. The concept of the political middleman, while applying in general terms to all the leaders, particularly helps explain the role of the local reds. And Chamberlain's ideas on the important role of the red outsider in military matters and as the "entering wedge" help in analyzing changes in the proportions of local as against outside reds over time.

Local Whites: Democratic Personages and KMT-era Generals. A large number of local whites played a part in the administration of the

36. Based on a personal letter from Huang Chen-hsia, June 16, 1973.
37. Vogel, *Canton*, p. 119.

Southwest region during the period of regional government. In fact, locals in general (both whites and reds) figured heavily in this administration.[38] (See Table 3.) This is at odds with Chamberlain's finding that, of the three cities he studied, consolidation or "the assignment to leadership positions in the community of those with few ties thereto" was the outstanding strategy in personnel placement in Canton, the city furthest from Peking of the three.[39] For if this same strategy obtained throughout China, there should have been even fewer insiders in the Southwest, which is considerably more distant from the capital. Possibly, the isolation and autonomy the Southwest provinces had enjoyed under the Republic meant that there was a more salient need here to accommodate the local population and the pre-1949 leaders than in most other sections of the country.

The locals whose personal histories could be traced were categorized as either whites or reds.[40] Whites were further broken down into two distinct groups of individuals by background. (See Table 1.) The overwhelming proportion of the whites were turncoat KMT-era generals.[41] These men turned over, or peacefully surrendered to the Communists, as the advancing PLA armies spelled certain collapse of KMT rule in the closing months of 1949. It should be noted here that these officials generally had not been supporters of the KMT, but were accustomed to independence at home and noninterference by outsiders. The Nationalist government's intrusions into the Southwest in the 1930s and 1940s were deeply resented by them.

The remaining whites in the Southwest were so-called "democratic personages": men who had been professors, editors, scientists, or members of political parties in protest against the KMT before 1949.

There was a difference in the type of posts assigned to these two groups of whites. The democratic personages tended to be

38. Of the sample of 139 individuals, the provincial origin of ninety-four could be traced. Of these ninety-four, fifty-seven were born in the Southwest provinces: well over one-half.

39. Chamberlain, "Transition and Consolidation," pp. 254, 301.

40. Of the fifty-seven locals, backgrounds were identified for thirty-nine. Twenty-three of these were whites and sixteen were reds.

41. Seventeen out of the twenty-three identified whites were KMT-era generals. Many of these were local warlords before 1949 with only tenuous connections with the KMT. The remaining six were "democratic personages."

granted positions as ordinary members on the various committees under the Military Administrative Committee—such as the
Culture-Education Committee, or the Finance-Economic Committee. These were positions that called for particular skills but
had little to do with power. The ex-KMT group, however, was
awarded a wide variety of jobs: five were made Vice-Chairmen of
the Military Administrative Committee and seven were appointed
heads of departments. The departments they chaired ranged
from the Water Conservancy Department to the Judicial Department and the Supervisory Commission; others served as deputy
heads for the Agriculture-Forestry, Culture-Education, and
Labor Departments. These jobs required skill as well as some
linkage to power centers in Southwest society.

How can the relatively high proportion of these local "whites,"
particularly of ex-KMT turncoat generals, within the leadership
ranks of the new regional regime in the Southwest be interpreted?[42] The concept of "cooptation" has direct bearing on this
issue. This pertains to "the process of absorbing new elements
into the leadership or policy-determining structure of an organization as a means of averting threats to its stability or existence."[43]

There are at least two types of cooptation: one kind is used
when the organization has a need either to establish the legitimacy of its authority or to further the administrative accessibility
of the coopted group. Another type is employed where there is a
need to adjust to pressures from specific power centers within the
community.[44] Kao, in his study of Wuhan, uses similar terms to
explain the use of whites there.[45] He notes their roles in communication with and control over certain sectors of the population.

In the Southwest, where tens of thousands of KMT troops had
recently surrendered and still resided, and where local secret
societies had connections with the former warlord generals,

42. One-third (twenty-three) of the identified personnel (seventy) were local
whites. This is the same number of men as those identified as belonging to the
Second Field Army among the Southwest leadership.
43. Philip Selznick, "Coöptation," in Robert K. Merton, *Reader in Bureaucracy*
(1952), p. 135.
44. *Ibid.*
45. Kao, "Urban Bureaucratic Elite," p. 225.

power considerations apparently played more of a part in the case of the ex-warlords than they did for the democratic personages. Apparently members of the latter group were given jobs more in order to ensure the accessibility of their talents and know-how. The ex-KMT group, however, did obtain some posts carrying at least the trappings of power, such as the heads of the Judicial Department and of the Supervisory Commission. Moreover, the visibility of this group was probably felt to be especially crucial in this area, where the chief enemies of the new regime were the allies and subordinates of these ex-KMT generals.

Turning once again to Liu Chin, his analysis of the employment of the ex-KMT generals sheds further light on the subject. Despite a need for caution in taking at face value all he says, there may be some validity to his interpretation. He alludes to these factors in explaining the use of the ex-KMT generals: a type of psychological warfare toward Chinese overseas (presumably including people on Taiwan); the need to pacify and placate these men in an attempt to assure quietude among their subordinate troops; and the possibility of setting them up as idols for the local Southwest population.[46]

Thus, in the case of this category of "white" or non-Communist KMT-era personnel, somewhat different considerations applied than in the case of the democratic personages. For by honoring these men, it was apparently hoped that the potentially most troublesome elements in Southwest society would be appeased, and that the counter-revolutionary suppression in this area could thereby be facilitated.

In general, the whites—local non-Communists of prestige—stood as the third link in the chain uniting certain power centers of society and politics in the Southwest with the new central government. As representatives of the pre-1949 order in the various Southwest provinces, their presence at the newly formed regional level meant that key segments of the leadership in the localities were being aggregated at the supraprovincial level. And in their association at that level with Communists both from the Southwest and from outside, they completed the blending of individuals from various layers of administration, from various

46. Liu Chin, *Ch'uan K'ang*, see pp. 158-160, 166, 169, and 174-175 for treatment of high-level turncoats, especially Teng Hsi-hou, Liu Wen-hui, and P'an Wen-hua.

political groupings, and from various locales that was required for an overall integration here. In this sense, the competing political centers of the more local levels of society and of the new central government were bridged through use of a variegated leadership group (Proposition 5.1).

The Leadership in the Provinces

This section will take a brief look at the nature of the personnel assigned to govern the Southwest provinces after 1949, in order to determine how this group compared with the regional leadership. The analysis is based on lists of the provincial governors and vice-governors, and of the military commanders and political commissars, and their respective deputies in the provinces.[47] (See Tables 4 and 5.) Interestingly, the pattern in the provinces was quite similar to that at the regional level.

Thus, in Kweichow, Yunnan, and Szechwan, outsiders were governors. These men belonged to the Second Field Army in the cases of Kweichow and Yunnan, and to the First Field Army in Szechwan. This resembles the situation in the region, insofar as the three most important regional leaders all entered the Southwest with the invading Field Armies; there also, two were Second Field Army officers and one was a First Field Army officer. As noted above, two of these, Liu and Teng, were native Szechwanese, but Ho and the several others who took on more power after 1952 were all outsiders. Vice-governors, on the other hand, tended to be locals.[48] This too compares with the arrangement on the Military Administrative Committee and the Administrative Committee, where seven of the nine vice-chairmen were natives of a Southwest province. On both the regional and provincial levels, there was a tendency to pair an outsider with a local deputy.

Moreover, among these locals in the provincial governments, at least one Yunnanese vice-governor was a Communist, and Sikang's governor also was a Communist. The remaining two vice-

47. For government leaders in the provinces, see *SCMP*, No. 474 (1952), pp. 15-16. For military personnel in the provinces, see Liang Po-ming, "Chün-ch'ü," p. 42. See also Appendix.

48. All three in Kweichow were natives of the province; three of Yunnan's four vice-governors were native Yunnanese; and two of Szechwan's four were native Szechwanese. In Sikang, the governor and two of his five assistants were from Sikang.

TABLE 4
Provincial Origin (1) and Background (2) of Provincial
Governors and Vice-Governors

Position	Kweichow	Yunnan	Szechwan	Sikang
Governor	(1) Hunan (2) Second Field Army	Hunan Second Field Army	Kiangsi First Field Army	Sikang Underground in SW
Vice-Governor	(1) Kweichow (2) ?	Yunnan With PLA in N. China	Szechwan Second Field Army	Sikang ex-KMT
2nd Vice-Governor	(1) Kweichow (2) ?	Yunnan ex-KMT	Shensi Second Field Army	Shansi Second Field Army
3rd Vice-Governor	(1) Kweichow (2) ?	Yunnan ex-KMT	Szechwan ?	Sikang ?
4th Vice-Governor	—	(1) Shantung (2) ?	—	?
5th Vice-Governor	—	—	—	(1) Honan (2) ?

SOURCE: *Survey of China Mainland Press*, No. 474 (December 17, 1952), pp. 15-16.
NOTE: — indicates position unfilled. ? indicates data unavailable although the post was filled.

governors in Yunnan were turncoat generals, as was one of Sikang's vice-governors. Thus at this level again, one finds the mixture of leaders from different background pools now working together, as in the Military Administrative Committee and the Administrative Committee.

A further similarity between the two levels is apparent in the appointment of officials to the provincial Military Districts. Among the nine officials of the Southwest Military Region whose provincial origin is known, eight were outside reds. All but one of these men were members of the First or Second Field Army. In the individual provinces, it was possible to trace the provincial

TABLE 5

Provincial Origin(1) and Background (2) of Officers in the
Provincial Military Districts in the Southwest

Position	Kweichow	Yunnan	Szechwan	Sikang
Commander	(1) Hunan (2) Second Field Army	Hunan Second Field Army	Hupeh First Field Army	Sikang SW Underground Worker
Political Commissar	(1) Hunan (2) Second Field Army	Hupeh Second Field Army	Kiangsi First Field Army	Sikang Same person as Commander
Deputy Commander	(1) ? (2) Second Field Army	Hupeh ?	? Second Field Army	Sikang ?
Deputy Political Commissar	(1) ? (2) Second Field Army	? ?	Shensi Second Field Army	? ?

SOURCE: Liang Po-ming, "Chung-kung chün-ch'ü piao-chieh," *Chung-kung wen-t'i*, No. 1 (May 1954), p. 42.

NOTE: ? indicates data unavailable.

background of a total of eleven military personnel. Only in Sikang were natives employed in the Military District at all; in the other provincial districts, as in the regional Military Region, the "wielders of the instruments of coercion" were Communists from outside.

Thus, there was no basic difference between the provincial and regional leadership in terms of composition. The only difference between the two levels lay in the fact that the local whites at the regional level were more outstanding in local society; and that the Communists in the regional administration held higher posts in the Field Army military hierarchies than those assigned to the provincial Military Districts. The overall effect at both levels was to weave the entire area together by scattering members of distinct elites throughout the government in a patterned fashion.

In general in the Southwest, posts carrying real power were

bestowed on the military, most of whom were outside reds. Non-Communist natives at both provincial and regional levels were coopted to provide legitimacy and accessibility, as well as to placate those who had held positions of power in the pre-1949 local society. And the native Communists were the go-betweens for these two groups, and, in a symbolic sense, for the local and the national, the old and the new.

Military Deployment and New Units for Control

Military pacification was crucial in creating order in the Southwest after takeover. Accordingly, the deployment of the troops of the two Field Armies in the Southwest was the means used to create new units for control. Chapter One pointed out the recurring importance of structural devices in establishing new arrangements of power and control in China. In the early 1950s in the Southwest the military played a central role in this process.

The degree of regional military control varied among regions and even among provinces in the early post-liberation years. Among the six Great Regions, the most extensive control was exercised in the Northwest and Southwest, where hostile ethnic minority groups resided, where many KMT troops had surrendered, and from which areas the military advance on Tibet was planned. Thus, in these two regions, the provincial and regional governments were heavily dominated by the military.[49]

The military's connection with control in the regions dated back to the period of takeover. In the Southwest, as in the rest of China, the civil war campaigns of the late 1940s sketched out the area for the Great Administrative Region there.[50] In the Southwest, the fact that it was the troops of the First and Second Field Armies that were the liberators may not have been purely a matter of chance. As noted above,[51] the conquest here was planned and deliberately worked out: it was undertaken by specific armies moving from various corners of China to converge on the Southwest. Quite possibly, the particular troops chosen to take part in the advance were selected because their commanders

49. John Gittings, *The Role of the Chinese Army* (1967), pp. 270-271.
50. *CB*, No. 170 (1952), pp. 3-4.
51. See Chapter Three.

had previously had some experience in this long isolated, autonomous, and problematic area.

The troops of the Second and First Field Armies took over and
then occupied the Southwest. The Second, however, had been
fighting together with the Third Field Army since the Huai-hai
Battle of December 1948, and the two forces moved into East
China together in the spring of 1949. In fact, Liu Po-ch'eng and
his troops temporarily took over the government and military
control of Nanking in April 1949, and Liu served briefly as
Chairman of the Military Control Commission there. Apparently
those who planned the subsequent Southwest campaign felt it
desirable that Ch'en Yi and his Third Field Army remain in the
east while Liu Po-ch'eng proceeded westward.

Moreover, when the Second Field Army moved first south and
then westward after leaving Nanking, it was aided by units from
the Fourth Field Army. But these units, rather than staying in the
Southwest, withdrew to the neighboring Central-South area.
And, instead of Liu Po-ch'eng's troops being left in total command of the Southwest area, they were supplemented by the
forces under Ho Lung, coming down from the Northwest area.
Presumably, Ho's assignment to the Southwest, where he remained after takeover, was based on a decision that his talents
would be better used here, where he had spent some time in the
1930s, than in the Northwest with P'eng Te-huai and the rest of
the First Field Army.

Turning again to Liu Chin, he offers an interpretation of the
deployment of troops in the Southwest during takeover and
thereafter. Since this portion of his work deals largely with considerations before the takeover, when he may have been present
in the Southwest, his judgments may have somewhat more credi-
bility on this matter.

According to Liu Chin, before liberation, the CCP leadership
hoped for a peaceful liberation of the Southwest. He claims that
Szechwan and Sikang were considered the focal points in achieving this. Yunnan was not considered to be a problem (possibly
owing to a stronger sympathy for the Communists there)[52] and

52. One gets this impression from Chang Wen-shih, *Yün-nan nei-mu* [Behind
the Scenes in Yunnan] (1949). See also George Moseley, *The Consolidation of the
South China Frontier* (1973), p. 34, on local guerrilla activity in support of the
CCP in Yunnan from 1948 on; and Chapter Two, the section entitled "Politics:
Local Leadership and Groups."

the troops in Kweichow were feeble.[53] At another point, Liu contends that neither Kweichow nor east or south Szechwan was considered to require an army (*ping-t'uan*) to control it.[54]

Apparently, only north and west Szechwan and Sikang were seen as being problematic, according to this account. The military strategy behind the liberation campaign in Szechwan, then, was purposely to give over both north and west Szechwan to the KMT, to entice its troops voluntarily to draw back and become concentrated in those areas.[55] Ho Lung and his forces had been positioned on the Shensi-Szechwan border, and after feinting for a time, they gradually descended into north and west Szechwan and took the KMT by surprise. The KMT fell into the trap laid for them, and many thousands of troops, recognizing their plight, chose this area in which to surrender. Ho Lung was then put in control of the most difficult and potentially troublesome areas in the Southwest, leaving the less challenging locales for Liu.

Thus, partitioning of the Southwest after liberation was based on the final stages of the campaign in a purposive manner, with the commanders of the different armies taking charge over the military districts they occupied at the close of the war. The result was a division of the provinces in the Southwest according to the amounts of area it was convenient for one corps to administer.

According to Huang Chen-hsia,[56] immediately after takeover the Southwest was divided among the various occupying armies in the following manner (see Table 6): the Third Army of the Second Field Army was split up, with two of its three corps (the 10th and 11th) stationed in south Szechwan and one (the 12th) in

53. Liu Chin, *Ch'uan K'ang*, pp. 171-173.
54. *Ibid.*, pp. 7-10 and p. 42. Liu explains the deals the CCP had made with KMT General Lo Kuang-wen, whose troops controlled south and east Szechwan and with Kuo Ju-kuei in south Szechwan, respectively. Communist accounts of the takeover agree on this strategy. See my Chapter Three on the takeover.
55. *Ibid.*, p. 4; see also footnote 19 on the takeover of the Southwest in Chapter Three.
56. The following is based on a letter from Huang Chen-hsia, July 10, 1973. See also Whitson, *High Command*, pp. 190-192. For a slightly different and probably later deployment, see Fang Chün-kuei, "Chung-kung ti ye-chan chün" [The Chinese Communists' Field Armies], *CKWT*, No. 1 (1954), p. 49.

east Szechwan.[57] Its Fourth Army was stationed largely in Yun-nan, and most of its Fifth was in Kweichow. The Eighteenth Army, which was composed of the men referred to here as the

TABLE 6

Military Deployment in the Southwest, Immediately After Takeover (1) and After December 1950 (2)

Ping-t'uan (Army)			
Eighteenth Army	Fifth Army	Fourth Army	Third Army
60th *Chün* (Corps)	16th *Chün*	13th *Chün*	10th *Chün*
(1) West Szechwan	(1) West & South Szechwan	(1) Kunming	(1) South Szechwan
(2) Korea & local Szechwan units	(2) Korea & Kunming	(2) Yunnan	(2) Deactivated & Korea
61st *Chün*	17th *Chün*	14th *Chün*	11th *Chün*
(1) North Szechwan	(1) Tsunyi	(1) West Yunnan	(1) South Szechwan
(2) Deactivated & Korea	(2) Deactivated & Independent in Kweichow	(2) Yunnan	(2) Deactivated & Independent & Korea
62nd *Chün*	18th *Chün*	15th *Chün*	12th *Chün*
(1) Sikang	(1) Tibet	(1) West & South Szechwan	(1) East Szechwan
(2) Korea & Yunnan	(2) Tibet	(2) Korea & Independent	(2) Local regiment in Szechwan & Korea

SOURCES: Personal letter from Huang Chen-hsia, dated July 10, 1973; and William W. Whitson, *The Chinese Communist High Command* (New York: Praeger, 1973), Chart C, p. 124.

57. Whitson, *High Command*, pp. 140-141. Here Whitson notes that most of the "Szechwan faction" of the Second Field Army elite was assembled in the early 1930s. Ch'en Hsi-lien was in this group. During the early 1930s Ch'en was fighting in northeast Szechwan, in an area which later fell under his control as part of the new East Szechwan Military District in 1949. See footnote 58 below.

First Field Army group in the Southwest, was divided up, its three corps (the 60th, 61st, and 62nd) going to west Szechwan, north Szechwan, and Sikang respectively.[58] One corps (the 16th) from the Fifth Army and a part of one corps (the 15th) from the Fourth Army occupied a section of land on the Szechwan-Sikang border.

This arrangement suggests that the design for military occupation in the Southwest had several facets. First, no one province was to be dominated by any one entire army. Second, each army was to be split up, which would have prevented its establishing a stronghold in any one locale. Third, the Field Army groups were probably located in areas where they were considered most effective. Fourth, the military control work required at the first stage of liberation called for the policing of relatively small blocs of territory by separate army groups.[59] This justified a balancing of the two Field Army groups which may have made sense in political terms as well.

The overall significance of the partition of the Southwest was that it led to the institution of new patterns of control in the localities of the Southwest, based on the structure of certain First and Second Field Army units. The superimposition of units of the PLA, a national organization, onto the lower levels of society in the Southwest made for a juncture of the local and the national and of the old and the new. In this regard, troop deployment served the same liaison function as personnel assignments in the Southwest did.

With the Korean War, certain shifts were made in the disposition of troops in the Southwest, as certain troops were transferred to the battlefield; but the basic pattern of dividing the Southwest up by army corps continued (see Table 6). Here again, as in the

58. Szechwan was divided into four administrative offices in 1949. The pattern of leadership assignment corresponded with the military deployment; thus the North and West Szechwan offices were headed by Hu Yao-pang and Li Ching-ch'üan, respectively, both with First Field Army backgrounds. The South and East offices' Chairmen were Li Ta-chang and Yen Hung-yen, respectively, both of whom belonged to the Second Field Army system. Officials of these offices are listed in *JMST* 1951, p. 卯 37.
59. See Chapter Three, the section on the Military Region.

case of personnel, some see these shifts in terms of an increase in the power of the First Field Army.[60]

Thus, Huang Chen-hsia, in his biographies of Wang Chin-shan and Ch'en Hsi-lien, notes that the crack troops of the Second Field Army were the first to go to the war. These included Liu Po-ch'eng's basic ranks, and Huang claims that their departure made Liu very sad.[61] Both Ch'en Hsi-lien and Ch'en Keng, the commanders of the Second Field Army's Third and Fourth Armies respectively, were sent off with the People's Volunteer Army. In fact, the war claimed troops from all the corps of the Second Field Army but the 13th, 14th, and 18th. Of these, the 13th and 14th were stationed in Yunnan and, besides pacification duties at home, were involved in supporting the Vietminh against the French, according to Huang.[62] The 18th corps, under Chang Kuo-hua, had liberated and was garrisoning Tibet. Huang claims that the emergency transfer of 80 percent of the regular forces from Szechwan and Kweichow at this time left what he terms the "Ho Lung-Li Ching-ch'üan [First Field Army] clique" with a free hand in military matters in the Southwest after 1952.[63]

However, whether or not Ho's hand was in fact strengthened by these maneuvers, the thesis presented here is unaltered. The remaining troops, those that had not gone to Korea, Vietnam, or Tibet, were deactivated. Of these, some divisions were given independent status and remained in position; others were redesignated local troops and were responsible for local security in Szechwan and Sikang.[64] But in general, the original division of power at the lower levels persisted: most of the units remained stationed in basically the same areas they had been in when formally under their Field Army commands.[65]

Thus, as before, the overall arrangement meant that each

60. Based on personal letters from Huang Chen-hsia dated June 16, 1973 and July 10, 1973; Huang Chen-hsia, *Chung-kung chün-jen*; Whitson, *High Command*, pp. 190, 193; Office of Military History, *Liu Po-ch'eng*, p. 31.

61. Huang, *Chung-kung chün-jen*, see his biography of Ch'en Hsi-lien.

62. Letter from Huang Chen-hsia, July 10, 1973.

63. Letter from Huang, June 16, 1973.

64. The above is drawn from Whitson, *High Command*, pp. 190-193; and letter from Huang, July 10, 1973.

65. See Whitson, *High Command*, Chart C, p. 124.

province, and consequently the Southwest region as a whole, was realigned on a new basis. Each subprovincial area was portioned out to a separate corps, responsible for establishing control on a local basis.[66] Moreover, the system dictated that troop units were dispersed, giving Ho Lung's forces, though fewer, military power over more critical areas, and Liu Po-ch'eng's troops, which were more numerous, control over a larger area. With time, Liu's forces were thinned out, strengthening the position of Ho, the outsider. And, despite the division of power in the localities between troops of two Field Armies, at the top of the military hierarchy, leaders from both Field Army systems came together in the Military Region. In this way, the entire Southwest became a new unit in military terms, a part of the national system. At the same time, its component provinces were drawn together as they had not been in the past.

The linkage between Integration I and II in a large, developing, and malintegrated nation—such as China was in 1949—can feasibly be made at the regional or intermediary level, positioned between the center on the one hand and the provinces and localities on the other. For if integration as a general process is to proceed at all, it must involve the joining of competing centers of political activity—in this case, the new central government in Peking and the subprovincial areas in the Southwest.

This chapter has dealt with these issues. First, it has shown that the personnel at the regional level represented a mixture of the following types of leaders: men native to the Southwest (local whites), coopted mainly in order that their various skills might be made accessible to the new leadership; Communist military leaders with previous ties to the Southwest (local reds), who could act as political middlemen in relating Southwest society to the new organs of power throughout China; and Communist military leaders from outside the Southwest (outside reds), who served as an "entering wedge" in instituting the new order in the Southwest.

---

66. Liang Po-ming, "Chün-ch'ü." On pp. 36-39 he explains the subdivision of provinces and how these subdivisions corresponded with Field Army armies, corps, and divisions. It is likely that in Szechwan at least such an arrangement would have interfered with the pre-takeover *fang-ch'ü* system of military control discussed in Chapter Two.

Also, this chapter has described the centrality of military problems in the Southwest after liberation; and it has pointed out that the creation of new units for control was basically a matter of military deployment, through a division of the Southwest into smaller areas controlled by sections of the two Field Armies there.

Both in personnel appointments and in the disposition of troops, there was the same attempt to connect Southwest society with new forms of control and with new national structures of power. Moreover, in both realms, natives to the Southwest were removed as time went on. In this way, Integration I was furthered. And this development coincided in time with the Southwest's loss of its specialness in the eyes of the central government, described in Chapter Three, and with the shift of control over regional administrative matters away from the region and to the central government, discussed in Chapter Four.

Finally, at the same time that the Southwest was being linked administratively with national power organs—the CCP and the PLA—the subprovincial localities were being united within the Southwest by the new regional organs. This was done in part through blending leadership groups in the Military Administrative Committee, and through bringing together the two occupying Field Armies in the Military Region. The next two chapters will discuss in more detail this aspect of integration, referred to here as Integration II.

CHAPTER VI

Integration II: Strategies Used toward Trade, National Minorities, and Counter-revolutionaries in Creating Integration within the Southwest Region

This chapter will deal with the policies geared at attaining Integration II, the process by which the localities within the Southwest became administratively connected with each other.[1] Instead of viewing this as one undifferentiated process, the discussion will focus on the policies dictated toward three different problem areas: trade, minority nationalities, and counter-revolutionaries. It will demonstrate how, in each case, the strategy advocated to achieve integration was linked to the nature of the problem at hand; and how the form integration was to take vis-à-vis that problem was related to the strategy chosen. Moreover, the type of role the regional-level organs were to play in solving the difficulties in each case was closely related to the type of strategy favored in integration. Thus it will be shown that in the early years after takeover in the Southwest, there was not one uniform approach taken toward all problems; instead, different approaches designed for different problems led to different roles for the regional administration during Integration II. It should be pointed out here that the analysis presented in this chapter is one that the author has superimposed upon the events recorded in the Southwest press. Whether or not the leadership of the

---

1. The focus here is on policy itself; Chapter Seven examines the successes and failures in implementation of the policy.

People's Republic of China (PRC) actually operated on the basis of such a model is a moot point for our purposes here.

Previous chapters have suggested that integration as an administrative process is a matter of linkages: of creating new relationships between levels. This chapter is concerned not only with unification within the Southwest region (Integration II), but also with the interrelationship between Integration I and II over time. Chapters Three and Four described how the geographical integration that had been effected within regions nationally by late 1952 gave way to a more functional integration in 1953 and 1954. Related to this development, the nature of Integration II also began to shift in 1952. During that year and thereafter, hierarchy and structure came to play bigger roles in linking the localities into the Southwest subsystem. These changes will be dealt with in this chapter.

The focus here will be on the three problem areas of trade, minorities, and counter-revolutionaries, in order to follow through on themes introduced earlier. In the Introduction, regionalism was defined as being a matter of local distinctiveness combined with local control of local economic and military resources and local decisional autonomy. It was also pointed out that regional associations fall into three broad categories: economic, cultural, and political. Here the thread laid down in Chapter Two's discussion of the pre-1949 Southwest will be picked up, and the typical problems of regionalism in the Southwest in these three broad categories will be traced over time, by investigating how they were handled by the Communists.

Chapter Two explained that the three problem areas analyzed there—trade, minorities, and local leadership and groups—were particularly characteristic of the types of integration and malintegration that marked local life in the Southwest before 1949. It showed that the small concentrations of population and territory in the Southwest were relatively cut off one from the next, in matters of political groupings and trade relations; and that many different and separate minority tribes were scattered across the landscape. Thus these three areas best represented the problems of regionalism (local distinctiveness plus local control) in politics, economics, and culture, respectively, in the Southwest as of 1949. Moreover, these issues were the principal concerns of the new regime in dealing with the Southwest after 1949. And in focusing on these three topics and their treatment, in a more general sense the analysis here will examine the approach toward problems of local separatism and diversity adopted by the PRC just after takeover.

This chapter will be divided into two sections. The first section will consider the relationship between the nature of each problem area, the strategy chosen to deal with it, and the type of integration envisaged for that area during Integration II from takeover until 1952. The second section will be concerned with the shifts in strategy and mode of integration that occurred in Integration II after 1952, as the nature of Integration I was also changing on a national basis.

Strategies and Propositions

This section presents two model strategies for handling regionalism and achieving integration. These two strategies, labeled here "direct" and "indirect," respectively, have been gleaned from literature on regionalism. The section then offers four propositions relating these strategies to the process of Integration II.

As indicated in the Introduction, each strategy entails an administrative approach to dealing with personnel, units of rule, and concrete policy measures. Basically, the direct approach seeks to install outsiders to the region in positions of power within the region to avoid favoritism toward the local population. It erases traditional "natural" administrative boundaries, or establishes new units, organs, and hierarchies of control, thus shaking up old and habitual administrative patterns. Finally, it imposes a uniform policy toward substantive issues in all localities, regardless of local conditions. It attempts to level disparities and refuses to compromise with traditional practices. The aim here is to achieve a forced consensus through controls and manipulation.

The indirect model, alternatively, involves retention of old personnel and traditional administrative boundaries, and entrusts to these officials the adaptation of national policy to circumstances in the localities. The purpose is to raise local initiative, enthusiasm, and consequently allegiance by permitting locals to participate actively in their own governance. Such participation, it was noted earlier, is authorized only within a centrally controlled mandate.

These two model strategies need not be viewed as mutually exclusive. Rather, they can be considered as two poles of a continuum, so that a given policy might, for example, be more direct than indirect, but still contain some elements of each strategy.

Several authors, in discussing political integration, suggest a similar dichotomy of methods. One writer lists two "public policy strategies for the achievement of national integration": the first, the "assimilationist" strategy, is used to eliminate the distinctive cultural traits of minority communities into a "national" culture. The second, called the "unity in diversity solution," is to establish national loyalties without eliminating subordinate cultures. Also, this author describes two modal strategies for integrating values: one stresses the importance of consensus and is concerned with maximizing uniformity through coercion or exhortation. The other emphasizes the interplay of individual and group interests.[2] In both cases, the first alternative parallels the direct model described above, and the second coincides with the indirect model.

Also, Emerson, from whom the terms direct and indirect were borrowed,[3] extends this distinction to the realm of nation-building in Africa. He notes that at the extremes, tribalism can be handled in two ways in the course of nation-building. First, tribes as such can be used as the building blocks of the nation (indirect). Alternatively, they can be eradicated as completely as possible, and replaced with a populace having a single national solidarity (direct).[4]

Finally, a third writer states that "if ethnic or territorial groups cannot be assimilated, fully integrated, or eliminated [direct], the principle of recognition of diversity can be applied [indirect]."[5]

2. Myron Weiner, "Political Integration and Political Development," *Annals of the American Academy of Political and Social Sciences* [hereafter *Annals*], No. 358 (1965), pp. 56, 59.
3. See the Introduction.
4. Rupert Emerson, "Nation-Building in Africa," in K. W. Deutsch and W. J. Foltz, eds., *Nation-Building* (1963), p. 105.
5. Ivo D. Duchacek, *Comparative Federalism* (1970), p. 95. See also Cynthia H. Enloe, *Ethnic Conflict and Political Development* (1973), pp. 3-5. Here she points out that "ethnic identity can be a building block, but also a potential stumbling block, on the road to modernity." She deals too with the "ways in which institutions and jurisdictional patterns foster national integration" and with the "discrepancy between conditions of unity and requisites for modernization." See Enloe, pp. 84-85, and her Chapters 4 and 6.

All three writers, then, posit two contradictory methods of handling diversity during political development and nation-building; and all draw the same basic distinction between these two methods as is drawn here in administrative terms, in deline-ating the two model strategies used in the present analysis.

In fact, one or the other of these approaches has been followed to some extent in many of the major countries attempting to create unified nations out of culturally diverse territories. It was from a study of the policies adopted in these countries that the two model strategies were composed. The propositions that follow were also based upon data showing how these other countries handled problems of regionalism.

For example, India,[6] Yugoslavia,[7] and Nigeria,[8] all nations where groups with pronounced cultural differences live in sepa-rate regions of the country, have generally applied an indirect strategy in handling diversity. Thus, each has permitted ethnic-ally distinctive regions to retain their identities in various ways: India's creation of linguistic states in 1956 has reinforced ethni-city; and Yugoslavia's six republics and Nigeria's strongly feder-alist state system (particularly up to 1966) both use local ethnic divisions as the basis for political representation in national politics.

Thus, in Fisher's interpretation, the goal in Yugoslavia has been "to obtain integration through controlled differences or ordered local diversity under an indirect mechanism of federal supervision."[9] Also, since cultural homogenity or increased uni-

6. On India, see Selig S. Harrison, *India: The Most Dangerous Decades* (1960); and Joan V. Bondurant, *Regionalism Versus Provincialism* (1958).

7. On Yugoslavia, see Gary K. Bertsch, *Nation-Building in Yugoslavia* (1971); Jack C. Fisher, *Yugoslavia—A Multinational State* (1966); Nicholas R. Lang, "The Dialectics of Decentralization," *World Politics* 27, No. 3 (1975), pp. 309-335; and Gary K. Bertsch and George M. Zaninovich, "A Factor-Analytic Method of Identifying Different Political Cultures," *Comparative Politics* 6, No. 2 (1974), pp. 219-243.

8. On Nigeria, see R. L. Sklar and C. S. Whitaker, "Nigeria," in G. M. Carter, ed., *National Unity and Regionalism in Eight African States* (1966), pp. 7-150; Charles R. Nixon, "Self-Determination: The Nigeria/Biafra Case," *World Politics* 24, No. 4 (1972), pp. 473-497; and Robert Melson and Howard Wolpe, "Mod-ernization and the Politics of Communalism," *American Political Science Review* 64, No. 4 (1970), pp. 1112-1130.

9. Fisher, *Yugoslavia,* p. 6.

formity appeared politically impossible, it was decided to stabilize and control the existing diversity by increased participation of the individual in economic and political life.[10] The plan here was to utilize a uniform administrative system based on the commune along with Party control to bolster unity while preserving six ethnic republics.

In India, according to Watts, from 1947 to 1967 the Congress Party fostered cohesion between ethnically diverse localities on the one hand and the central government on the other, and provided a context for intergovernmental cooperation.[11] Whatever integration was thereby achieved must have been valuable indeed. As an example of the power of the localities, local (state) leaders in India were so vocal in opposing the appointment of nonresident, centrally recruited civil servants into their states during the reorganization of the states in 1956 that the scheme had to be dropped.[12]

In Nigeria the power of regional groups was so strong that not only were the large ethnic groups and their leaders left in control of their traditional territories at the time of independence, but when the constitution was written, the central government was assigned a very small range of exclusive powers.[13] The hope was to try to promote responsible self-government at the regional level by extending regional autonomy and curtailing the power of the central government.[14]

On the other hand, Ethiopia under Haile Selassie[15] and France after the Revolution[16] both employed a direct strategy in leveling local disparities and establishing strong, unitary centralist states. In Ethiopia centralization was attempted through one dominant ethnic group. Here fourteen provinces, of which some corresponded only roughly to older regional divisions (and some did

10. *Ibid.*, p. 25.
11. Ronald L. Watts, *Administration in Federal Systems* (1970), p. 13.
12. Harrison, *India,* p. 91.
13. Watts, *Administration,* p. 70.
14. Sklar and Whitaker, "Nigeria," p. 118.
15. On Ethiopia, see Robert L. Hess, "Ethiopia," in Carter, *National Unity,* pp. 441-538.
16. On France, see R. K. Gooch, *Regionalism in France* (1931); and Norman Furniss, "The Practical Significance of Decentralization," *Journal of Politics* 36, No. 4 (1974), pp. 958-982, especially p. 964.

not correspond at all), were ruled by appointed men, in order to undermine the power of regional leaders; and borders were shifted to destroy the cohesion of older political entities.[17]

In France, where centralization and unification were also regime goals after the Revolution, the historical provinces were eliminated, as were their organs of government. Their place was taken by a new hierarchy of administrative divisions, governed by appointed outsider officials, and regional traditions and languages were ignored.[18] In each of these countries different considerations, based on such factors as regime goals and ideology, the amount of internal cultural diversity, and the balance of power between the center and the localities seem to have dictated different strategies.

The objective here is to show the particular determinants of the choice of one strategy as against the other in one part of one country at a given point in time. Another aim is to reveal how the strategy chosen for each problem related to integration. Such an analysis should clarify certain key causative factors, since one of the factors alluded to above, regime goals and ideology, will be held constant. Thus, it should be possible to gauge the effects of the other two factors noted above: cultural diversity and variations in power. In order to do this, four propositions will be stated and illustrated in light of data on how the People's Republic of China (PRC) handled the three problem areas in the Southwest.

It should be kept in mind that these propositions, though designed with the experience of a number of states in mind, pertain particularly to China and its leaders' goals and ideology at a given point in time. During the first five years of the PRC, as pointed out in Chapter One, the regime had an ideological commitment to centralization, tempered by some concern for adaptation to suit local circumstances. Also at that time, the leadership in Peking was bent on rapid modernization and industrialization, and thus was heavily influenced by the centralized, hierarchical administrative structure used in governing the Soviet Union. At the same time, however, attempts had to be made to placate certain groups in order to ensure acceptance of the new regime. Therefore, we should be cautious in attempting to apply these

17. Carter, *National Unity,* pp. 495-496, 552.
18. Robert E. Dickinson, *Regional Ecology* (1970), p. 152.

propositions to other nations whose ideology or goal structure might differ. It cannot even be assumed that these same propositions would hold for later years in the history of the PRC—when local initiative had a greater or lesser role to play, when rapid industrialization was no longer a priority, or when the regime was less concerned with winning legitimation. The propositions are as follows:

Proposition 6.1. The strategy chosen for achieving integration in particular problem areas is a function of these four factors, all of which relate to cultural diversity or power:

a. local cultural differences
b. the degree of threat posed to the new regime and its values
c. the value of the group-in-question's potential support to the regime
d. the resource costs of control or suppression.

Accordingly, the following associations can be made:

a. the greater the local diversity, the more likely an indirect strategy
b. the greater the threat, the more likely a direct strategy
c. the greater the value of the group-in-question's support to the regime, the more likely an indirect strategy
d. the higher the resource costs of control (or suppression), the more likely an indirect strategy; alternatively, the lower the costs of control relative to the costs of laissez-faire, the more likely a direct strategy.

This proposition can be illustrated first, by analyzing the nature of each problem in order to establish, according to these four criteria, whether the problem ought to have called for a mainly direct or a mainly indirect strategy. The policy actually advocated in dealing with this problem can then be examined to find whether it was in fact the predicted strategy, based on the description of the direct and indirect models given above.

Proposition 6.2. The type of power (normative, coercive, remunerative)[19] emphasized in controlling problem areas is related to an

19. Based on Amitai Etzioni's three-fold classification. See Amitai Etzioni, "A Basis for Comparative Analysis of Complex Organizations," in A. Etzioni, ed., *A Sociological Reader on Complex Organizations* (1969), pp. 59-76.

assessment of the primary nature of the problem involved. That is, using the same factors as in Proposition 6.1 above:

a. if the relevant population primarily poses a physical threat, predominantly coercive controls are used
b. if obtaining the group's support is seen as possible and valuable, mainly normative control tends to be relied upon to obtain that support
c. if the issue principally involves regime control or loss of control over material resources, remunerative controls are the ones mostly applied.

In exploring this, the type of organs assigned to deal with the problem and the sort of work they did will be investigated. Based on the definitions of the two model strategies, we should expect to find more coercive controls being used with a direct strategy, and more normative controls being used with an indirect strategy.

Proposition 6.3. The structure of the integration aimed at is related to the strategy—direct or indirect—predominantly used.[20] Thus:

a. a vertical type of integration tends to accompany a direct strategy
b. an atomized integration (through a loose linkage of atomized—largely autonomous—units by a regional-level body) is connected with an indirect strategy
c. a horizontal-type integration is associated with a mixed strategy.

Thus, where localities are largely left alone, as under an indirect strategy, a loose type of integration would occur. Alternatively, where central controls are involved, as in the direct model, a vertical principle would structure intragovernmental relations. A mixed strategy might produce an intermediate amount of integration, with somewhat atomized units linked laterally, rather than through strict controls imposed at higher levels.

In presenting this third proposition, the functions of different levels in the administrative hierarchy in coping with the problem

20. For a discussion of various types of integration in an administrative system, see Frank Sherwood, "Devolution as a Problem of Organizational Strategy," in Robert T. Daland, ed., *Comparative Urban Research* (1969), pp. 60-87.

at hand will be considered, and the interrelationships between these levels will be analyzed.

Proposition 6.4. The choice of strategy (indirect or direct) affects the role of the region (or other intermediary structure) vis-à-vis the locality with respect to the problem at hand. Thus:

a. a direct strategy (coupled with vertical integration) means an increased role for the region
b. an indirect strategy (plus atomized integration) decreases the role of the region
c. a mixed strategy (with horizontal integration) gives the region some role but not a large one.

This can be shown by examining the role of the regional organs with respect to each of the three problem areas.

By means of this set of propositions, each of which builds on those before it, it is possible to come to an understanding of the overall process termed Integration II. In short, this is an attempt to determine the connections between the nature of each specific problem and the role the regional organs were to play in integrating the localities into the region with respect to that particular problem.

The reader should keep in mind that the above propositions do not attempt to establish strict causal linkages. Rather, in each case, they posit an association between the various factors cited. Furthermore, the data in the following discussion will be presented in the form of illustrations of the propositions, and should not be taken as constituting their definitive proof. In short, this is an attempt to show that these propositions, as they stand, do hold for the case at hand.

Three Problem Areas and Integration II, 1949-1952

Problems: Counter-revolutionaries

According to the Communists, the special characteristics of the counter-revolutionary groups in the Southwest were these: they "utilized feudal sects for cover, spread rumors, murdered and poisoned, incited rebellion and chaos, and sneaked into the people's government organs to steal intelligence and plotted to organize armed power.[21] This group included all persons whom the new regime felt were opposed to its programs and policies: the secret society leaders; landlords; ex-KMT personnel, troops, and generals; bandits, and some tribal headmen. All these groups were alluded to in Chapter Two.

If this group is analyzed according to the four determinants of strategy listed in Proposition 6.1, the following can be concluded: first of all, the Communists perceived few local or cultural differences among those who made up the target group here. The only important distinctions between them concerned the severity of their crimes, especially whether or not they were ringleaders. The analysis here will focus on the ringleaders, as they were the ones perceived as counter-revolutionaries par excellence. According to L. E. Willmott, a Canadian resident of Chengtu in the early 1950s, "those condemned to death all had been guilty of causing the death of revolutionary workers" either before or after liberation, or "had been leaders of counter-revolutionary armed bands or terrorist agents of the KMT, or local gangsters working with secret societies and landlords."[22] In other words, this group as a whole, whose members all were involved in violence, was considered relatively homogenous.

Second, the threat such individuals posed to the institutionalization and consolidation of Communist power and values was great. Not only were their own deeds destructive, but their power to command subordinates multiplied by many times the danger they posed to the new regime. Third, the regime had no hope of eliciting their support. Thus, adopting a milder means of control than extermination would not have provided additional adherents to the CCP program, from the point of view of the authorities. Finally, the costs in terms of resources of eliminating the minority who were the ringleaders were not prohibitively high.[23]

21. *Hsin-Hua jih-pao* [New China Daily] (Chungking) [hereafter *HHJP*], November 22, 1950.

22. L. Earl Willmott, "Tentative Manuscript for Diary of a Revolution," (unpublished manuscript), entry for August 15, 1951, quoted by permission of the author. Also, the directives on counter-revolutionary work draw distinctions according to nature of crime, and not by different types of groups. See footnotes 27 and 28 below.

23. Chapter Three tells us that, by the end of 1952, one million "bandits" had been killed in the Southwest. This was less than one and a half percent of the population of the area.

In fact, the costs of leaving these people alone would have been higher to the state than the costs of suppressing them.

Thus, all the conditions favoring a direct strategy existed here. There was no important local diversity among members of the target group; their threat was great; their support was not valued; and the relative costs of suppressing them were not heavy. And, in fact, it can be shown that the basic policy toward the leaders of this group most closely approximated the model of the direct strategy.

The basis for the policy toward counter-revolutionaries after 1949 was set down in the Common Program of the Chinese People's Political Consultative Conference, in Article Seven:

The People's Republic of China shall suppress all counter-revolutionary activities, severely punish all KMT counter-revolutionary war criminals and other leading incorrigible counter-revolutionary elements who collaborate with imperialism, commit treason against the fatherland, and oppose the cause of the people's democracy. Feudal landlords, bureaucratic capitalists, and reactionary elements in general, after they have been disarmed and have had their special powers abolished, shall, in addition, be deprived of their political rights in accordance with law for a necessary period. But, at the same time, they shall be given some means of livelihood and shall be compelled to reform themselves through labor so as to become new men. If they continue their counter-revolutionary activities, they will be severely punished.[24]

Thus, the initial statement on treatment of this group in the main mandated severe measures and strict controls.

Then, in Mao's speech to the Third Plenum of the Seventh Central Committee of the CCP on June 6, 1950, he outlined a policy "combining suppression with leniency, that is, the policy of punishing the principal culprits and not bringing to book those who were forced to become accomplices; and awarding those who do meritorious work."[25] A harsh statute, the "Directive on the Suppression of Counter-Revolutionary Activities," was passed a little over a month later (on July 23, 1950), embodying this principle.

Next, at the time of a meeting of the Supreme People's Court

24. "Common Program of the Chinese People's Political Consultative Conference" [hereafter "Common Program"], 1949, in Albert P. Blaustein, ed., *Fundamental Legal Documents of Communits China* (1962), p. 37.
25. *Current Background* [hereafter *CB*], No. 1 (1950), p. 4.

and its regional branches in October 1950, "boundless magnanimity [leniency]" was termed the characteristic of judicial practice throughout China.[26] This one-sided tendency was condemned, and Mao's principle from the Third Plenum restated.

Two other directives fleshed out these basic principles: one a "Statute on Punishment for Counter-Revolutionary Activity" of February 20, 1951;[27] and one stating "Temporary Regulations for the Surveillance of Counter-Revolutionary Elements" of June 27, 1952.[28] Neither deviated in doctrine from these earlier pronouncements.

The Common Program's spirit of no-compromise suppression of obstinate counter-revolutionaries was only apparently tempered by the tactics implied in Mao's speech to the Third Plenum. In accord with Mao's speech, "bandits" were treated with a two-pronged approach. This consisted of "military extermination," apparently aimed at the chief offenders, coupled with "political disintegration."[29] Among those who were to be punished, four grades of penalty were specified, depending upon the offense.[30] Political disintegration involved winning over the followers through propaganda, and utilizing them to isolate and capture the ringleaders. Thus the regime hoped to eliminate, and thus not have to deal with, the most die-hard opposition, and attempted at the same time to salvage some support from the underlings among this opposition.[31]

On the basis of these directives, it is possible to evaluate which strategy was involved. To do this, we must consider the approach taken toward personnel, policy, and administrative units. Thus,

26. Both these last two directives are translated in *CB*, No. 101 (1951).
27. *Ibid.*, pp. 9-11. Also, translated in Blaustein, *Legal Documents*, pp. 215-221. Original in *Jen-min shou-ts'e* [People's Handbook] 1952 [hereafter *JMST*] (1952), pp. 39-40.
28. *CB*, No. 193 (1952). Also translated in Blaustein, *Legal Documents*, pp. 222-226.
29. *HHJP*, November 21, 1951. Also, Liu Chin, *Ch'uan K'ang i-shou ch'ien-hou* [Before and After Szechwan and Sikang Changed Hands] (1956), p. 144; and *Survey of China Mainland Press* [hereafter *SCMP*], No. 783 (1954), pp. xix-xxi.
30. *HHJP*, November 21, 1951. These were: the death sentence, suspended sentence, prison, and mass surveillance.
31. Liu Chin, *Ch'uan K'ang*, pp. 144-152. He describes this method. See also G. William Skinner, "Aftermath of Communist Liberation in the Chengtu Plain," *Pacific Affairs* 24, No. 1 (1951), pp. 66-68.

in terms of personnel, this attempt to eliminate the principal culprits meant that the Communists hoped to destroy the leadership of the groups in opposition to them. In policy, a uniform policy applied to all the chief offenders, with no adaptation made to account for local or cultural differences. And with respect to administrative units, it will be shown below that a new system of public security units and courts was meant to counter the dominant position in local society that those called counter-revolutionaries had held before 1949.[32] So indeed a direct strategy was mandated, as expected, at least insofar as the diehards were concerned.

Proposition 6.2 deals with the nature of the controls exercised against the target group. Since the primary nature of the counter-revolutionary problem involved physical threat, it is to be expected that coercive controls were the most important ones applied. The controls applied can be understood by looking at the types of organs involved in suppressing counter-revolutionaries.

The effort to suppress counter-revolutionaries was joined by several sorts of organs working cooperatively. Public security units of the Southwest Military District, in close coordination with frontier defense units of the army, served as the backbone of the military campaign. These forces were aided by the militia formed in the countryside under the aegis of the peasant associations.[33] Moreover, various organs of the local governments were also involved. These included the public security and judicial organs, along with the procuratory organs.[34] Finally, people's tribunals, with the support of the courts, were to match up their work with

32. This accords with Lieberthal's findings for Tientsin. He states that the CCP there had a tripartite strategy in attempting to break up the pre-1949 coolie associations, which were the "front" organizations through which secret societies controlled the transport industry in Tientsin. The strategy involved: (1) as to personnel, driving a wedge between the bosses and the workers; (2) as to policy, using a uniform, national surrogate organization, the trade union, to substitute for the coolie associations; and (3) as to units, changing the size of the basic unit in transport to remove the territorial basis of identity of the most durable level of secret society organization. See Kenneth Lieberthal, "The Suppression of Secret Societies in Post-Liberation Tientsin," *China Quarterly*, No. 54 (1973), p. 252.

33. *SCMP*, No. 775 (1954), pp. xi-xiii; and No. 793 (1954), pp. ix-xi; *HHJP*, November 10, 1950, p. 1.

34. *HHJP*, November 23, 1951.

the key campaign of the moment, and be prepared to handle cases arising in the given campaign.[35]

These organs were all involved in the use of coercive power.[36] This is what was expected according to Proposition 6.2; and this also accords with the nature of a direct strategy. For a direct strategy was characterized as one that seeks through controls and manipulation to arrive at a forced consensus. In this case this was to be accomplished by the physical elimination of the ringleaders.

Given that a direct strategy was used to handle counter-revolutionaries, how did this affect the type of integration built up in this realm of policy? What was the structure of the apparatus created to mete out justice to this group?

According to the third proposition (6.3), a direct strategy should involve a vertical type of integration, or one entailing the strict application of controls by higher levels in the administrative hierarchy. A look at the work of the levels involved in handling counter-revolutionaries, and at the linkages set up between them, will illustrate this.

Suppression of the counter-revolutionaries was organized down to the lowest level of society. Mass security defense organizations for suppression used the neighborhood (hu-k'ou-tuan) and the natural village as units.[37] The PLA worked on the principle of "localization of army units with unification of leadership" since its public security units were highly dispersed.[38] Further, people's militia and security committees at the basic levels (ch'ü or district and hsiang or township) were instructed to subject counter-revolutionaries and unlawful landlords to stringent control.[39]

However, counter-revolutionary cases could only be handled by people's tribunals[40] or judicial and public security organs at the hsien (or county) level or above. Organs below this level were not empowered to sentence these criminals.[41] The lower levels were

35. HHJP, December 24, 1951, p. 2.
36. According to Etzioni, coercive power is control based on the application of physical means. See Amitai Etzioni, Modern Organizations (1964), p. 59.
37. HHJP, October 21, 1951.
38. SCMP, No. 205 (1951), pp. 12-17; and No. 793 (1954), pp. ix-xi.
39. SCMP, No. 846 (1954), pp. xiii-xiv.
40. These were special courts set up to deal with cases arising in the land reform movement. See CB, No. 101 (1951), p. 2, and No. 44 (1950).
41. HHJP, December 24, 1951, p. 2.

entitled only to make recommendations to the *hsien*-level organs for review and approval.[42] An incident is described in the press in which the *ch'ü* government called a meeting to collect the opinions of the peasants' representatives in the *hsiang* under its control. At the meeting, the "bad elements" denounced were sent to the *hsien* people's tribunal for trial.[43] From these several pieces of information it can be inferred that, whereas the military aspects of suppression occurred at all levels of society, the *hsien* was the organ responsible for disposing of the routine judicial work connected with passing judgment on counter-revolutionaries.

More serious cases had to be handled at the levels above the *hsien*. Province-level courts were to lead and supervise the work of the *hsien*-level tribunals, and judicial organs at the provincial level and above were to evaluate the work reports of the organs at the *hsien* level. These *hsien*-level organs were to report monthly to the provincial court, and the provincial court designated key point *hsien* tribunals to report directly to the Southwest Judicial Department and the Southwest Regional Court.[44]

However, while provinces had some authority, they were clearly subservient to the region. Thus, all provinces were permitted to draw up enforcement measures in handling counter-revolutionaries according to local conditions, but had to submit them to the Military Administrative Committee for approval.[45] And when it came to executing leading counter-revolutionary criminals, the Southwest Regional Court of the People's Supreme Court was in charge.[46]

Here it is clear that a definite hierarchy of control was designed to deal with counter-revolutionaries. At its apex stood the Judicial Department of the Military Administrative Committee and the Southwest Regional Court.[47] Although it can be assumed that the

42. *CB*, No. 193 (1952), p. 2, Article 11 of "Provisional Measures [Temporary Regulations] for the Control [Surveillance] of Counter-Revolutionaries" [hereafter "Provisional Measures"], July 21, 1952.

43. *HHJP*, November 3, 1950, p. 3.

44. *HHJP*, December 24, 1951, p. 2.

45. "Provisional Measures," Article 11.

46. *SCMP*, No. 92 (1951), pp. 29-30. As Chapter Three notes, there was also a military court under the Military Region that had the power to execute top ringleaders.

bulk of suppression and judicial work happened at the *hsien* level or below, the new organs above the province stood as the ultimate authority in the field of criminal control.[47]

Overall, this creation of a hierarchy of control meant that, as Proposition 6.3 predicted, a vertical form of integration was envisioned in the military-judicial system that controlled the most heinous of the counter-revolutionaries. And, as Proposition 6.4 foresaw, the direct strategy and the vertical integration associated with it meant a relatively large role for the region. For in this problem area, the region was responsible for final judgments and ultimate punishments; its power was superior to and of a different nature from that of the levels below it.

In sum, the counter-revolutionary problem was met with suppression: a coercive policy coupled with a direct strategy. Since a hierarchy of increasing control at higher levels was required to enforce this coercive policy, a vertical type of integration was the aim, with the responsible regional organs exercising specific and weighty powers over the relevant units below.

Problems: Minorities

According to the discussion in Chapter Two, the outstanding quality in the minorities issue was that many separate tribal groupings, each with different customs and beliefs, made a cultural jigsaw puzzle of the Southwest provinces. Representing somewhere from one-eighth to one-fourth of the Southwest population,[48] the minorities with their diverse life-styles and foreign habits were a problem for the Communists involved in instituting programs of social reform. Also, the inveterate hatred

47. The final authority for ratification of the death sentence was the governor of the provincial people's government or the chief of the administrative organ at the special district administrative office level in the newly liberated areas; and the provincial government or Great Administrative Region Chairman in the old liberated areas. See *CB*, No. 101 (1951), pp. 4-5, in the "Directive [Statute] on Suppression [Punishment] of Counter-Revolutionary Activities" of July 23, 1950.

48. "Hsi-nan ti-fang ching-chi ti-li" [Economic Geography of Southwest China], ed. by Sun Ching-chih (1960). Translated in U.S. *Joint Publications Research Service* [hereafter *JPRS*], No. 15069 (1962). On pp. 19-20 they are listed as comprising 12 percent of nearly 100,000,000 people in the Southwest, according to the 1953 census. However, in *SCMP,* No. 709 (1953), p. 36, the figure given is "about one-fourth of the more than 70,000,000 people."

many of these groups entertained for the Chinese made winning their support a challenge.

Analyzing this group in terms of the four components of Proposition 6.1, then, there were large local disparities among minorities. Second, although some tribal chieftains were counted among the counter-revolutionaries, the threat the average minority tribe posed to institution of the new regime and its values was not severe.

Third, in terms of support, as will be noted below, the policy toward minorities was informed by a desire to make of China "one big cooperative family"—that is, to obtain the collaboration of all the peoples living in China in building a new socialist state. Also in this vein, the minorities' aid could be enlisted in coaxing productivity out of their barren and mountainous homelands. Another reason why the regime courted the minorities' support was its stated hope that these peoples would "oppose imperialism and their own public enemies." A crucial fact about these peoples was that many óf them lived on China's strategic national borders or in the mountainous areas to which fleeing counter-revolutionaries had escaped during the closing days of the civil war. Thus they were situated in a prime position for aiding in the suppression of these elements, as well as for fighting off imperialist encroachments. In the Southwest in particular, the anti-Communist guerrillas in Yunnan were based in the hill areas where minorities lived, and counter-revolutionaries were most active in the mountains along the frontier.[49]

In fact, several articles on minorities in the Southwest press reflect these concerns.[50] These articles mention that the population living on the national defense borderland is almost wholly composed of these peoples; and that the homes of some even straddle this border, so that these tribes live in part within neighboring countries. One piece spells out explicitly that many remnants among the KMT troops had fled to minority districts, and that imperialist elements on the national defense line joined with these "bandits" to incite the minorities against the new

49. George V. H. Moseley, *The Consolidation of the South China Frontier* (1973), pp. 35-37; see also *HHJP*, September 29, 1952, and *Hsin-Hua yüeh-pao* [New China Monthly] (Peking) [hereafter *HHYP*], No. 23 (1951), p. 1024.

50. *HHJP*, October 1, 1951; September 29, 1952; and December 8, 1952.

Chinese regime. The article goes on to note that this situation has made minority problems in the Southwest "very complicated" and has caused them to take on a "special importance."[51] For these various reasons, minority support was seen as valuable by the leadership.

Fourth, the large numbers of minority people in the Southwest meant that the costs involved in forcibly eliminating them would probably have been too high.

Thus, here are all the conditions tending toward an indirect strategy, according to Proposition 6.1, at least insofar as the average minority elements were concerned: great local diversity; relatively low degree of threat; a high value placed on the group's support; and high costs associated with suppression. The policy toward minorities was in fact directed toward the average minority tribespeople, and will be examined with these factors in mind.

The policy toward the minority groups living scattered throughout China was stated in two basic documents. These were the Common Program of 1949 and the August 1952 General Program for Regional Autonomy.[52] The pertinent tenets of the Common Program are as follows:

Article 50: "All nationalities within the boundaries of the PRC are equal. They shall establish unity and mutual aid among themselves, and *shall oppose imperialism and their own public enemies,* so that the PRC will become *a big fraternal and cooperative family* composed of all its nationalities. Greater nationalism and chauvinism shall be opposed. Acts involving discrimination, oppression, and splitting the unity of the various nationalities shall be prohibited." [Emphasis added.]

Article 51: "Regional autonomy shall be exercised in areas where national minorities are concentrated and various kinds of autonomy organs of the different nationalities shall be set up according to the size of the respective populations and regions. In places where different nationalities live together and in the autonomous areas of the national minorities, the different nationalities shall each have an appropriate number of representatives in the local organs of political power."

Article 53: "All national minorities shall have freedom to develop their dialects and languages, to preserve or reform their traditions, customs, and religious beliefs. The people's government shall assist the masses of

51. *HHJP,* September 29, 1952.
52. Moseley, *Consolidation,* p. 39.

the people of all national minorities to develop their political, economic, cultural, and educational construction works."[53]

In this document, the principles set down for dealing with minorities were clearly characterized by appeasement. Minorities were to be treated equally, it dictates. At the same time they were permitted to establish "various kinds" of regional autonomy organs, depending upon the locality; they would be afforded the freedom to develop, preserve, or reform their own traditional cultural forms; and they would receive special types of aid not granted to the Han peoples.

The measures promulgated in August 1952 left unchanged the basic principles of the Common Program, but made the political structure of the autonomous areas more systematic.[54] They preserved the spirit of the Common Program in that they instructed higher-level governments to "adequately estimate the special characteristics and concrete conditions in the various areas . . . and see that directives and orders issued are in conformity . . . with such special characteristics and concrete conditions."[55] These higher-level governments were also to "utilize different appropriate forms to introduce to people of various regions the experiences and conditions of political, economic, and cultural construction in the advanced regions."[56] Thus, accommodation to the individual attributes of the minority groups remained the touchstone of policy toward these peoples during the early 1950s.

From the principles decreed in these documents, a program of "nationalization" was designed. This notion of "nationalization" of autonomous areas was a key tenet in dealing with the minorities. The policy involved using the minorities' own cadres, own languages, and own national forms in the management of the internal affairs of each nationality group.[57] A concerted effort

53. In Blaustein, *Legal Documents,* pp. 51-52.

54. S. B. Thomas, *Government and Administration in Communist China* (1955), pp. 95-96; Moseley, *Consolidation,* pp. 44 and 48-49; *CB,* No. 264 (1953), pp. 12-22; full text translated in Blaustein, *Legal Documents,* pp. 180-192. See also the section in the following text on shifts in strategy and mode of integration after 1952.

55. "General Program for Regional Autonomy," Article 31, translated in Blaustein, *Legal Documents.*

56. *Ibid.,* Article 34.

57. *CB,* No. 264 (1953), p. 4.

was made in the Southwest to train minority cadres. This involved setting up training classes at the local levels[58] and sponsoring several provincial minority academies and one at the regional level. By October 1952, 25,000 minority cadres had been trained.[59]

Besides training new cadres, a special attempt was made to include "representative personages" of the minority tribes in government councils;[60] and the tribespeople were to be consulted in the delimitation of autonomous areas.[61] Two scholars have noted that, in fact, many of the new administrative areas set up for the minorities corresponded closely to the old domains of the *t'u ssu* (native chiefs).[62]

Furthermore, frequent injunctions were made to Han cadres to respect the customs of the minorities;[63] and measures were taken to aid the minorities in compiling, improving, and forming their written languages.[64] Behind this policy of appeasement lay an element of expediency. The Communists realized that by winning over those leaders with prestige among their peoples[65] they could use such leaders to resolve the differences that existed between the wishes of their tribespeople and the directives from above.[66]

Here then is a tendency to realize the indirect strategy: in terms of policy, there was a preservation of local cultural disparities; and in dealing with units and personnel, traditional political forms and leaders were retained. Each area, under the guidance of a local committee, was permitted to adapt national strategy to local conditions; traditional leaders, where malleable, were made use of, albeit while being "trained"; and customary boundaries

58. *HHJP*, November 27, 1950.
59. *HHJP*, September 29, 1952; see also Moseley, *Consolidation*, pp. 111-112.
60. *HHYP*, No. 23 (1951), pp. 1021-1024; *HHJP*, December 13, 1952.
61. *HHYP*, No. 23 (1951), pp. 1021-1024; and *SCMP*, No. 409 (1952), pp. 25-26.
62. Inez de Beauclair, *Tribal Cultures of Southwest China* (1970), p. 33; Moseley, *Consolidation*, p. 47.
63. For example, *HHJP*, October 9, 1950; *SCMP*, No. 614 (1953), p. 17.
64. *SCMP*, No. 843 (1954), pp. 7-8.
65. Wiens claims that *t'u-ssu* who were unpopular with their tribesmen were eliminated. See Herold J. Wiens, *China's March Toward the Tropics* (1954), p. 258.
66. *Ibid.*, pp. 258-259.

were drawn for administrative purposes, within limits. This shows that Proposition 6.1 appears to hold for this problem.

The second proposition dictates that, since obtaining the support of the minorities was crucial to the Communists, normative controls would be an important component of the strategy used to obtain that support. To test this, one must look at the types of organs involved in working with minorities and at the nature of their work.

According to Etzioni, normative controls are those used in the process of encouraging compliance through the use of symbols such as prestige, esteem, love, and acceptance. Normative power, then, is the use of such symbols for control purposes.[67] So the organs dealing with the minorities ought to have depended heavily on these methods of control if normative power was the sort employed.

The organs most generally involved in control of the minority problem were the nationalities affairs committees of the government councils at various levels of administration.[68] The next most important organ in this realm was probably the PLA.[69] However, the PLA's work with the minorities differed greatly from its role with the counter-revolutionaries. Rather than using coercive power, as it did with the counter-revolutionaries, its principal purpose with the minorities was to induce their loyalty to the state. Its troops brought daily necessities to the tribespeople, helped them in farming, offered medical services, assisted them in establishing militia forces, built roads and schools for them, and did propaganda work.

Further, when thirteen regional-level organs (including the organs for finance, culture, agriculture, water conservation, politics, and industry) were coordinated to form a minority work corps, their main task was propaganda work.[70] Trade units were also concerned with work in the minority areas; in developing commerce among these peoples, their job was to take into account the special characteristics of each area and to set up special forms

67. Etzioni, *Modern Organizations*, p. 59.
68. Wiens, *China's March*, p. 259.
69. Moseley, *Consolidation*, pp. 106-110; also, for example, *SCMP*, No. 766 (1954), pp. 29-30.
70. *HHJP*, October 9, 1952.

to accommodate these traits.[71] Thus, in work with minorities remunerative appeals, or the use of material benefits, were combined with a largely normative approach.

In examining the organs that participated in working with minorities, it is apparent that regardless of the type of organ, the nature of its work was dictated by a policy of caution, concessions, and cooptation. Further, the concern with propaganda to win over the minorities, which was shown by all the various organs engaged in this work, indicates that normative control was meant to be a prime component in the controls used here.

The work of these organs can be analyzed further. In line with this policy of concessions and caution, a sort of courting of the minorities took three general forms in the Southwest. Minorities were exempted temporarily from mass movements of social and economic "reform" carried out among the Han population of China; a large-scale and many-faceted program of assistance was developed for the minorities; and representatives from various minority groups were frequently fêted by governmental organs at higher levels.

Governmental directives issued in the Southwest typically contained a proviso exempting the minorities or tempering the application of the general rule when dealing with minorities. For example, a method for resolving quarrels about debts in the rural areas, passed in late 1950, was not to apply to the minority districts.[72] Caution was mandated in the implementation in these districts of the movement to ban opium.[73] Special consideration was to be taken in confiscating forests where minorities lived.[74]

As to the rent-reduction and land-reform movements, "carrying them out exactly the same in minority as in Han districts was wrong," and exceptions could be made for one district or even one family if this seemed desirable.[75] Careful precautions had to

71. See *SCMP*, No. 720 (1954), p. 38; No. 791 (1954), pp. 41-42; *CB*, No. 152 (1952), pp. 2-4; *HHJP*, September 29, 1952.
72. *HHJP*, November 13, 1950.
73. *HHJP*, November 19, 1950.
74. *HHJP*, December 5, 1950.
75. *HHJP*, January 31, 1951; September 29, 1952; Chang Chi-ch'ün, "Kuan-yü hsi-nan ch'ü chien-tsu wen-t'i ti pao" [On Questions in Rent Reduction in the Southwest], in *Cheng-fu kung-tso pao-kao hui-pien* [Compendium of Government Work Reports] (1951), p. 1009; U.S. *JPRS*, No. 15308 (1962): *Szechuan*, translation of a Russian language book by Ye. A. Afanas'yeskiy (1962), p. 71.

be taken in instigating these movements among the minorities. Finally, caution was stipulated in monetary work and the tax burden of the minorities was to be lightened.[76] The impulse not to offend these peoples or to unduly disrupt their social systems was apparent.

Besides abstaining from social reform work among the minorities, the regime also offered these peoples many forms of assistance. Specifically, education, albeit tempered with patriotic propaganda, was promoted by establishing schools at all levels throughout the minority areas; health care was offered gratis; trade was boosted through improved transport and a favorable price policy; and agricultural production was pushed by means of loans, investment, free tools, and instruction.[77]

Finally, the third type of special treatment was fêting the minorities. This involved holding banquets for their representatives and sending them off on free travel tours of the major cities of China.[78] Obviously, through use of such methods the minorities were made to feel grateful and hopefully allegiant to the new regime.

In sum, the combination of normative and remunerative controls that were to be relied upon in this area of work approached the indirect end of the continuum. For, as noted above, the aim in an indirect strategy is to raise local initiative and enthusiasm, and consequently allegiance. Some use of normative controls to accomplish this was predicted by Proposition 6.2.

Given that a largely indirect strategy was to dictate work here, how could scattered minority groups be integrated together in the Southwest? Proposition 6.3 holds that an atomized integration should result from an indirect strategy—a loose linking of atomized or generally autonomous units through a regional-level body with a minimum of guidance coming from above. To find out whether this was the case, the relations specified between administrative levels in minority work can be examined.

76. *HHJP*, December 31, 1952.
77. *SCMP*, Nos. 496 (1953), p. 18; 538 (1953), p. 13; 716 (1953), pp. 26-27; 720 (1954), p. 38; 791 (1954), pp. 41-42; 843 (1954), pp. 7-8; *HHJP*, October 1, 1951; September 29, 1952; December 8, 1952; December 31, 1952; *HHYP*, No. 23 (1951), pp. 1021-1024; *CB*, No. 152 (1952).
78. For example: *HHJP*, November 11, 1950; September 29, 1952; November 1, 1952; November 12, 1952; November 28, 1952; December 1, 1952.

According to the general policy of matching the rules applied in each minority region to the specific traits and stage of development of the peoples living there, autonomous areas were set up at the subcounty levels, at least at first. And at each level, a conscious effort was made to suit local characteristics. Thus, even if authority was vested at the *hsien* level and higher, that authority was supposed to be modeled to fit the traits of the subordinate populations.

Both the location of the tribe and its social structure and customs affected the treatment it received. In Yunnan, for example, a distinction was drawn between minorities living in the interior and those residing on the frontiers. Among the interior peoples, land reform had been carried out by mid-1955; among the frontier peoples it had not.[79] This is in accord with Moseley's observation that the frontier areas were the first to be organized into autonomous areas.[80] Apparently those groups whose support was most crucial to the regime—those on the frontier—were the first to be integrated. It was also these groups that were given the greater exemptions from radical social movements, at least for a time.

In Kweichow, policy toward the individual minorities varied with the class structure of the particular minority group. The Miao people had no significant class distinctions among themselves and the majority of their people were middle peasants owning their own land. As of early 1952, except for the few landlords among them, most of the people continued to work their own land.[81] Among the Chung, however, "feudal" relations were more pronounced, and a landlord class existed, whose members, according to the Communists, promoted civil strife among their people. In dealing with the Chung, the Communists made use of class divisions and mobilized the Chung masses after 1949 to track down "bandits."[82]

The "I" people's land was tilled by tenant peasants who were exploited and harshly punished before 1949, according to the Communists. By 1952, the systems of demanding the payment of

79. *CB*, 356 (1955), p. 59.
80. Moseley, *Consolidation*, p. 49.
81. *CB*, 150 (1952), p. 8.
82. *Ibid.*, p. 10.

rents in free labor and of exacting money from the peasants were abolished. Oppressive headmen (*t'u-mu*) were arrested and killed and others had begun to lower their rents.[83] Thus, the Communists tried to mold their policy toward particular peoples in light of the existence or nonexistence of class divisions among the peoples.

In Szechwan these same "I" people had ruled a large area before 1949 in the Ta Liang Shan (on the borders of Yunnan, Sikang, and Szechwan). Here they were still living under their ancestral slave system until the mid-1950s. Land reform was not begun in this region until 1956 and 1957, when slavery and serfdom were abolished there.[84] The strength and sophistication of the ancient political and tribal regime among the "I"'s of this region of Szechwan was no doubt an impediment to quick institution of Communist programs there.[85] Definitely, careful consideration was given to a number of factors in determining the method of dealing with individual minorities in the localities in the first years after takeover.

Even though the various localities were each governed differently in minority areas, the lower-level organs were to form the base of an administrative hierarchy that reached up to the Military Administrative Committee at the regional level. But although the higher-level autonomous areas apparently had certain powers over the areas below them, these higher-level governments had to guarantee the lower levels the "right of autonomy."[86] Thus, it was frequently the areas at the special district level, such as the Hsi-shuang Pan-na area in Yunnan and the Tibetan area in Sikang, which were responsible for helping people of smaller minority groups within their areas to implement area autonomy.[87]

In the press, there are examples of the type of relationship that existed between the provincial level and the autonomous

83. *Ibid.*, p. 14.
84. U.S. *JPRS* 15308 (1962), p. 71.
85. See Lin Yueh-hua, *The Lolo of Liang Shan* (1961), especially Chapters 7 and 8, on the traditional social and political structure of the I.
86. *CB*, No. 264 (1953).
87. *SCMP*, Nos. 629 (1953), pp. 29-30; 505 (1953), pp. 22-24; 589 (1953), p. 28; 93 (1951), p. 35.

regions within its territory. The posture of the province vis-à-vis its minorities was quite different from its role toward its counter-revolutionaries.

Toward the counter-revolutionaries, as shown above, the provincial authorities had certain judicial and law enforcement powers. In the case of the minorities, however, the province-level organs arranged consultations between local peoples with respect to the administrative division of their territories;[88] they organized work teams to help the minorities develop production and enforce regional autonomy;[89] they sent teams to carry out propaganda work and help organize governments;[90] and they transferred cadres to support construction and perform medical services in minority areas.[91] Thus, the principles of appeasement and assistance laid down in the Common Program were meant to inform the work of the upper-level governments in handling the problem of cultural diversity.

Moreover, the provincial level had no law enforcement powers over the lower-level autonomous units. Rather, it had a coordinative function, as it unified the services and the ideological training to be given to discrete units below. This role can be viewed as one of ensuring the atomized type of integration that Proposition 6.3 predicted would accompany an indirect strategy.

What role then did the regional government play in this indirect strategy with its atomized integration? Proposition 6.4 specifies that it ought to have been a relatively small one, as compared with the part it played in managing counter-revolutionaries. The regional-level organs in fact had an even less direct responsibility toward the resolution of the minorities problem than did the provincial level. It was at the regional level that conferences were held on the minorities question, under the aegis of the Military Administrative Committee's Committee for Nationalities Affairs. The role of these conferences was to emphasize policy toward the minorities, to stress the tasks of implementing autonomy and organizing autonomous areas;[92] to

88. *SCMP*, No. 409 (1952), pp. 25-26.
89. *SCMP*, No. 349 (1952), p. 33.
90. *SCMP*, No. 589 (1953), p. 28.
91. *SCMP*, No. 877 (1954), p. 35.
92. *SCMP*, No. 71 (1951), p. 22; No. 88 (1951), p. 30.

ensure that "nationalization" was effected and that the minorities' standard of living was being raised;[93] and to encourage production in the minority areas.[94]

Apart from holding these conferences, only two other activities that were carried out by the Military Administrative Committee and the Administrative Committee toward the minority groups were mentioned in the press. First, at times the Military Administrative Committee's Nationality Affairs Committee, combined with such other organs at the regional level as the Military Administrative Committee's Finance–Economic Committee, its Culture–Education Committee, and others, transferred cadres to form a minority work corps. Such a corps would visit autonomous districts and propagandize the policy toward minorities, promote the establishment of political power organs, and assist in the development of work to improve the minorities' economic and cultural situations.[95] Second, it was at the regional level in the regional capital at Chungking, that most of the fêting of minority representatives took place.[96]

Apparently, the bulk of the work in handling the minorities was to be done at subprovincial levels. Given the fact that the basic thrust of the policy in this area in the early 1950s was to suit the locality and to carry out work that would be appropriate to local conditions, the role of the highest levels in the region could not have been decisive.

Thus, since the lower-level minority units were more or less autonomous in the first years after takeover, most of the regional organs' work on this problem was geared toward linking up the units in terms of policy and propaganda, rather than exercising power over them. In fact, this role was a lesser one as compared with the region's role in counter-revolutionary work, as Proposition 6.4 predicted.

Hence, this discussion has indicated the connections between certain elements of the minorities issue, the type of strategy adopted to handle these people, the type of integration that was to result from this strategy, and the role of the regional adminis-

93. *HHJP*, December 8, 1952, p. 1.
94. *HHJP*, December 31, 1952, p. 1.
95. *HHJP*, October 9, 1952.
96. See footnote 78.

tration in effecting this integration. The overall principle was laissez-faire coupled with assistance, and the anticipated goal was the inclusion of the minorities into the new Communist state.

Problems: Trade

As explained in Chapter Two, trade in the Southwest was crippled by topographical impediments, by a gaping insufficiency in transport, and by the controls over commerce in certain goods exercised by powerful local groups. Related to the transport problem in the Southwest, the linkage was weak between small and medium-size cities on the one hand, and large cities on the other.[97] And "due to the difficulties of transportation, the exchange of commodities encountered great difficulties as products could not be marketed in remote areas and goods could not be imported cheaply."[98] Also tied in with transport were problems with local and special products, in which the Southwest abounded.[99] These goods, largely unmarketable before 1949, tended to accumulate, causing losses to the peasants.[100]

How did trade appear in relation to Proposition 6.1's four determinants of strategy? First, the characteristics of trade in the Southwest differed from locality to locality, and, on a larger scale, were different from those in other parts of the country. In this regard, the trade problem, like the minorities problem, had to be handled at the most local levels. Also, as was true in the case of the minorities, the trade situation did not initially pose a major threat to national unification and Communist rule.

However, as in the case of the counter-revolutionaries, the support of the groups manipulating local commerce was not seen as valuable or desirable in the long run, in light of the region's ultimate goals of socialization and nationalization of wealth in the country. Moreover, the costs involved in redirecting and control-

97. Wang Wei-tsu, "Hsi-nan kung-shang-yeh i nien lai ti chin-pu ts'e-hsieh" [Emphasizing a Year of Progress in Southwest Industry and Commerce], *Ching-chi chou-pao* [Economic Weekly] (Shanghai) [hereafter *CCCP*] 12, No. 8 (1951), p. 18.

98. *SCMP,* No. 355 (1952), pp. 17-19.

99. "Local and special products" of the Southwest include such items as tung oil, hog bristles, raw silk, hemp, medicinal herbs, hides, and skins.

100. *HHYP,* No. 17 (1951), p. 1119; Huang Fu-chung, "Hsi-nan ch'eng-hsiang kuan-hsi ti hsin mien-mao" [The New Appearance in Urban-Rural Relations in the Southwest], *CCCP* 12 (1951), No. 18, p. 16.

ling trade would have been less than the costs to the regime of failing to establish some control. Some of these concerns appear in the official statement of policy on domestic trade, as stated in the Common Program:

Article 37: "All legitimate public and private trade shall be protected. . . . Freedom of domestic trade shall be established under a unified economic state plan, but commercial speculation disturbing the market shall be strictly prohibited. State-owned trade organs shall assume the responsibility of adjusting supply and demand, stabilizing commodity prices, and assisting the people's cooperatives."[101]

Thus, state control over trade was projected from the start, as was outlawing of private manipulation of the market.

Given these concerns, a mixed strategy should have been used toward trade, since some aspects of the trade situation satisfied the conditions for an indirect strategy and some satisfied those for a direct strategy, according to Proposition 6.1. Whereas local diversity and low threat dictated the indirect approach, the lack of desire for Southwest merchants' support and the relatively low costs of control relative to the costs of laissez-faire called for elements of the direct approach.

In order to determine which approach was mandated, it is useful to consider how trade policy dealt with traditional markets and merchants, and with local diversity.[102] In general, the aim in trade policy was to enliven but to control old patterns of trade relations that had dried up, as well as to establish new linkages at all levels of society.[103]

In line with this aim, the rehabilitation of local markets was an important aspect of the trade policy.[104] This mainly involved strengthening the leadership of the state-operated trade sector over these markets.[105] This strengthening meant that new forms of commercial relations were promoted and new state-sponsored organs were created to enforce these relations. Thus, goods

101. Blaustein, *Legal Documents,* p. 48.
102. These three factors—markets, merchants, and local diversity—parallel the three elements toward which each strategy is directed, i.e., units, personnel, and concrete policy.
103. *HHYP,* No. 22 (1951), p. 868. See also *Jen-min jih-pao* [People's Daily] (Peking) [hereafter *JMJP*], March 13, 1951, p. 2.
104. *HHJP,* September 29, 1952.
105. *HHJP,* December 13, 1952; December 14, 1952, p. 2.

exchange meetings, a new approach in trade, were promoted down to the *hsiang* level, under the aegis of local governments and Party committees.[106] It appears that local, traditional markets were used to organize these exchange conferences, because references were made to the *ch'ang-chen*, an urban market at a level below the *hsien*.[107] However, the *hsien* capital, an administrative seat, was also a common site for such events.[108] Moreover, state-operated supply and marketing cooperatives were to penetrate down to the level of elementary (*ch'u-chi*) markets, though here too, the *hsien* was the territorial unit for directing local cooperative work.[109]

Thus, while use of traditional markets was encouraged, these markets were now under the control of new Communist organs and Party personnel; and the *hsien*, an administrative unit, was utilized in the guidance of the bulk of local commerce.[110] This indicates that a mixed strategy was in use.

Where personnel were concerned, private merchants were exhorted to participate in joint operational bodies with native products companies created by the state;[111] and these companies' personnel were ordered to join ranks with the private merchants.[112] Here again there was a mix of the direct and indirect principles: those local personnel willing to cooperate with regime policies were retained, at least for a time; but the new state and Party controls over these individuals gradually changed the nature of their activities considerably.

Finally, in policy terms, there was the same double-edged approach at work. One prong of the policy was to accommodate the locality. Thus in selling industrial goods to the rural areas trade organs were frequently enjoined to research the needs and

106. *HHJP*, October 29, 1951; September 14, 1952; November 9, 1952.
107. *HHJP*, December 13, 1952; December 14, 1952.
108. *HHJP*, September 14, 1952; September 25, 1952; December 13, 1952; December 14, 1952.
109. *HHJP*, December 2, 1951.
110. Donnithorne explains that the official machinery of trade has been aligned primarily with administrative units even where they do not coincide with natural economic areas. She points out that this is representative of a desire for tight political control of trade. See Audrey Donnithorne, *China's Economic System* (1967), pp. 307-308, 317.
111. *SCMP*, No. 348 (1952), p. 32.
112. *HHJP*, September 24, 1952.

demands of the villages for these goods.[113] Also, an emphasis was placed on creating outlets for stopped-up native products.[114] In 1951, for example, organizing the flow of local products was proclaimed as the central task in finance and economic work in the Southwest.[115]

However, viewing these policies from another angle, commerce could not continue, much less be active, without a clear awareness of the types of products the peasants were willing to buy. Further, local products were supported in the Southwest because these constituted so large a share of the total income from all agricultural production in the area: by the autumn of 1951 they accounted for 35 to 40 percent of this income.[116] Thus, the very nature of trade, which required a concern for the local demand and supply situation, caused the policy to have an indirect component. And the use of state-operated organs to promote this policy meant that traditional trade in the localities was modified to suit regime goals, as a direct strategy would dictate.[117]

Apparently then, in terms of traditional forms of commerce and the personnel engaged in it, and as regards leeway for the locality, a mixed approach characterized trade work. This is what Proposition 6.1 implied would happen.

Since the primary nature of the trade problem was a matter of the management of material resources, the controls associated with this policy ought to have been remunerative ones,[118] according to Proposition 6.2. And, in fact, not surprisingly, the organs

---

113. *HHJP,* October 1, 1950; November 28, 1950; December 11, 1950; January 25, 1953; June 11, 1953; Wang, "Kung-shang-yeh," p. 18.

114. *HHJP,* October 29, 1951; November 24, 1951, p. 2; December 13, 1951; September 29, 1952; October 20, 1952; *HHYP,* No. 11 (1950), p. 1064; No. 17 (1951), pp. 1116-1118, 1119-1120; No. 22 (1951), pp. 868-869; U.S. *JPRS,* No. 10761 (1951), "Kweichow of the Fatherland," translation of portions of *Tsu-kuo ti kuei-chou* (1955), p. 14.

115. *HHYP,* No. 17 (1951), p. 1116.

116. *HHJP,* October 29, 1951.

117. Policy toward trade was also mixed during these years insofar as officially set prices were combined with a free market; and government companies exercised control over the supply of key commodities while most goods were allowed to be traded freely. See Dwight H. Perkins, *Market Control and Planning in Communist China* (1966), pp. 13, 30, 32-40.

118. Utilitarian (remunerative) power is defined by Etzioni as the use of material means for control purposes. See Etzioni, *Modern Organizations,* p. 59.

involved in this work were all ones concerned with financial and economic affairs.

At the hub of the bureaucracy set up in the regions to handle trade after 1949 were the regional and provincial trade departments. It was their duty to supervise and coordinate the operations of the state trading companies in the areas under their jurisdiction, to fix the prices for companies at smaller centers, and to control private trade.[119] Each of these trading companies monopolized the trade in a particular commodity, and facilitated price control by furnishing the government with reserves of key goods. These companies also mobilized food and raw materials for the cities, and, through supply and marketing cooperatives, collected industrial goods for the rural areas.[120]

In rural areas, the state's chief tools of control were these supply and marketing cooperatives. The co-ops, after contracting with the state companies, bought from the peasants on behalf of the state and sold them consumer goods, production equipment, and supplies in exchange.[121]

Other organs were also involved in trade work. Small groups sent to the countryside to spur the sales of industrial products were composed of personnel from banks and private commercial firms, as well as from state trading companies.[122] And a report on trade work in the autumn of 1952 indicated that the following governmental departments were involved in this work: tax collection, insurance, banks, transport, and industry as well as commerce.[123]

These organs were all involved in the use of remunerative power. While their work contributed to improve the material lives

119. Donnithorne, *China's Economic System*, p. 275. See also "Government Administrative Council Decisions on Procedures Governing the Unification of State-Operated Trade in the Nation," of March 10, 1950, translated in Chao Kuo-chün, *Economic Planning and Organization in Mainland China: A Documentary Study (1949-1957)* (1960), 2:20-23. This document lays out the functions of the specialized state trading companies, the powers of the Central People's Government Ministry of Trade, and the responsibilities of the regional and provincial trade departments.

120. T. J. Hughes and D. E. T. Luard, *The Economic Development of Communist China, 1949-1960* (1961), p. 25.

121. Donnithorne, *China's Economic System*, pp. 274-275, and 279; A Doak Barnett, *Communist China: The Early Years: 1949-1955* (1965), pp. 177-180; *China News Analysis*, No. 7 (1953), pp. 2-4; *CB*, No. 106 (1951).

122. *HHJP*, December 11, 1950.

123. *HHJP*, September 29, 1952.

of the people in the Southwest, they were at the same time able to achieve control over commerce. Not only was the state able to monopolize the trade in crucial goods and to control prices, but it could also determine the total amounts of various products, their producing centers, and their marketing areas. This enabled the state to fix the rate of profit in trade and to control output.[124] The authorities could also regulate the division of labor in commerce, eliminate shortages, and create incentives for an increase in production through their trade promotion policies.[125] These methods of serving state goals while rewarding the masses materially were the hallmark of the trade policy in this era.

In granting material benefits to the Southwest population, trade was at the same time enlivened there. In this way, the regime advanced toward its goal of unlocking the material resources hidden in inaccessible land pockets. The principal means used to bolster trade in the Southwest provinces were the improvement of transport, and the rationalization and adjustment of freight rates and pricing policy, to take into account the obstacles to trade posed by geography. Improving transport included opening ports;[126] mobilizing carts for transporting goods from mountainous districts;[127] reorganizing junk transport facilities;[128] building new roads, highways, and rail lines, the most outstanding of which was the Chengtu-Chungking Railway;[129] and organizing new forms of joint transport to link up various transport modes from one locality to the next.[130]

These developments in transport, particularly the Chengtu-Chungking Railway, were vital tools in contributing to spatial

124. *Far Eastern Economic Review* [hereafter *FEER*] 14, No. 8 (1953), pp. 230-232.
125. Hughes and Luard, *Economic Development*, p. 106.
126. *SCMP*, No. 11 (1950), p. 13.
127. *SCMP*, No. 90 (1951), p. 31.
128. *SCMP*, No. 105 (1951), p. 60; No. 108 (1951), p. 40.
129. *SCMP*, No. 266 (1952), pp. 16-17; No. 368 (1952), pp. 29-30; No. 355 (1952), pp. 17-19; No. 580 (1953), p. 21; *HHYP*, No. 54 (1951), p. 169. As the railway was being built, connecting highways were also constructed, linking up localities that were formerly not serviced by direct transport. Thus, although the rail line itself only passed through the Szechwan Basin, these connecting roads permitted the line to have an effect on neighboring provinces.
130. *HHJP*, October 31, 1951; December 13, 1951. On October 31, 1951, a "Southwest Regional Joint Transport Company" was established, whose job was to organize various kinds of new and old transport facilities and to coordinate their routes by plan, so that urban and rural areas, or production and marketing areas, would be rationally linked.

integration in the Southwest. Not only were commercial products given an outlet, but industry and agriculture in the area served were both promoted as demand rose along the new transport routes.

These new forms of transport were made more readily accessible with the abolition of old excessive transport fees and lowered shipping rates;[131] lowered interest rates for private merchants;[132] and regulated prices. For example, as freight rates were cut for shipping local produce down the Yangtze, their exchange was stimulated.[133] The new price policy also involved lowering the costs of daily necessities which could then be imported into remote areas of the Southwest more easily.[134] Further, prices were adjusted depending on the distance goods had to travel. They were also regulated according to differences among districts, seasonal variations, and disparities in quality.[135] In general, the effort made in the Southwest to eliminate the isolation and market exploitation that marked pre-1949 commerce conferred material benefits on the Southwest people while increasing the financial revenue of the state. This was the impact of the remunerative controls predicted in Proposition 6.2.

What sort of integration was sought through this mixed strategy, which both favored local needs and products and also strengthened the role of the state in trade? According to Proposition 6.3, the combination of atomization, associated with an indirect strategy, and the verticality of control of the direct strategy might produce a horizontal type of integration. That is, while local units retained some autonomy, higher-level organs could have an intermediate amount of control over their activities. Lateral linkages were then depended upon to connect units, rather than strict controls imposed at higher levels.

In fact, horizontal ties—localized trading patterns centered on units at the same administrative level—were stressed throughout the system. For example, there was an emphasis on promoting

131. *HHJP*, December 16, 1950; *SCMP*, No. 11 (1950), pp. 11-16; No. 88 (1951), p. 36; *CB*, No. 146 (1951), p. 19.
132. *HHJP*, September 29, 1952; December 13, 1952.
133. *SCMP*, No. 88 (1951), p. 36.
134. *HHJP*, December 16, 1950; September 29, 1952.
135. *HHJP*, October 20, 1952; March 6, 1953.

urban-rural exchange within a given area.[136] Also, goods exchange meetings were convened between units at the same administrative level, from the most local-level units all the way up the administrative hierarchy to the regional level.[137] The most basic link in developing trade was the elementary market. Beginning at that level, trade was spurred among equivalent units all the way up the hierarchy of places, reaching the regional level at the top. There was no one level at which the bulk of the activity was focused, nor did the role of any one level differ greatly from that of the next, except insofar as the volume of trade handled at higher levels was necessarily greater.

What, if any, special duties were assigned to specific levels? It was noted above that the *hsien* capital as well as lower-level markets were commonly used sites for holding local trade meetings and that supply and marketing cooperatives were organized at the *hsien* level to guide lower-level coops. The special district, which included several *hsien*, was important as the organizational level for branches of the state-operated trade companies. It was also at this level that mobile teams were created in the Southwest to buy up local products and push the sales of industrial goods. These teams sold and bought on commission in order to organize purchase, shipping, and marketing in remote regions of the Southwest.[138]

The provincial-level organs' role was to coordinate the commerce within their borders, and to facilitate linkages between the trade there and that in neighboring provinces. For example, at provincial goods exchange meetings, the provincial-level supply and marketing cooperatives, banks, and trading departments purchased native and special products from the masses in their province and supplied the peasants with the means of production from other provinces, and vice versa.[139] Here again, trade was

136. As, *HHJP*, October 31, 1951; October 2, 1951; November 24, 1951, p. 2; September 29, 1952; November 2, 1952, p. 1; *HHYP*, No. 11 (1950), p. 1064; Huang, "Ch'eng-hsiang kuan-hsi," pp. 16-17.

137. *HHJP*, September 14, 1952; September 25, 1952; October 6, 1952; November 9, 1952; December 14, 1952; *SCMP*, No. 378 (1952), p. 27; these meetings are described in detail in *FEER* 14, No. 8 (1953), pp. 230-232.

138. *HHYP*, No. 17 (1951), pp. 1116-1118; *HHJP*, November 28, 1950.

139. *SCMP*, No. 583 (1953), pp. 3-5; No. 70 (1951), p. 24; No. 340 (1952), p. 20; No. 571 (1953), p. 39; No. 86 (1951), p. 26.

coordinated between units on the same level, but without rigorous vertical controls.

Thus, commerce was organized at increasingly inclusive administrative levels as one moved up the hierarchy, while the functions at each level were basically the same. The important point was that trade could be boosted initially only through promoting exchange at every level between units at that same level. A horizontal type of integration was the intended result, as Proposition 6.3 suggested.

Given this horizontal integration, how did the regional organs function? The regional-level organs were meant to oversee and coordinate trade at the levels below. The relevant organs at the regional level were the Military Administrative Committee or Administrative Committee Trade Department and its Cooperative Affairs Bureau. These organs held conferences at the regional level,[140] issued policy instructions to lower-level units,[141] sent out investigation teams to check on the work of these units,[142] and coordinated trade with other regions.[143]

The function of regional conferences, aside from reviewing and planning work and promoting new directions in work, was to provide a forum for Southwest state trading companies, industrial departments, and cooperatives to buy and sell.[144] Investigation teams organized at the regional level, whose main duty it was to examine the implementation of policy, also engaged in selling goods in which commerce had been slack.[145]

Probably most important in terms of linking up all of China into a vast trade network was the work of the regional organs in coordinating trade with other regions. At one regional trade meeting for managers of special goods companies across the nation, held in March 1951, local products contracts were signed

140. *HHYP*, No. 17 (1951), pp. 1114-1116; *HHJP*, January 23, 1954; *SCMP*, Nos. 342 (1952), p. 29; 378 (1952), p. 27; 791 (1954), pp. 41-42; 816 (1954), pp. xx-xxii.
141. *HHJP*, October 12, 1950, p. 2 (two articles); September 24, 1952; November 2, 1952; January 25, 1953; January 23, 1954.
142. *HHJP*, December 11, 1950; September 24, 1952; October 27, 1952; May 8, 1953.
143. *SCMP*, No. 399 (1952), p. 20; *CB*, No. 146 (1951), p. 19; *HHYP*, No. 17 (1951), pp. 1119-1120; No. 22 (1951), p. 868.
144. *SCMP*, No. 378 (1952), p. 27.
145. *HHJP*, December 11, 1950.

between Southwest companies and those in the other six Great Areas.[146] The Southwest Trade Department also set up trade organs in Hankow, Canton, Shanghai, and other places, to promote the sales of native products, and organized native produce delegates to visit trade exhibits in the other regions.[147]

Thus, the regional organs' role vis-à-vis trade was different from their functions with respect to counter-revolutionaries and minorities. Regional organs constituted a sort of court of last appeal, the peak of the control apparatus in the regions, in handling counter-revolutionaries. Toward the minorities, regional organs had only a loose advisory function in promulgating policy toward the autonomous areas. In the case of trade, however, the overall emphasis was on creating horizontal linkages. In this sense, the trade units at the regional level formed the highest layer in a series of planes, each more inclusive in its commercial dealings than the one below it. In the field of trade, then, there was not an increase of control and authority as one ascended up the hierarchy; rather, there was an extended network for the same types of commercial relations as existed at lower reaches of the system. Thus, as Proposition 6.4 held, the mixed strategy planned for commercial affairs gave the regional organs only a moderate role in this problem area.

In sum, the relationships established in commerce grew out of the mixed nature of the regime's considerations on this issue. While the regime held gaining control over the commercial sector as a long-term goal, in the short run trade could only grow through the promotion of policies that suited and benefited the localities. Remunerative controls and a horizontal integration were relied upon; and the regional organs coordinated the trade relations at the regional levels just as lower-level organs supervised the trade at their respective levels.

Each of three problems in the Southwest has now been analyzed in accordance with the four criteria set down in Proposition 6.1—local distinctiveness, threat to Communist rule, value of support for the regime, and costs of suppression—and it was found that a different strategy for each area went along with variations in the nature of each.

146. *HHYP,* No. 17 (1951), pp. 1119-1120.
147. *CB,* No. 146 (1951), p. 19.

It was shown also that the type of strategy adopted in each case seemed to have a strong bearing on the structure of integration that was projected; and, consequently, on the role of the regional administration. Thus, the more a problem called for an indirect strategy, the more the localities themselves had to take on powers of control; and the less could organs at the all-region level deal with it. In such cases all-region integration was necessarily weaker. Thus, the region's role was minimal toward minorities, larger in the case of trade, and largest of all for counter-revolutionaries; and integration in the Southwest was meant to be increasingly tight as the regional organs' role increased.

But the role of the region varied in different problem areas in ways other than the size of that role. Once the nature of the regional organs' relation to each area is known, this sheds light on the type of integration sought vis-à-vis each area. The Nationalities Affairs Committee (under the Military Administrative Committee or Administrative Committee) was merely a guarantor of a policy—autonomy, assistance, and appeasement—that left the minorities as more or less the sheet of loose sand they had been before 1949. This committee, then, through ensuring unified policy toward minorities in the Southwest, merely served to link up the atomized autonomous areas, each of which was adapting this policy to its own area.

In trade, however, the regional Trade Department aimed at uniting the local markets under its jurisdiction into a coordinated network. Here the stress was on horizontal linkages: urban-rural, private-public, cooperatives-state companies, *hsien-hsien*, province-province, and, ultimately, region-region across the country. This pattern of liaison by layers, then, was consolidated by an organ at the apex that differed in degree but not in kind from its lower-level layers. In short, the form of integration designed for commerce was a horizontal one.

Finally, the military and judicial organs at the regional level represented a court of last appeal in the regions for counter-revolutionaries. In this area of political control and military coercion, the regional organs had authority to amalgamate vertically the power of lower-level courts and troops; they surpassed the power of the lower levels in degree and in kind. Counter-revolutionary control, then, was to be worked out through a vertical integration.

In sum, there was no uniform approach to local problems of diversity and separatism in the Southwest just after 1949; rather, in each case the methods and policies employed had a clear connection with the nature of the problem at hand. Although this was more or less the case throughout the entire period of regional government, policies toward the various issues began to have somewhat more in common after 1952.

Shifts in Strategy and Mode of Integration after 1952

This study has suggested in various places that Integration I and II were interrelated processes—that integration *within* the subsystem (Integration II) was somehow connected to the integration of the subsystem *into the national system* (Integration I). So, if this is true, one would expect some modifications in the handling of the three problem areas as Integration I changed from being based on a geographical principle to being based on a functional principle in 1952. The functional integration that marked the era of the Administrative Committees tended to operate through vertically organized functional branches, from the center downward, as Chapter Four indicated. Thus it seems likely that hierarchy and vertically organized structures would come to play at least a somewhat larger role in handling problems across the board with the demise of the Military Administrative Committee in late 1952. This section will examine developments in each of the three problem areas from 1952 onward to determine whether this was in fact the case.

Counter-revolutionaries

The approach toward the counter-revolutionaries had from the start been one stressing strict coercive, hierarchical controls. However, if two statutes on the counter-revolutionary problem are compared, one from early 1951 and one from mid-1952, a marked difference emerges in the way powers were granted to responsible organs to deal with the problem.

The February 1951 "Statute on Punishment for Counter-Revolutionary Activity" stated in Article 20: "During the period of military control, the affairs of persons who have committed crimes specified in this statute are subject to consideration by military tribunals set up by the headquarters of the Military Regions, military control commissions, or organs combatting banditry."[148] This regulation was vague in specifying the interrelationships between levels and the exact authority each held.

Alternatively, the "Temporary Regulations for the Surveillance of Counter-Revolutionary Elements" of June 1952 were far more exact on these matters.[149] They contained three articles—Numbers 11, 13, and 14—dealing with the jurisdiction for establishing surveillance over criminals. These articles set out, respectively, the competent local-level organs in ordering surveillance and the authority for confirming the order; the responsible organ in enforcement; and the duty of the provinces to draw up specific local instructions, subject to confirmation by the Military Administrative Committees. Thus, by mid-1952 precise provisions had been drawn up, tightening the vertical linkages in enforcing control of counter-revolutionaries.

Minorities

Although it was specified above that the August 1952 "General Program for Implementation of Regional Autonomy for Nationalities"[150] retained the basic spirit of the Common Program, some new elements were introduced into it. De Francis, writing in 1951, noted that while there were different levels of nationality areas practicing regional autonomy, there was no system of gradations comparable to the Soviet terminological hierarchy.[151] This irregularity was brought to an end with the General Program of 1952.

First, a new stress was put on the subordination of autonomous areas to higher-level governments. Article 2 illustrated this trend in stating that "The autonomous organ of each national autonomous region is a local government led by the people's government of the next higher level, under the unified leadership of the Central People's Government." Also, according to Article 23, any special regulations drawn up by an autonomous organ were subject to approval by the next two higher-level governments.

148. *JMST*, 1952, p. 40.
149. *CB*, No. 193 (1952). Also translated in Blaustein, *Legal Documents*, pp. 222-226.
150. "General Program for Regional Autonomy," Article 31, translated in Blaustein, *Legal Documents*.
151. John de Francis, "National and Minority Policies," *Annals*, No. 277 (1951), p. 152.

And Article 31 ruled that it was up to these higher-level governments to ensure that their directives to the areas below conformed both to the general policy line and to the special conditions in the locality. This emphasis on the upper levels carried with it an increase in the importance of vertical control over minorities.

Moreover, Article 5 authorized the inclusion of some Han Chinese in setting up future autonomous areas. This naturally worked to water down the purely ethnic composition that previous areas had had. Finally, Article 7 decreed that the administrative status of autonomous regions should correspond to that of equivalent units in the regular governmental hierarchy. Thus, the lack of structure that de Francis had noticed in 1951 was being rectified, and a regular hierarchy of organs was being set up.

Moseley claims that the effect of the General Program was to promote use of one or more *hsien* for autonomous area units after 1952.[152] The *hsien* was a convenient unit because it contained an administrative seat with a concentration of Han Chinese. This meant that previously formed units comprising individual *hsiang* or *ch'ü* tended to be discarded or amalgamated into larger units; and thus that small and scattered groupings of non-Han peoples lost their own autonomous units.

This trend of deemphasizing the more extreme form of autonomy of the first few years after liberation continued into 1953. Thus, a *Jen-min jih-pao* editorial following the Third Conference of the Nationalities Affairs Commission of June 1953 stated that "The nationalization of autonomy organs cannot be separated from a strengthening of the leadership of the autonomy regions by the CCP and the people's governments at higher levels."[153] And in the report at that conference, participants were told that "Respect for national forms is not to be carried to the stage of the preservation of even such national forms as obstruct the progress of development."[154] So, even minority work, which earlier had been geared expressly toward suiting each tribe and each locality, was to be given more structure and more uniformity across the country.

152. Moseley, *Consolidation*, p. 49.
153. *CB*, No. 264 (1953), p. 6.
154. *Ibid.*, p. 20.

Trade

A series of measures pertaining to trade promulgated in 1952 and 1953 changed the mixed character of commercial policy to a more totally direct one. First the "five-anti (*wu-fan*) campaign" (against bribery, tax evasion, stealing state property, cheating on government contracts, and stealing state economic intelligence), begun in early 1952, subjected private enterprise to severe attack.[155] In the same year, local Federations of Industry and Commerce were organized to impose further controls on businessmen.[156]

Then, in late 1953, the "general line of the state" was announced, which carried with it the ultimate goal of socialist transformation of private commerce.[157] And at the same time, measures were issued unifying the purchase and supply of grain. This set of policies included: planned purchase of grain from grain-surplus peasants in the rural areas; planned supply of grain to urban and rural inhabitants who were short of food; strict controls over the grain market and prohibition of private merchants from engaging in free grain trading; and division of the work of grain control between the central government and local authorities under the unified control of the former.[158]

These measures changed the nature of commerce in China in two important ways. First, with this order, the supply and marketing cooperatives achieved a monopoly in dealings in many important commodities. For, according to this plan, the coops together with the commercial departments of the state became the sole authorized buyers of many specified commodities.[159] Second, with the introduction of these measures, the traditional periodic rural markets almost ceased to exist for a time.[160] Here it appears that as time went on, commercial affairs were also operated on a more uniform basis nationally, as private capital fell under state control, businessmen were organized into federations, and trade transactions came more and more into the hands

155. See Barnett, *Early Years*, pp. 132 and 190.
156. *Ibid.*, pp. 195-196.
157. Thomas, *Government and Administration* (1955), p. 135.
158. See *JMJP*, March 1, 1954.
159. Donnithorne, *China's Economic System*, p. 279.
160. *Ibid.*, p. 291.

of state-operated organs. Thus the policy toward trade, which had been mixed, veered toward a direct strategy in 1952 and 1953.

In all three areas, then, as central direction increased with time and as the Military Administrative Committee gave way to the Administrative Committee, the lower levels of society and administration were gradually subordinated to and regulated by upper-level organs. The result was that, as similar structures were synchronized to perform similar functions throughout the country, local differences came to be seen as less important. Consequently, it seemed possible to build uniform hierarchies in all problem areas across the country, as the functional integration associated with the Administrative Committee was consolidated.

What can be said by way of conclusion about the connection between Integration I and II over time? It has been shown how through the use of various strategies the regional organs were to unify the area under their jurisdiction in different ways for different issues by 1952. To the extent that progress was made in this direction, the Southwest was by that time an area geographically or internally integrated. Then, as the localities in this Southwest subsystem became integrated in various ways—horizontally, vertically, and in an atomized fashion—it then was seen as possible to bring this subsystem into the larger, national system.

Presumably, the Southwest, as one subsystem more or less integrated internally, had been organized along similar lines for similar problems as were the other Great Administrative Regions by 1952, so that all organs dealing with the same problem across the nation were using similar methods. According to this mode of analysis, internal subsystem integration—Integration II—was the prerequisite for national integration (Proposition 6.5).

However, the matter may be viewed in another light as well. Apparently, the whole process of integration was set in motion and monitored at the central government level. Chapter Three described how the Southwest was enticed along a path laid out in Peking, and dictated largely by Peking's economic goals, despite the Southwest's frequent lack of total readiness to go forward at various steps along the way. Thus, not only did Integration II have an effect on Integration I; there was also a mutual interaction between the two processes. For it was central-level decisions to increase centralization and unification at various points in time which shaped the nature and the speed of subsystem integration (Proposition 6.6).

There is no sure means of determining the exact direction of cause and effect between Integration I and II; and in fact it appears that each had an influence on the other. The overall effect by late 1952, however, was that the region had gradually become just one more level in the national administrative hierarchy, and was no longer to be the focal point of subsystem integration.

CHAPTER VII

Integration II: Its Evaluation from the

Perspective of the Chinese

The last chapter discussed policies and strategies advocated in attempting to integrate the Southwest internally (Integration II) with respect to three problem areas. Here an attempt will be made to determine whether or not the leadership viewed these policies and strategies as successful in achieving this integration. Earlier chapters (One, Three, and Four) tended to stress the goals of economic development in explaining the fate of regional government. That is, they emphasized that the Military Administrative Committee's powers were diminished in 1952, and that the Administrative Committee was abolished in 1954 largely because economic construction demanded centralization. This chapter will consider specific problems the leadership perceived in regional government itself, in its makeup and functionings, and will look at the difficulties encountered in overcoming regionalism.

The flaws to be described are those shortcomings and weaknesses recounted in the Southwest press in articles pinpointing successes and problems in work. The interpretations placed on these problems have been accepted at face value and have been categorized so that they fit in with the previous line of analysis taken here. Thus, although the Chinese themselves do not refer to the problems as barriers to integration, we will consider them as such here, to retain the consistency of the argument. The focus is on problems which, as stated in the press, show the leadership's views of what was a malfunction in the system. Further, the discussion will also consider leadership interpretations of the causes of these malfunctions. In short, this chapter evaluates difficulties in work, based on the official Chinese perspective.

Of course, the explanations for deviations in work that appeared in the press may not be the only ones with validity. For example, in some cases lower-level cadres may have done as they were told, but, since the policies themselves provoked adverse reactions from the people, cadres were criticized in the press. Similarly, it was often convenient for the upper levels to shift the burden for failures onto the shoulders of their subordinates.

Finally, the nature of what was considered a noteworthy deviation was often redefined depending on the central policy concerns at a given point in time. For example, concern with "bureaucratism" was heightened by the national movement against bureaucratism, commandism, and alleged violation of laws and discipline that began in February 1953. Similarly, bourgeois habits became a focal point in late 1951 after Mao called for a campaign to increase production and practice strict economy.

The point here is that in analyzing deviations, one should be aware of the more general political context. However, for the purposes of this chapter the question is only whether or not the system was working, according to the leadership's views and values, and the answer will be phrased in the terms this leadership used to describe the problems that did occur. Moreover, the overall concern with integration that guides this study will inform this analysis as well.

The first part of this chapter discusses those cadre deviations in work that were most frequently cited in the press. It analyzes them in relation to the personnel policies and bureaucratic arrangements instituted to integrate the Southwest. It will be shown that the deviations were at least in part caused by tensions these policies and arrangements created in the administrative system in the Southwest.

The second part will use this analysis to take a second look at Integration II in the Southwest. Here, as in Chapter Six, the focus will be on the three salient problem areas there: counter-revolutionaries, minorities, and trade. The success of the policies instituted to combat separatism within the Southwest will be weighed by investigating the behavior of two key sets of actors: the Southwest cadres and the local population groups affected for each problem. Cadre behavior will be examined in light of the general deviations in work outlined in the first part of the chapter. The actions of target population groups will be considered as reactions to the strategies and policies used in dealing with these groups. The overall picture of Integration II in the Southwest, from the Chinese point of view, should emerge from combining the findings of Chapter Six—on policy and its intended outcomes—with the findings here.

The Deviations

The analysis in Chapter Six implied that administrative integration in the Southwest was a matter of establishing solid, dependable linkages. It was shown that for each problem a different sort of integration was attemped, but that for all three, a smoothly running bureaucracy was essential to ensure the vertical, horizontal, or policy ties that were required to create integration.

Second, and perhaps more basically, internalization of CCP ideology and policy and a keen awareness of how to put them into practice were necessary in guaranteeing that the strategy (direct or indirect) and the controls (remunerative, coercive, or normative) appropriate to each problem area were exercised properly. These considerations somewhat parallel Lewis's discussion of correct leadership in China: he points out that there should be "direct, open channels of communication to the lowest levels of information and opinion"; and that "a high value is put on regularized procedures."[1] In short, administrative reliability and efficiency and careful attention to implementing policy were crucial in achieving integration.

Despite the concern with integration, some aspects of the very personnel policies and bureaucratic arrangements instituted to control the area created tensions in the system that hindered integration. This is not surprising. In large bureaucracies, such as the one set up to administer China, the methods used to handle certain problems often themselves lead to new and different types of difficulties. Several writers on Western-style bureaucracies have come to this conclusion in studying large organizations in the West. Thus, one analyst holds that the causes of what he

1. John W. Lewis, *Leadership in Communist China* (1966), p. 73.

terms "bureaupathological" behavior are to be found in the structures and conditions within the organizations themselves.[2] Similarly, another study uses the concept of "dilemma" to illustrate the inevitability of conflict in organizations. Thus it notes that "the innovations instituted to solve one problem often create others because effectiveness in an organization depends on many factors some of which are incompatible with others."[3]

In the Southwest regional administration, certain tensions grew out of the nature of personnel assignments in the area. It was noted in Chapter Five that the policy toward personnel involved introducing outsiders—particularly members of the First and Second Field Armies—in large numbers into leading posts in the Southwest. Problems cropped up because these outsiders were unfamiliar with the Southwest.[4] Personnel policy also included retention of ex-KMT officials born in the Southwest, both because of a shortage of Communist cadres and as part of a deliberate attempt to coopt these individuals and to present the local population with officials with whom they could identify. The outcome of this policy was that difficulties were created in dealing with work styles and mind sets left over from the past.

Some bureaucratic arrangements also had the effect of thwarting integration. A new administrative hierarchy and new organs of power were utilized in the institution of a regional level of power. It is likely that many bureaucratic problems occurred at least in part because the regional administration was far removed from the lowest levels of society and could not establish dependable communication linkages or otherwise exercise effective control over these lower levels.

Each of two conditions needed for integration—bureaucratic efficiency and bureaucratic discipline in correctly implementing policy—depended on proper handling of certain strains introduced into the system by the policies and arrangements alluded to above. First, an efficient bureaucracy required that the out-

2. Victor A. Thompson, *Modern Organization* (1961), p. 166.
3. Peter Blau and Richard Scott, *Formal Organizations* (1962), p. 250.
4. References to cadres' lack of familiarity with the Southwest were made in several places. See, for example, *Hsin-Hua yüeh-pao* [New China Monthly] (Peking) [hereafter *HHYP*], No. 7 (1950), p. 22; No. 11 (1950), p. 1063; and *Hsin-Hua jih-pao* [New China Daily] (Chungking) [hereafter *HHJP*], October 3, 1951.

sider cadres become sufficiently familiar with the region to govern it. At the same time they had to be able to coexist with those whose knowledge of the Southwest exceeded theirs. This will be referred to as the commonly recognized tension between *insiders and outsiders.*[5] Bureaucratic effectiveness also called for maintaining well-working relationships between the organs at all levels in the administrative hierarchy. For convenience, this tension will be regarded as one between the *upper and lower levels.*

The proper implementation of policy, the second requisite for integration, in operational terms meant adoption of the appropriate strategies and controls for each problem tackled. This depended, as the Party leaders saw it, on a correct "work style"[6] and on firm adherence to doctrine. The relevant problems here were those that arose between *the old and the new* and between *theory and practice.*

The old-new problem was especially salient in the Southwest because large numbers of ex-KMT hangers-on from the pre-1949 regime remained there after takeover. This meant that intractable habits and attitudes had a continuing influence on policy implementation. Tensions between theory and practice, on the other hand, were the concern of the Party members. These tensions were manifested in deviations from prescribed "work style" and were caused by insufficient attention to the ideological aspects of policy. They were at least partly attributable to the extreme shortage of Party cadres in the area.[7]

In sum, then, all of the deviations to be considered can be subsumed under one of these four categories of tension: between insiders and outsiders; between upper and lower levels; between the old and the new; and between theory and practice. In the

5. This problem is handled thoroughly by Chamberlain. See H. B. Chamberlain, "Transition and Consolidation in Urban China: A Study of Leaders and Organizations in Three Cities, 1949-1953" (1971).

6. "Work style" for the Chinese refers to the nature of the cadre's performance in his or her daily interactions with the masses. For a full discussion of this term, see Lewis, *Leadership*, pp. 83-86.

7. According to *Jen-min jih-pao* [People's Daily] (Peking), July 1, 1950, p. 1, of the more than 5,000,000 Party cadres nationwide, the Northeast, East, and North Great Administrative Regions together housed 3,400,000 Party members. This means that only 1,600,000 members were located in the Central-South, Northwest, and Southwest Regions combined. See also Chapter Three's discussion of the First Plenum of the Southwest Military Administrative Committee.

following discussion, deviations will be seen as creating problems in integration, either because they led to bureaucratic inefficiency or because they amounted to failures in implementing policy. Each deviation will be considered under the tension that best explains its occurrence. Each of the four tensions will be related to problems in integration by a proposition that points out the connection between the tension and the aspect of integration affected. These hypotheses are stated so that they apply specifically to the context of Southwest China, 1949–1954. However, as will be apparent from the discussion, each can be generalized to a wider context.

Tensions: Insider-Outsider

Proposition 7.1. If the bureaucracy were to work efficiently, regional-level cadres (most of whom were outsiders) had to become familiar with the area under their control. In the absence of this condition, deviations in work resulted.

In the Southwest this condition was particularly difficult to fulfill. For various reasons indicated elsewhere, outsiders had to be relied upon but often lacked knowledge of the area. There was no quick way of changing an outsider, useful for his ties to Peking and the Party, into an insider with deep understanding of the Southwest and its social problems in the first few years after takeover. And yet the efficiency of the bureaucracy and thus the effectiveness of any integration in the area was intimately related to cadres at the upper echelons being knowledgeable about the territory under their jurisdiction.

Because this need for a sizable number of cadres with ties to the Southwest was largely unsatisfied, difficulties cropped up in running the administrative system there. Cadres' lack of understanding of the lower levels was a frequent charge in the press. Apparently the problem affected departments of government across the board and led to policies that were inappropriate for the localities.

For example, in trade, because the state companies lacked understanding of the local rural markets, the goods they sold did not meet the people's needs.[8] The cooperative stores also were

8. *HHJP,* November 28, 1950.

not stocked according to the peasants' requirements.[9] Because of this ignorance of local consumption habits, some goods accumulated while others were out of stock.[10] The conclusion drawn by the lower levels was this: "the leadership is high above, divorced from reality."[11]

In farming, the upper levels "lacked understanding about the private and scattered nature of the small peasant economy." Therefore they set targets too high and demanded uniformity.[12] The tendency of not proceeding from the present state of the small peasant economy led to reckless "adventurism" in the cooperative movement.[13]

In tax collection, since the leadership did not know enough about the situation in the localities, it was forced to rely on simple collective reports that hid many facts.[14] Likewise, during a spring famine, upper-level cadres considered only the overall nature of the harvest at the *hsien* level, and had no knowledge of the disaster situation in individual villages.[15]

In the Water Conservancy Department, "almost no one could grasp the Southwest situation." In fact, although there was partial understanding of Szechwan, in the other three provinces the cadres were even unfamiliar with the circumstances in the one province they ruled.[16]

Finally, some interesting episodes that occurred in the Southwest Forestry Industry Management Bureau were described in the press.[17] There also the leadership did not understand the situation at the base. First, the Bureau arbitrarily sent out more than 200 workers to a *hsien* to do felling and shipping. After the workers had brought their tools and food to the forest district, they realized that the area had few trees and was too steep for

9. Wang Wei-tsu, "Hsi-nan kung-shang-yeh i nien lai ti chin-pu ts'e-hsieh" [Emphasizing a Year of Progress in Industry and Commerce in the Southwest], *Ching-chi chou-pao* [Economic Weekly] [hereafter *CCCP*] 12 (1951), No. 8, p. 18.

10. *HHJP*, June 11, 1953.

11. *HHJP*, May 28, 1953.

12. *Survey of China Mainland Press* [hereafter *SCMP*], No. 583 (1953), pp. 3-5.

13. *Ibid.*, and *SCMP*, No. 626 (1953), pp. 21-22; and No. 674 (1953), pp. ii-iv.

14. *HHJP*, March 29, 1953.

15. *HHJP*, March 24, 1953.

16. *HHJP*, March 14, 1953.

17. *HHJP*, May 15, 1953.

felling work. The next month, the Bureau instructed the same *hsien* to ship out stored wood to Chengtu. In fact, no roads were open in this area, while the amount of stored wood actually existing there was only one-third of the amount requested.

It is likely that this persistent unawareness of affairs at the lower levels would not have been so pronounced had more reliance been placed on native Southwest people in administering the region. But at the same time, reliance on insiders alone would have meant that other goals in integration would have been sacrificed. And yet, as these examples indicate, the use of outsiders lacking knowledge of the Southwest impeded the smooth operation in administration that was essential to integration. This was the prediction of Proposition 7.1.

Tensions: Upper-Lower Levels

Proposition 7.2. In using the several-tiered administrative system associated with regional government, it was difficult to achieve coordination and cooperation between regional and lower levels in the bureaucracy. But without such coordination, problems in work occurred.

The question of the coordination of the upper and lower levels in the bureaucracy lay at the heart of the problem of administrative integration. Problems in effecting such coordination are endemic to large organizations and have been noted by many analysts of Western bureaucracy and organization.[18]

While each analyst attributes difficulties in administrative coordination to different factors, all of them find the underlying causes in the inherent nature of bureaucratic arrangements. Simon speaks of problems of communication, and holds that information tends to be filtered upward selectively—that is, only when it will not have unpleasant consequences for the transmitter. So, a major problem for the higher levels is that much information needed in their decision-making may not ever reach these levels.[19]

Another student of bureaucracy agrees that the output of "problem information" is likely to be restricted by lower-level personnel who are anxious to please their superiors and to pre-

18. For an analysis of the role of bureaucracy in Chinese politics, see Harry Harding, Jr., "The Organizational Issue in Chinese Politics, 1959-1972" (1973).
19. Herbert A. Simon, *Administrative Behavior* (1960), p. 163.

serve their tried routines in work.[20] Yet another believes that merely adding levels to a hierarchy compounds distortion. This author also notes that declining "marginal efficiency" is naturally associated with increasing size, such that coordination becomes more and more difficult.[21] And according to Downs, a high volume of messages alone will lead to delay, poor coordination, and a waste of resources and personnel.[22] Thus all these analysts see problems of communication and coordination as attendant upon large organizations generally.

Others draw attention to the phenomenon of red tape that tends to impede efficiency and obstruct cooperation between levels in organizational life. Both attribute its appearance to an emphasis on routine procedures, and blind adherence to rules.[23]

Finally, still another writer finds that a desire to please superiors creates personal insecurity at the lower levels in large organizations. This leads to the worker's concentration on the quantitative aspects of his or her job that can be measured and observed by upper-level bureaucrats.[24]

In an essay on bureaucracy, Mao demonstrates his own awareness of the malfunctions of bureaucracy. Among those which draw his disapproval, and are also relevant to this section, are the following: "divorce from reality"; routinism; lack of responsibility; formalism and red tape; and lack of unity ("the top is divorced from the bottom").[25] Other criticisms of his pertain to a later section.

And yet, despite these seemingly inevitable shortcomings in bureaucracy, it remained necessary to establish a working liaison between levels. The functioning of the bureaucracy in China required that lower-echelon cadres make thorough investigations of conditions at the base and report them accurately to upper levels; it also required informed decision-making by the upper-

20. Harold L. Wilensky, *Organizational Intelligence* (1967), p. 43.
21. Gordon Tullock, *The Politics of Bureaucracy* (1965), pp. 150-152.
22. Anthony Downs, *Inside Bureaucracy* (1967), p. 130.
23. Walter R. Sharp, "Procedural Vices: La Paperasserie," in Robert K. Merton, ed., *Reader in Bureaucracy* (1952), pp. 407-410; and Robert K. Merton, "Bureaucratic Structure and Personality," in Merton, *Reader*, pp. 361-371.
24. Thompson, *Modern Organization*, pp. 160-161.
25. "Chairman Mao Discusses 20 Manifestations of Bureaucracy," in "Selections from Chairman Mao." U.S. *Joint Publications Research Service* [hereafter *JPRS*], No. 90 (1970), pp. 40-43. See also Martin King Whyte, "Bureaucracy and Modernization in China: The Maoist Critique," *American Sociological Review* 38, No. 2 (1973), pp. 149-163.

level organs and their sensitive supervision of the implementation of these decisions.[26] In short, as Western analysts have noted,
cooperation and coordination were called for at every step.
Where they were lacking, efficiency, and consequently, integration suffered.

Examples of the deviations connected with dislocation between
levels reminiscent of Western critiques abound in the Southwest
press. First, "bureaucratism" plagued the upper levels, while
confusion marked the base in many instances. "Bureaucratism"
had several manifestations, all of which amounted to examples of
the failings noted above that are common to all large bureaus.
Here, by far its most common symptom was upper-level failure to
investigate and research conditions below.[27] Moreover, the upper
levels neglected to pass down rules;[28] and province-level cadres
were opposed to sending cadres to the lower levels and refused to
examine and consider plans sent up to them from below.[29] These
shortcomings are related to problems in coordination noted by
Western authors.

Other examples of this "bureaucratism" all have analogues in
Western studies. "Quantitative compliance" occurred in the Finance Department. In their hurry to complete the job, upper-
level finance cadres quickly estimated the grain output, rather
than carefully calculating the amount.[30] When it was time to
undertake general planning, cadres reverted to an old habit of
simply "adding on figures," rather than doing careful planning
work.[31] And because of their general ignorance of the localities,
upper levels had to rely on summary statistics.[32] As a result, they
demanded too much, in a time limit that was too short,[33] and they
inflexibly insisted on task fulfillment regardless of actual condi-

26. Lewis, *Leadership*, pp. 72-74; and Mao Tse-tung, "On Methods of Leadership," *Selected Works* (1954-1956) 4:111-117; "On Setting Up a System of
Reports," *Selected Works* (1961) 4:77-79; "On Strengthening the Party Committee System," *Selected Works* (1961) 4:267-268.
27. For example, *HHJP,* October 1, 1950; December 9, 1951; September 28,
1952; May 21, 1953; and May 28, 1953.
28. *HHJP,* October 6, 1950.
29. *HHJP,* June 3, 1953.
30. *HHJP,* December 11, 1950.
31. *HHJP,* June 3, 1953.
32. *HHJP,* March 14, 1953, and March 24, 1953.
33. *HHJP,* June 4, 1953.

tions.[34] Here it appears that there was frequently a lack of liaison between levels.

Other articles described inconsistent handling of problems because of the poor communication between various levels mentioned by several Western analysts.[35] Thus, plans at one level diverged from those at the next and rules were altered frequently.[36] Upper levels failed to offer guidance and aid to their subordinates,[37] refused to answer requests for instructions,[38] and were tardy in introducing mass movements to lower-level units.[39] Lower echelons complained that investigation work was not well coordinated between levels and that no attention was given to staff or workers' criticisms.[40] Thus the lack of coordination and overall communication left the lower levels frustrated.

Finally, bureaucratism in the Southwest entailed the "red tape" pointed to above: holding frequent meetings and reading reports,[41] "leading work by empty speeches and directives,"[42] and becoming enmeshed in a ceaseless passing around of documents.[43] This busyness stultified work and alienated the lower levels.

However, confusion at the lower levels was also responsible for disruptions in the bureaucracy. This confusion took several forms. At a given level in the hierarchy, organs that ought to have worked cooperatively were often uncoordinated. This was manifested in a lack of adequate liaison between the trade and finance organs,[44] finance and food grains,[45] various transportation units,[46] and local control commissions and the departments they were meant to oversee.[47] In basic construction, each office admin-

34. *SCMP*, No. 677 (1953), pp. xx-xxi.
35. *HHJP*, October 6, 1950.
36. *HHJP*, June 4, 1953.
37. *Ibid.*
38. *HHJP*, May 15, 1953.
39. *HHJP*, September 28, 1952.
40. *HHJP*, May 28, 1953.
41. *HHJP*, March 4, 1953.
42. *SCMP*, No. 611 (1953), pp. 17-18.
43. *HHJP*, June 4, 1953; May 19, 1953; June 11, 1953.
44. *HHJP*, November 2, 1950.
45. *HHJP*, November 10, 1950.
46. *HHJP*, October 30, 1952.
47. *HHJP*, November 30, 1952.

istered its own affairs without general coordination.[48] During a spring famine, the failure of the banks to join in work with the supply and marketing cooperatives meant that the peasants could not purchase supplies after they had received loan and relief funds.[49] Such horizontal discontinuities necessarily created obstructions in work at the base independent of the failures of superiors.

The misuse of personnel and materials which Downs predicts further affected the work of those at the basic levels. Thus, in geological work, technical cadres were given administrative chores.[50] In building construction, only one-third of the machinery was used and only one-fifth of the designing personnel were qualified for their work.[51] Haphazard distribution of the labor force meant that capital construction was hampered.[52] Again, chaos in management by the base was unrelated to the problems at higher levels.

Certain lower-level cadres and organs exhibited a basic sense of irresponsibility, as Mao has charged. Several instances were reported of these cadres taking action without obtaining approval from the appropriate administrative organ. These included unauthorized hiring and firing of personnel,[53] units under the Machinery Bureau mobilizing production capital and buying equipment at will,[54] and local finance committees arbitrarily disbanding general goods company teams.[55]

Along these same lines, cadres in the basic construction industry saw planning as merely "a problem of getting money from the upper levels," and felt that "in basic construction the nation invests," so that there was "no need to make payments to the upper level."[56] Cadres in a local granary hoped that the upper level would force the *ch'ü* government to share the responsibility for the bad grain these cadres had collected, and they handed the grain over early in an attempt to get rid of the responsibility.[57]

48. *HHYP*, No. 40 (1953), pp. 119-120.
49. *SCMP*, No. 588 (1953), pp. 7-8.
50. *HHJP*, December 25, 1952.
51. *HHJP*, May 21, 1953.
52. *SCMP*, No. 677 (1953), pp. xxxi-xxxiii.
53. *HHJP*, September 7, 1952; September 20, 1952; October 14, 1952.
54. *HHJP*, November 17, 1952.
55. *HHJP*, January 25, 1953.
56. *HHYP*, No. 40 (1953), pp. 119-120.
57. *HHJP*, November 10, 1950.

These examples of lower-level lack of responsibility show that basic-level cadres at times tended to ignore their duties as part of a hierarchy.

Another suggestive article indicating this lack of responsibility commented on the work of reducing taxes and exempting peasant households from taxation. It mentioned cadres taking a "sounding-out attitude" toward the upper levels. Either the cadres engaged in "egalitarianism," reducing everyone's taxes or no one's out of a fear of offending people, or they bargained with the masses, discussing with them the amount of taxes that should be reduced.[58] Apparently cadres in some units at the lower levels saw their roles as antagonistic to those above them, and so tried to organize work on their own initiative. Behavior of this type loosened the essential links between levels in the bureaucracy.

A final category of problem at the base was traceable to the flaws of those above. In water conservancy, for example, cadres were unclear as to lines of responsibility: they did not know who was supposed to take care of soil conservation.[59] And among labor units, staff were confused as to which level they were to report to, and consequently reported to the wrong level.[60] Here one is reminded of the claim of one analyst that simply adding levels decreases efficiency in large organizations.

In sum, the distance between levels created by negligence and indifference at the top simply encouraged any tendencies among those at the base to withdraw from authority. When the upper-level cadres failed to keep themselves informed, when their work was uncoordinated with that of their subordinates, and when they did not offer guidance, those below were, in effect, presented with a shield behind which they might fail to coordinate organs, misuse materials, and act upon irresponsible attitudes. The overall result was that faulty coordination affected work, as Proposition 7.2 suggested it would.

Tensions: Old-New

Proposition 7.3. In implementing policies, the habits and attitudes prevalent among the KMT before 1949 had to be eradicated. Where they persisted, policy execution was impaired.

58. *HHJP*, November 11, 1952.
59. *HHJP*, March 14, 1953.
60. *HHJP*, September 22, 1952.

Persistence of KMT habits in work was bound up with the retention of old personnel who had served under the former regime. Although the implementation of CCP policy could have been more nearly ensured had more CCP cadres been available, the Southwest administration was severely handicapped by the small numbers of Party personnel in the area. And the enforcement of policy was definitely influenced by the attitudes and work styles of these KMT officials.

Although these old officials served in several areas of work and allegedly affected the work of the relevant organs,[61] the most interesting examples of this problem appeared in articles on the judicial organs.[62] There, the way old personnel were trained under the KMT, along with their long-ingrained habits and biases, created obstacles to the institution of a Communist legal system.[63]

Thus, they twisted the law to obtain bribes, delayed, hindered, or refused to carry out "the people's" litigation, procrastinated, were perfunctory in work, and mixed up right and wrong, as defined by the Communists.[64] These charges indicate that judicial workers under the KMT had no dealings with the lower classes, those who after 1949 were termed "the people." Their limited experience hindered the application of Communist policy.

Moreover, their work style was characterized by an attitude of "sitting in judgment" and interrogating, rather than carrying out investigation and research; by passing subjective, arbitrary judgments; and by relying only on verbal reports.[65] Even as late as December 1952 this situation persisted, as the Southwest area was still plagued by an acute shortage of judicial cadres.[66] Here there was no simple solution to the contradiction between the need to recruit those with some experience in legal matters in the Southwest and the fact that their ties to the past greatly tempered their value to the new regime. The effect of employing these people in

61. See *HHJP*, November 23, 1951, on teachers; December 15, 1951, on the Tax Bureau; December 17, 1951, on industry; October 19, 1952, on the building industry; and November 17, 1952, on the machinery industry.

62. *HHJP*, November 23, 1951; September 28, 1952; December 14, 1952.

63. Old judicial cadres were said to retain the "phony" *Liu fa* viewpoint in legal work. This was a code used under the KMT.

64. *HHJP*, September 28, 1952.

65. *HHJP*, December 14, 1952.

66. *Ibid.*

the regional administration was that policy enforcement was hampered at times.

Tensions: Theory—Practice

Proposition 7.4. In implementing policies, cadres' work had to conform to CCP work style and embody CCP ideology. When their work style deviated from the prescribed style and when insufficient attention was paid to ideology, policies were wrongly applied.

At times cadres failed to exhibit the proper Communist work style in dealing with the masses or working with their comrades. Many articles in the Southwest press highlight typical flaws in style that thwarted policy execution. The errors that were most frequently pointed out included commandism,[67] discrimination,[68] fearing troublesome work (*p'a ma-fan*),[69] the bourgeois-capitalist work style,[70] departmentalism,[71] and a general neglect of policy or political education.[72] These types of flaws in work style have been documented by analysts of Chinese administration as well as by theorists of Western bureaucracy.

Thus, in Lewis's discussion of the Chinese mass line style of work, the theoretical guide to good practice among the masses, he lists several deviations from the line. Most of these deviations involved cadres becoming too far removed from the people. Lewis notes here "commandism," "isolationism," "bureaucratism," "sectarianism," and "subjectivism."[73] In his piece on bureau-

67. *HHJP*, January 3, 1951, on rent reduction; November 23, 1951, on the Resist-America-Aid-Korea movement; October 7, 1952, among cooperative cadres; March 29, 1953, on tax collection; November 10, 1950, on grain collection; *SCMP*, No. 561 (1953), pp. 25-26, on extending loans; No. 583 (1953), pp. 3-5, on setting farming targets; No. 674 (1953), pp. ii-iv, on the cooperativization movement.

68. *HHJP*, April 3, 1954, and March 18, 1953, on loans to the poor; March 24, 1953, on giving relief funds; June 11, 1953, on the urban viewpoint in trade work; and *SCMP*, No. 887 (1954), pp. xvi-xvii, on selecting Party members.

69. *HHJP*, October 18, 1952; December 14, 1952; December 20, 1952.

70. *HHJP*, December 15, 1951; December 17, 1951; December 19, 1951; November 17, 1952.

71. *HHJP*, October 20, 1952, on personnel departments; December 17, 1952, on goods maintenance in factories; October 27, 1952, among state trade companies.

72. *HHJP*, October 7, 1951, on the land reform; October 7, 1952, on trade cooperatives; January 25, 1953, on goods interchange; October 12, 1950, on trade; November 4, 1950, on the Party.

73. Lewis, *Leadership*, p. 78.

cracy, Mao too refers to several deviations related to failures in work style and lack of attention to ideology and policy. Thus, he speaks of authoritarianism, overlords, laziness, "back-door deals," official airs, embezzlement and speculation, sectarianism, and not grasping policy.[74]

Western sociologists also find such phenomena in the organizations they study. Merton attributes commandism, or a "domineering attitude" as he calls it, to the bureaucrat's tendency to act as the representative of the power and prestige of the organization.[75] Another writer holds that when the official is caught between the demands of the "rights" of clients and tight administrative controls from above, dissociation from the clients and disinterest in their problems may seem to be the only way out of the dilemma.[76]

What the Southwest press refers to as the *p'a ma-fan* attitude may be explained by Downs' analysis of taking shortcuts in work. He says that such irregularities are related to uncertainties in work, changing environments, large expenditures of money, and heavy pressures from external agents.[77] And for the cadre in the Southwest after liberation, far from Peking and the national policy-makers and new to his job and often his work site, uncertainty was definitely present. The constant flow of directives from above and the rapid pace of societal reform movements below meant that the environment in which the cadre operated was in great flux. Further, pressure for performance and investigation of results caused frequent strains on the cadre in the region. The shortcuts he was likely to take, as will be shown, tended to be ones that made him appear to be neglecting the ideological components of policy directives.

Finally, what the Chinese term "departmentalism" or "sectarianism" is dealt with by several Western writers. Merton speaks of an "esprit de corps" which induces personnel to defend their entrenched interests. He says that this behavior tends to arise whenever there is an apparent threat to the integrity of the group.[78] Downs stresses self-interest as an important motive

74. U.S. *JPRS*, No. 90 (1970), pp. 40-43.
75. Merton, "Bureaucratic Structure," p. 369.
76. Thompson, *Modern Organization*, p. 162.
77. Downs, *Inside Bureaucracy*, pp. 71-72.
78. Merton, "Bureaucratic Structure," p. 367.

behind the diversion of organizational goals as policy filters downward.[79] And Selznick points to the concern for self-maintenance that accompanies the development of organizations into value-laden institutions over time.[80] Then, a last observer maintains that specialization per se encourages rivalry between units, and that this results in the lines of organization becoming lines of loyalty and security.[81]

Given these tendencies for flaws in work style to develop, what were some examples of these flaws that amounted to a divergence of practice from theory and hindered policy execution? First, commandism was often associated with an overemphasis on completing the job.[82] This follows Downs' observation that pressure put on workers in an organization often leads them to follow short-cut methods. Thus, speed and uniformity were typical manifestations of the commandist style.[83] Probably related to the same causes, cadres were charged with being afraid of taking responsibility, hitting snags, or running into trouble (*p'a ma-fan*) and therefore neglecting important aspects of their tasks.[84]

Another shortcoming that related to commandism and affected policy implementation was discrimination. Discrimination was largely directed against poor peasants, the rural areas, and the minorities. Cadres were reluctant to distribute loans to poor peasants whom they feared would not return the money,[85] general goods companies' supplies were managed with an urban bias,[86] and minorities were intentionally given the worst land, or, in some cases, got no land at all.[87] Although Communist cadres were to blame in these instances, apparently old ways of thinking and reacting had an impact on their behavior.

A deviation committed by Communist cadres but reminiscent of a pre-1949 cast of mind was working in a style characterized by

79. Downs, *Inside Bureaucracy*, p. 134.
80. Philip Selznick, *Leadership in Administration* (1957), especially pp. 20-21.
81. Wilensky, *Organizational Intelligence*, p. 48.
82. *HHJP*, March 29, 1953, and November 10, 1950.
83. *HHJP*, November 10, 1950; and *SCMP*, No. 583 (1953), pp. 3-5, respectively.
84. *HHJP*, October 18, 1952; December 14, 1952; December 20, 1952.
85. *HHJP*, April 3, 1954; March 18, 1953; March 24, 1953; *SCMP*, No. 887 (1954), pp. xvi-xvii.
86. *HHJP*, June 11, 1953.
87. *SCMP*, No. 718 (1953), pp. 17-19.

a bourgeois-capitalist mentality. Such organs as the Tax, Industry, Machinery, and Trade Departments were particularly affected. It was suggested in the press that where revolutionary cadres showed this trait it was owing to influences received from the old society.[88] It was difficult to absorb the old personnel successfully without some of them contributing to corrosion of the work style which the Communist cadres were meant to carry over from the Party's revolutionary period before takeover.

"Departmentalism" symbolized a failure to cooperate for the benefit of the state, a tendency to show excessive concern for the interests of one's own unit. This cropped up in personnel departments, hampering national construction;[89] in various factory units;[90] and in trade departments in dealings with private merchants.[91] Apparently, its causes in the Chinese context were no different from those noted in the West.

Finally, cadres' neglect of policy and political education was in many cases a variant of commandism, for both deviations resulted from an overemphasis on completing the job. Typical manifestations included citing only economic and not political reasons in mobilization for land reform;[92] emphasizing supplies, but not politics, in trade cooperatives work;[93] and omitting to offer ideological leadership in goods exchange meetings, so that the meetings "flowed by themselves," without direction.[94] Thus cadres relied on shortcuts, on whatever seemed to produce results, rather than carefully explaining the theoretical motives behind a policy.

This section has taken an overview of flaws in the system and related these to failings in the workings of the bureaucracy and to imperfections in policy implementation, both of which affected integration. In the course of the discussion it was suggested that the nature of the personnel appointed to govern the Southwest and the bureaucratic arrangements made in the wake of takeover

88. *HHJP,* December 15, 17, 19, 1951, and November 17, 1952.
89. *HHJP,* October 20, 1952.
90. *HHJP,* December 17, 1952.
91. *HHJP,* September 24, 1952; October 27, 1952.
92. *HHJP,* October 7, 1951.
93. *HHJP,* October 7, 1952.
94. *HHJP,* January 25, 1953.

placed certain demands upon the system, and that these demands help to explain the deviations in practice.

Four propositions were presented, relating the deviations commonly recounted in the press to specific tensions built into the administrative system. The first two propositions predicted that bureaucratic efficiency demanded that upper-level cadres be familiar with the region; and that the upper and lower levels in the bureaucracy be well coordinated, respectively. The second two propositions dealt with policy implementation. These specified that the adoption of appropriate strategies and controls in work depended, respectively, on eradication of the habits and attitudes prevalent before 1949, and on internalization of the CCP work style and ideology. When any of these conditions was absent or imperfectly fulfilled, a chain of events was set in motion that ultimately impaired integration.

For each proposition, data were used to illustrate the types of deviations that resulted from tensions between one of the following pairs: insiders and outsiders, upper and lower levels, old and new personnel; and theory and practice. In each case, examples showed that in fact the deviations did contribute to failures of bureaucracy or policy, and that integration consequently suffered. It is interesting to note that personnel and institutional devices installed to promote integration actually hampered it in the end.

The foregoing discussion covered the whole range of deviations mentioned in the press, but did not concentrate on particular problem areas. The next section will analyze the three problems presented in Chapter Six in light of the above framework, in order to gauge the extent to which problems in achieving integration affected crucial policy areas. It will thus serve to fill out the picture drawn in Chapter Six, by showing how the plans for integration outlined there were limited. At the same time it will demonstrate the continuing difficulties in eliminating regionalism in the Southwest.

Three Problem Areas

The discussion here will concentrate on the types of deviations that obstructed bureaucratic and policy integration in the three salient localist issues in the Southwest—counter-revolutionaries, minorities, and trade. This section will look at the effects of deviations on these issues by considering two key groups: first, there will be a focus on cadres' mistakes; second, on the reactions of target populations in the Southwest.

Cadres' errors will be examined by utilizing the analysis above. Thus, cadre imperfections in handling these problem areas will be interpreted in terms of flaws in bureaucratic linkages and faulty policy implementation. However, newspaper criticism of cadres' work in these particular problem areas did not always refer to all four sets of tensions specified above. Therefore, in the discussion that follows, the criticisms that will be presented are those that the leadership felt to be most worthy of mention.

The second part of this section will assess the impact of the various policies on the population groups at which they were aimed in the Southwest. Here the framework and propositions developed above are not applicable, since mass behavior was not criticized in the press in terms of the standards set for cadres. In understanding the obstacles that target groups posed to integration, a new set of propositions will be presented. These will account for the behavior of each group by viewing the behavior as a response to regime policies and strategies toward that group.

Cadre Deviations: Counter-revolutionaries

What were the outstanding errors made by cadres in handling counter-revolutionaries? Did they concern bureaucratic failures or inadequate execution of the policies toward the offenders?

Few charges were made in the press about flaws in the hierarchy set up to control counter-revolutionaries. However, although the administrative linkages themselves were not said to be awry, there were allegations that the campaign to suppress these elements was "unthorough" in certain places and in certain respects.[95] This may indicate that cadres at some levels were remiss in pursuing their work with due vigor.

More important than bureaucratic problems, the lack of exhaustiveness in carrying out this movement was mainly discussed in terms of a failure to mobilize the masses fully. Additional problems were overleniency and extreme "leftism."[96] Because of these errors in work style, policy was being wrongly applied, and

95. For example, *HHJP*, October 1, 1951.
96. Overleniency was charged in *HHJP*, October 9, 1951, and November 8, 1950; a "left" deviation was criticized in *HHJP*, November 8, 1950.

the proper type of control over the counter-revolutionaries was not being utilized.

Thus, the most important deviations in suppressing counter-revolutionaries were not related to bureaucratic problems and vertical linkages, but rather to problems in work style and policy implementation. Lack of thoroughness meant that the opposition was not eliminated with sufficient rigor. Presumably, establishment of proper controls and correct work styles was crucial in so sensitive a problem area; bureaucratic linkages received less attention in the press than accurate disposal of each case.

Cadre Deviations: Minorities

Press coverage of work with minorities spanned a wider range of problems. The criticisms tended to fall into the four categories used above in describing tensions in the system. Both bureaucratic and policy issues were at stake.

Since the policy toward the minorities was based upon recognition of the differences between the various peoples, a well-running bureaucracy with access to knowledge of the localities was essential. However, probably owing to discrimination against the minorities as well as to upper-level cadres' desires to complete jobs without undue effort, the governments at higher levels tended to disregard differences in different areas, ignore the special characteristics of the various minority areas, issue generalized orders, and mechanically apply experience obtained in the Han areas in carrying out work among the minorities.[97] Moreover, some upper-level organs even refused to recognize county-level minority autonomy organs under their jurisdiction. Instead, they would issue orders and work plans directly to governments at even lower levels under the autonomy organs.[98] Most likely, these upper-level organs preferred to deal with basic-level (hsiang or ch'ü) Han governments rather than with organs staffed by minorities. As a result, a lack of familiarity with the localities and dislocation between levels affected minority work. In such cases, the designated bureaucratic linkages atrophied and informal arrangements subverted policy. This tended to impair integration in this problem area.

Policy implementation was also a problem. The chief compo-

97. HHJP, December 8, 1952; SCMP, No. 718 (1953), pp. 17-19; No. 816 (1954), pp. xx-xxii; Current Background [hereafter CB], No. 264 (1953), p. 15.
98. CB, No. 264 (1953), p. 21.

nent of the policy toward minorities was a stress on normative controls, or encouraging compliance through use of symbols, such as prestige, esteem, and acceptance.[99] But improper application of controls marked deviations in this area too. Han cadres tended not to respect the minorities' traditions, customs, and religions and often ignored their needs.[100] They also failed to carry out the policy of nationalization outlined in Chapter Six. By monopolizing tasks that belonged to the minority cadres, they did not permit these cadres to share in the control of their own affairs. Also, they did not honor the autonomy rights of the minorities as set down in policy documents, and did not use the minorities' own languages in work.[101] These failings were attributed to "remnant influences of Pan-Hanism,"[102] an ideological disposition to feel that Han Chinese were superior to the minorities. Thus, pre-1949 attitudes and a faulty work style marked minority affairs. The overall result was that policy was wrongly applied.

In minority work, therefore, integration was hindered both because of faults in the bureaucracy and because policy was misapplied. In the bureaucracy's upper levels, lack of familiarity with minority areas and general negligence in work impaired even the minimal coordination required. And in terms of policy, remnant influences from the pre-1949 society and deviations in practice vitiated a policy meant to operate principally through normative controls.

Cadre Deviations: Trade

In trade work also, newspaper accounts of deviations touched on both bureaucratic and policy problems. In bureaucratic terms, the concern was with failing to establish linkages of several sorts. In this area of work, the emphasis was placed on various kinds of horizontal connections—that is, on the relations of organs, enterprises, and groups at the same administrative level. Thus, public and private enterprises were to work jointly, state trade companies were to combine their business with the cooperatives, and

99. Amitai Etzioni, *Modern Organizations* (1964), p. 59. See Chapter Six.
100. See footnote 97.
101. *Ibid.*, especially *CB*, No. 264 (1953).
102. As, *CB*, No. 264 (1953), p. 14.

commerce in general was to develop liaisons between the cities and the countryside.

But these relationships did not always follow the formulas set out for them. For example, state companies, preoccupied with their own affairs, lacked leadership over private merchants;[103] and at least one instance occurred when employees of a state company were found to have collaborated with private "unscrupulous" merchants by supplying them with commercial information they had obtained in the line of duty.[104] An urban bias marked the trade in general goods while agricultural sideline products were ignored.[105] And state companies were charged with not relying enough on the supply and marketing cooperatives.[106] Since the new fabric of trade relations was designed to promote cooperation between all commercial groups, these omissions to establish appropriate horizontal linkages weakened the trade policy.

Hierarchical controls were also weak at times. It was noted above that certain upper-level trade organs failed to understand the needs of the peasants, and that a stockpiling of unwanted goods and a lack of necessities resulted.[107] Other problems also affected the vertical links between levels in trade work. For example, when a shopping rush occurred in a *hsien* because of various organs' sudden demand for charcoal, market confusion resulted. Here these organs were at fault in not obeying the *hsien* government's regulations on purchasing and distribution.[108]

Then, when the *hsien* and *hsiang* governments bought yarn on their own and arbitrarily selected the amount they wished to buy rather than obeying orders from above, price stability was affected.[109] Charges of lax leadership over goods exchange meetings at the *hsien* level have been noted above.[110] And because pricing policy was not coordinated in different places, the market connections between different cities suffered.[111] Apparently, the

103. *HHJP*, October 12, 1950.
104. *SCMP*, No. 260 (1952), p. 15.
105. *HHJP*, June 11, 1953.
106. *HHJP*, November 2, 1952.
107. *HHJP*, June 11, 1953.
108. *HHJP*, December 6, 1951.
109. *HHJP*, October 12, 1951.
110. *HHJP*, January 25, 1953.
111. *HHJP*, May 28, 1953.

localities in the Southwest were not accustomed to having commerce coordinated from above and reacted badly to the dictates of such a scheme. Thus, bureaucratic linkages tended to be weak both horizontally and vertically in trade work.

Trade policy in the early years of the PRC was oriented toward remunerative controls. However, the relative freedom granted to private merchants and local markets created difficulties in instituting Communist control. In the area of trade relations, old habits and certain deviations in work style were particularly pronounced.

The influence of old habits in trade cropped up in the form of "capitalist management thought," stressing high prices and profits, among supply and marketing cooperative workers. This was attributed in part to the "impurity" of the cooperatives, the lack of professionals.[112] Also, a "pure business" viewpoint in the state companies led to prices that were either too high or too low, resulting in poor handling of commercial relations.[113]

The persistence of the private merchants' influence was adduced at times to account for the deviation of departmentalism in work style. These merchants were allegedly responsible for a stress on retail, rather than wholesale, sales.[114] State companies also showed departmentalism in not wanting to promote the sales of stockpiled goods,[115] in competing for famous-brand goods, and in hoarding goods for the sake of convenience.[116] The outcome was that practice was divorced from policy and leadership was often ineffective.[117] Apparently, the tendency to conduct policy in a permissive direction through remunerative controls led to infractions connected with going too far in this direction.

In trade work, then, both horizontal and vertical ties were weaker than they ought to have been, so that bureaucratic integration suffered. And policy foundered in that some trade workers were influenced by old habits and were using faulty work styles. The result was that integration here was less than total.

112. *HHJP*, October 7, 1952.
113. Huang Fu-chung, "Hsi-nan ch'eng-hsiang kuan-hsi ti hsin mien-mao" [The New Appearance in Rural-Urban Relations in the Southwest], *CCCP* 12, No. 18 (1951), p. 17.
114. *HHJP*, September 24, 1952.
115. *HHJP*, January 25, 1953.
116. *HHJP*, October 27, 1952.
117. *HHJP*, June 11, 1953.

Apparently, the policies outlined in Chapter Six for the three problems were followed only imperfectly. Although Chapter Six showed that a separate form of integration was envisaged for each problem, the findings here are that different sorts of shortcomings inhibited success in each area, according to the perspective of the Chinese. Policy controls were the focus of criticism vis-à-vis cadres working with counter-revolutionaries. In minority and trade work, integration was impaired both by laxity in the bureaucracy and by inadequate execution of specific policies.

However, cadres' mistakes accounted for only one part of the problem in achieving integration. Even if cadres were properly applying policy, some of the policies themselves apparently had an adverse effect on target population groups. The reactions of these groups will be examined below.

Effects on Target Populations

The elimination of regionalism and thus the success of integration depended heavily on the reactions of concerned population groups to the strategies and policies directed at them. The press seldom indicated what these reactions were, and rarely offered any diagnosis of them. Accordingly, the most useful approach in analyzing mass behavior will be to consider it as a response to the particular strategies (direct or indirect) and controls (remunerative, normative, coercive) used to handle the group in question. These responses will be interpreted in the light of two propositions, formulated with the aid of some social science theory. The aim will be to account for negative mass reactions, and to show in what ways these reactions acted as limits on regime policies of integration.

Both Barnard and Simon speak of the limits of power in inducing compliance. Barnard holds that "authority fails because individuals in sufficient numbers see the burden involved in accepting necessary orders as changing the balance of advantage against their interest and they withdraw or withhold indispensable contributions."[118] Simon essentially agrees with this, stating simply that "if it is attempted to carry authority beyond a certain point [the individual's 'zone of acquiescence'], disobedience will

118. Chester I. Barnard, "A Definition of Authority," in Merton, Reader, p. 181.

follow."[119] Both, then, agree that authority can be restricted by those over whom it is exercised. But under what conditions is authority most likely to exceed its limits?

Etzioni suggests that the more identitive (or normative) and utilitarian (or remunerative) power is built up, the more successful integration will be. On the other hand, the higher the application of coercive power above a given level, the less unification is likely to result.[120] Accepting his view of coercive power, however, it is still possible that under certain conditions an excess of normative power may also tend to produce unwanted consequences.

For example, it has been observed that "the greater the degree of integration or self-sufficiency one finds in communities, the greater the probability that they will and can resist penetration attempts from the center."[121] In the analysis presented in Chapter Six, the indirect strategy, associated with normative controls, generally tends to be adopted in areas where local integration already exists. Thus, according to the above observation, where the indirect strategy further increases the integration *within* local communities it may thereby inhibit a larger integration. In these cases, centralized authority may be stymied where too much normative power is used or too great a reliance is placed on an indirect strategy.

Based on the above, the two propositions are as follows: Where regionalism is strong, the reactions of target populations to regime strategies of integration are conditioned by the nature of the strategy used in one of the following two ways:

Proposition 7.5. When a direct strategy (entailing reduction of local diversity and replacement of local leaders) is applied with great pressure and coercion, the probable political reactions are alienation, passive noncompliance, or rebellion.

Proposition 7.6. Where an indirect strategy (involving retention of local traditions, autonomy, and political elites) is utilized to the point where no controls are placed on the populace, this popu-

119. Herbert A. Simon, "Decision-Making and Administrative Organization," in Merton, *Reader,* p. 190.

120. Amitai Etzioni, *Political Unification* (1965), pp. 94-95.

121. Joseph La Palombara, "Penetration: A Crisis of Governmental Capacity," in Leonard Binder, ed., *Crises and Sequences in Political Development* (1971), p. 226.

lace tends to attempt to attain additional local power. This may be manifested in hoarding resources, subversion of national policy goals, a self-conscious refusal to conform, and the growth of "independent kingdoms."

To illustrate these propositions, the publicized popular responses to the direct and indirect strategies among the three target populations can be analyzed.

Counter-revolutionaries. As shown in Chapter Six, the strategy used in handling this group of individuals was direct: local differences were ignored, top leaders were killed, and a rigid hierarchy of courts and police exercised controls.

The reactions of counter-revolutionary groups—including secret society leaders, some ex-KMT personnel, and local gentry—reactions both to policies they opposed and to the regime's attempts to suppress themselves, took several forms. In the early period, these groups rose in open rebellion and refused to comply with the new regime's policies. As described in Chapter Three, for example, in early 1950 Szechwanese peasants led by secret society leaders rose in an insurrection which involved seventy *hsien*. The rebellion was quashed by military force and political measures to divide the rebels, but not before a large and unified revolt had swept literally all of the province's more well-to-do districts.[122] In Kweichow in the spring of 1950 the landlord class allegedly tyrannized the countryside, resisted the public grain collection, and supported bandits. Later in the year the leaders of the movement were ferreted out and killed during the rent reduction campaign.[123]

Thereafter, once the power of counter-revolutionaries was diminished through the death and arrest of their leaders, some of the "reactionary" individuals gave up. Others sneaked into peasant associations in an attempt to take over leadership of them,[124] and infiltrated state economic organs in order to subvert their operations and harm the state's economy.[125]

---

122. See Chapter Three, p. 85.
123. *China News Analysis* [hereafter *CNA*], No. 329 (1960), p. 2; *SCMP*, No. 205 (1951), pp. 12-17.
124. *HHJP*, November 3, 1950; November 22, 1950; October 9, 1951.
125. For example, *HHJP*, December 8, 1950; November 21, 1951.

The behavior of these elements over time is described in one article: after the people's government was established, they organized bandits, created chaos, burned, killed, robbed, destroyed communications, attacked cities, and plundered towns. Later, many surrendered voluntarily, turning over information, documents, and weapons; some repented before the people, some committed suicide out of fear, and some fled. The few remaining counter-revolutionaries continued to plot destructive activity and revenge from places of concealment, and special agents engaged in subversion.[126]

Connecting this with Proposition 7.5 about excessively direct strategies, it appears that the attempt to wipe out local opposition to state policies was fully successful only when it involved total elimination of the opponent. Otherwise, there were signs of the predicted alienation and rebellion. And as long as there continued to be individuals who were antagonistic to regime policies, they found means to obtain leverage over new administrative units and to work in other ways behind the scenes for the disruption of these policies.

Minorities. Minorities were supposed to be dealt with, at least in the early years of the PRC, with a policy that gave them rights of local control, an indirect strategy. However, as early as June 1953, leaders of the national Nationalities Affairs Commission in Peking realized that the minorities wrongly "thought that autonomy meant separation from the Han." Also, "ultra-nationalism" among the larger groups of minorities was still a problem. That is, because of chauvinism among the nationalities who were in the majority in certain areas, smaller populations living in these areas became anxious about discrimination by the larger groups.[127]

These signs of tension between the minorities' expectations and the regime's intentions did not develop into full-scale opposition and noncompliance until four years later. However, apparently the resistance that surfaced in 1957 was foreshadowed by misunderstandings going back to the period when autonomous governments were first instituted. The underlying problem was that from the start the minority peoples developed misconceptions

126. *HHJP*, October 1, 1951.
127. *CB*, No. 264 (1953), pp. 16-17.

about what autonomy would entail.[128] Thus the Miao of Kwei-chow "took autonomy at its face value and put it into practice." They resisted orders to come down from their mountains and to bring their superior cattle along with them.[129]

In this case, not only was a policy promulgated that proclaimed to be indirect, but its target population, the minorities, interpreted this policy as tantamount to a grant of full independence for them. Thus they reacted most noticeably by trying to exercise the rights that full autonomy would have entailed and by consciously refusing to submit to policy, as Proposition 7.6 predicted for groups in such a position.

Traders and Merchants. The strategy toward trade was one that combined direct and indirect components. Here the major problems with the strategy at different times can best be understood by looking at the nature of the adverse reactions to it.

The preceding discussion on trade implied that the deviations in this area of work were often tied up with permissiveness in the policy toward private merchants. The bulk of the criticism of these merchants' behavior was made during the first two or three years of the regime—before the *wu-fan* campaign in 1952 had brought private business under tighter control, and before the November 1953 measures to unify the purchase and supply of grain.[130] During that earlier period, charges of hoarding and departmentalism characterized the critiques of commerce. These practices amounted to attempts to increase local power and represented the type of reaction to an indirect strategy that was outlined in Proposition 7.6.

By the spring of 1954, however, a different sort of problem had cropped up in commerce. An editorial in *Jen-min jih-pao* reprinted in the Southwest press claimed that the market situation had changed with the introduction of unified purchase and unified supply.[131] After the original commercial network had been altered by the removal of grain and oils from the free markets and the prohibition of capitalist operations, goods inter-

128. *CNA*, No. 232 (1958), pp. 5, 7.
129. *Ibid.*, p. 5.
130. See Chapter Six, p. 206.
131. *HHJP*, April 13, 1954, p. 2.

change in the basic-level markets had become slack and listless, disrupting urban-rural exchange. Apparently, goods not centrally controlled were being withheld from the market. In this instance, the concern of the leadership shifted to dealing with the adverse effects of a direct strategy in trade, as these effects manifested themselves in the alienation which Proposition 7.5 predicted in such cases.

Thus, there were problems in all three target areas that could be associated with the strategies used in each area. By 1954, though progress had been made in each realm in accord with the policies specified in Chapter Six, the full support of minorities had not been enlisted, counter-revolutionary opposition persisted, and the state had not yet been able to obtain control over all commercial dealings to the extent desired.

Failures in integration have been attributed to two sets of causes. First, cadres were remiss in developing and building the organizational linkages necessary to carry out policy effectively; and flaws in their work styles meant that the right form of control was not always achieved. Second, local population groups reacted adversely to or took advantage of the strategies used to deal with them, so that unplanned negative responses occurred.

How can these two sets of factors be linked to arrive at a unified explanation? In the case of the counter-revolutionaries, their hostility and alienation was vented whenever possible, but, according to the Communists' explanation, it particularly found an outlet whenever the vigilance of cadres slackened. At such times, counter-revolutionaries "escaped the net" and were able to hide in state organs and create havoc.[132]

Even though the main cadre deviation in relation to minorities was failure to rely on normative controls and failure to show respect for minorities, the minorities still seemed to feel they deserved the indirect strategy and therefore acted independently. It was noted that this was the result of the minorities' misinterpretation of the policy. Apparently, their actions were based on what they had been told about the regime's professed aims on their behalf.

132. As, *HHJP*, November 21, 1951.

Finally, in the case of trade, while local markets were permitted and private merchants were tolerated, the regime had difficulties with a form of backlash characteristic of too much local control. Later, when more direct measures were instituted, the response correspondingly switched to one in line with a policy of this sort. In neither case was a solution achieved that unfailingly promoted an integration of part and whole such that local resources made the hoped-for contribution to the nation.

The outcome of the effort to integrate Southwest China hinged on a number of factors. First, the administrative system—the bureaucratic arrangements and the officials who operated within these arrangements—involved mixing several sets of incompatible personnel groups, and required the coordination of an array of hierarchical administrative levels. The attempt to achieve cooperation between these groups and levels posed a challenge that was not always met, and integration was hindered as a result.

Second, the individual cadres working in sensitive problem areas apparently found it difficult to extricate themselves from old habits and attitudes and to adhere consistently to prescribed policies without taking shortcuts. When cadres, under pressure for results, altered policies in their daily work, integration was unavoidably affected.

Third, at times the policies themselves were designed in ways that alienated certain key population groups or abetted a lack of cooperation from these groups. Where policies failed to enlist mass support or eliminate opposition, again integration was hindered. And where integration was imperfect, forms of regionalism persisted.

In this chapter, several propositions suggested the conditions under which integration was likely to succeed or fail. Data was presented to show that, in fact, where the specified conditions were not met, certain types of problems appeared that influenced integration. If one considers only the factors that were working to obstruct integration, a rather bleak picture emerges.

But the situation can also be viewed from another angle. Perhaps these problems were inevitable in consolidating a new regime. Perhaps the Military Administrative Committee and Administrative Committee served usefully as buffers, shielding the central-level government from encountering these questions of local-level integration at a time when the tasks at the center were especially heavy.

Further, the regional organs were set up at a level from which they could realistically attempt to alleviate these necessary evils. Through efforts to integrate some insiders into the new regime, they may have warded off some alienation; and by trying to utilize and control old KMT officials they obtained some insight into local society. Also, while some groups were discontented at times, the bulk of the population may still have been largely satisfied.

Finally, the mechanisms employed in integrating the area helped to overcome, at least in part, the ills of the bureaucracy. Here, the investigation and check-up teams described in Chapter Four tried to connect the localities more securely with the region; and the key point experimentation with new programs gave the regional leaders some grasp of the territory they ruled. On balance, then, the regional organs served as a useful if temporary expedient for attacking problems endemic to the governance of the country.

CHAPTER VIII

Conclusion: Reflections on
Regional Government
and Political Integration

Summary: Political Integration and Its Dynamics

The concept of political integration has been central to this study. The literature on this aspect of political development reveals the complexity of the integrating process. As discussed earlier, some scholars define this process as the attainment of control over and the extension of authority throughout an entire society. Accordingly, successful integration requires the active regulation of regionalism and the reconciliation of alternative political centers competing for the loyalty and allegiance of relevant populations. Its realization ought to lead to a decisive shift in the balance of power from regionalistic enclaves to the central government, divesting the region of any independent authority.

In administrative terms, political integration has both vertical and horizontal dimensions. Vertically, it entails the development of capacities to control at the national level and the fostering of habits of compliance at the subordinate levels. Horizontally, integration involves the building of cooperation between those living in a single territorial area. Both dimensions must be present in any fully integrated state. In this sense, national integration takes place through two interrelated processes, which we have labeled Integration I and Integration II. The first pertains to the macro-level process by which large areas become more fully enmeshed in the administrative structure of the nation. The second, on a more micro level, refers to integration occurring between small localities within these larger areas. In a large and diverse nation such as China, in the wake of the Communist takeover, these two processes could only occur through the use of structures intervening between the center and the localities, and with the aid of political middlemen working in these structures. We have explored these processes of administrative integration by examining one of China's six Great Administrative Regions, the Southwest.

In one sense, the regional administration's contribution to political development is obvious: it was able to deal with the localities with all their special characteristics much more efficiently than any national government could have done, at least initially. It could serve as a manageable conduit for sending information upward from the base, information which ultimately made possible the larger-scale coordination required to launch the First Five Year Plan by 1954. By forging the links for the regularized passage of central orders downward and monitoring their implementation, the regional institution permitted a greater degree of control than would otherwise have been possible. In regulating reforms in the localities according to centrally designed policies, it made the Southwest into a building block that eventually contributed to a stronger central government.

The Military Administrative Committee and Administrative Committee were the organizations that best bridged the pre-1949 gaps between province and center, and shifted mass loyalties away from the province or subprovincial places toward the center. Chapter Two described how the Southwest before 1949 comprised a myriad of semi-autonomous areas. Here in this nearly isolated corner of China, the world of the provincial warlord had revolved around two issues: the consolidation of his own rule within his province, and the exclusion of national authorities from the province. With the advent of Communist rule, the provinces were no longer permitted to remain the little kingdoms of old.

In ending this provincial independence, the new regional organs worked at tying subprovincial localities together for the first time. At lower levels, the organs of the Military Administrative Committee and the Administrative Committee were responsible for building up structures in various functional areas, in order to reorient local groups toward Peking. These structures ranged from minority autonomous areas to supply and market-ing cooperatives. As state-operated and state-sponsored bodies gained control over behavior patterns and over the disposal of resources in the localities, and as national policy was thereby able to penetrate to these areas, the balance of power gradually shifted from the regions toward the center. Chapter Six de-scribed the institutionalization of controls, compliance, and coop-eration that was to comprise the process of Integration II.

Chapters Three and Four focused on Integration I, the larger process by which the whole Southwest became linked with the nation. This process occurred in two steps: first a geographical principle ordered work, then a functional principle took over. As Chapter Three showed, the Military Administrative Committee, which existed from 1949 until late 1952, was largely concerned with the solution of local problems. Its function was to take note of the special features of Southwest society while guiding local development along the lines of central policy. It did this by promoting national programs within its territory with some adaptation to local conditions. Then, by the time conditions were claimed to be ripe nationally for planned, large-scale economic development, the Military Administrative Committee gave way to the Administrative Committee.

The Administrative Committee, as Chapter Three and Four illustrated, was involved in organizing the sectors of the South-west economy to fit in as one branch in a national economic system. As the transition from the Military Administrative Com-mittee to the Administrative Committee progressed, the format of regional conferences and the jargon in which regional goals were couched became more and more similar to the formats and the jargon being used at the national level and in the other regions throughout the country. At the same time, the locus of governmental decision-making changed as the central govern-ment directed more and more local work. Finally, Chapter Five described the position and role of the political middlemen and new administrative structures at the regional level, which were designed to link the Southwest region with the national CCP and PLA.

The particular contribution of this book lies in its analysis of the dynamics involved in the effort to build this integration. These dynamics can be clarified by posing a series of questions similar to those laid out in the Introduction. The answers to the questions will consist of a set of propositions, some of which have been stated explicitly in the text and some of which are implicit in the arguments of particular chapters.

The questions are as follows: How did the Southwest, a separatist, isolated region, become a contributing member of the larger nation, and through what stages did this process occur? What strategies were projected to cause the disconnected localities within the Southwest to cooperate, and what governed the choice of strategy for creating integration relating to specific problems? What was the role of regional government in these strategies? What determined the form and amount of integration attained at particular points in time and in particular problem areas? What were the respective parts played by the center and the localities in the overall process? What controlled the success or failure of given strategies for integration? What shaped the responses of the population to given strategies?

These questions go to the heart of the problems of achieving political integration in a developing society. They direct attention to the interactions between tiers of government in this one case in creating political integration, and they seek the causative factors in the process along with their effects. The propositions that follow in response to these questions constitute the findings of this work, and are numbered according to the chapter in which they first appeared. They also are hypotheses, generated from this one case study, which can be tested in other contexts.

1.1. In a large, diverse nation lacking integration, geographical integration of separate territories precedes and prepares for an all-national integration on a functional basis.

4.1 and 4.3. As functional integration proceeds—that is, as various types of work become directed in terms of functional sectors—center and provinces tend at the same time increasingly to take over control of work from the regional (geographical) administration.

4.2 The compliance and cooperation associated with integration require uniform ideological and organizational direction throughout the nation. With the growth of a political institution (the Party) capable of enforcing ideological norms on a nationwide basis, the role of separate, territorially based administration in integration (geographical integration) is diminished.

Thus, Integration I—here, the integration of the various Great Administrative Regions into the national system—occurs in two stages: a stage of geographical integration followed by one of functional integration. During this process, work is transferred from geographically oriented bodies to organs with a more functional focus. In China in the early 1950s this took place when the Administrative Committee took over from the Military Administrative Committee in late 1952.

5.1. In situations of regional government, those in the regional leadership groups act as political middlemen. These groups most effectively relate individuals from the localities in the region to individuals representing new national organs of power. In such cases, pivotal positions are filled by those who at once represent the locality and the new organs. Thus, the balance between and power of groups—locals versus outsiders, for example—within this leadership throws light on the nature of linkages being created between center, region, and locality.

In this connection, the organizational structure of the PLA units assigned to the Southwest was superimposed on the Southwest provinces, thereby relating this area to the national PLA. In the civilian administration, a mix of local non-Party leaders, CCP members native to the Southwest, and CCP outsiders took control. This joined representatives of the locality with outsider agents of the Party; and the gap between the two groups was bridged by political middlemen, the Southwest-born Party members.

6.1. The strategy chosen for achieving integration in relation to particular problem areas is a function of:

a. local cultural differences
b. the degree of threat posed to the new regime and its values
c. the value of the group-in-question's potential support to the regime
d. the resource costs of control.

Accordingly,

a. the greater the local diversity, the more likely an indirect strategy
b. the greater the threat, the more likely a direct strategy
c. the greater the value of the group-in-question's support to the regime, the more likely an indirect strategy

d. the higher the resource costs of control, the more likely an indirect strategy; alternatively, the lower the costs of control relative to the cost of laissez-faire, the more likely a direct strategy.

6.2. In controlling problem areas, the type of power (normative, coercive, remunerative) emphasized is related to an assessment of the primary nature of the problem involved. Thus, using the same factors as in proposition 6.1 above:

a. if the relevant population primarily poses a physical threat, predominantly coercive controls are used
b. if obtaining the group's support is seen as possible and valuable, normative control tends to be mainly relied upon to obtain that support
c. if the issue principally involves regime control or loss of control over material resources, remunerative controls are the ones mostly applied.

This proposition adds a dimension to the theories of Etzioni and Skinner on this same topic. Etzioni has attributed the choice of power type to two sets of factors: first, to the ranks of the participants to be controlled, and to the nature of the organization involved.[1] Second, in another place he states that the type of power used will be congruent with the kind of involvement the lower participants have for other reasons.[2] Skinner and Winckler note that certain kinds of goals tend to dictate the use of certain types of power. This is so because for each type of goal, one type of power is especially effective in generating the mode of involvement best suited to achieving the goal at hand.[3]

However, these formulations leave certain questions unanswered. For example, what determines the sort of organization that ought to be used to exercise controls? What are the especially relevant aspects of the lower participants' involvement and how do these mesh with the political goals of the regime? Finally, what

1. See Amitai Etzioni, *Modern Organizations* (1964), p. 60.
2. Amitai Etzioni, "A Basis for Comparative Analysis of Complex Organizations," in A. Etzioni, ed., *A Sociological Reader on Complex Organizations* (1969), p. 68.
3. G. W. Skinner and Edwin A. Winckler, "Compliance Succession in Rural Communist China: A Cyclical Theory," in Etzioni, ed., *A Sociological Reader*, p. 411

is the relationship between the goals of the regime and the political problems posed by particular groups? The above proposition, in linking power type utilized to the nature of the problem posed for the regime, is directed at dealing with these kinds of questions.

6.3. The type of integration aimed at is related to the strategy—direct or indirect—predominantly used in achieving it. Thus:

   a. a vertical type of integration tends to accompany a direct strategy
   b. an atomized integration (through a loose linkage of largely autonomous units by a regional-level body) is effected by an indirect strategy
   c. a horizontal-type integration is associated with a mixed strategy.

6.4. The choice of strategy (indirect or direct) affects the role of the region (or other intermediary structure) in relation to the locality with respect to the problem at hand. Thus:

   a. a direct strategy (coupled with vertical integration) means an increased role for the region
   b. an indirect strategy (plus atomized integration) decreases the role of the region
   c. a mixed strategy (with horizontal integration) gives the region some role but not a large one.

This set of four propositions deals with Integration II. Illustrations of these propositions in Chapter Six demonstrated that the nature of each of three problem areas dictated a different policy strategy (direct or indirect) and different types of controls (remunerative, coercive, normative) for each. Also, the strategy adopted in each case was intimately related to the type of integration aimed at—whether primarily vertical, horizontal, or atomized. The role of the region, as the focal point for subnational integration, was consequently different for each issue area.

6.5. Only after the localities have become integrated in various ways within the area, can the area be brought into the national system. Thus, Integration II—the integration of the localities within the area—lays the ground for Integration I, whereby the area as a whole becomes tied in to the nation.

6.6. But central-level decisions also shape the nature and speed of subsystem integration; or, Integration I (at the national level) determines Integration II.

Thus, there is a mutual interaction between two simultaneous processes; and there is no sure means of determining the exact direction of cause and effect between them.

7.1. If the bureaucracy were to work efficiently, regional-level cadres (most of whom were outsiders) had to become familiar with the area under their control. In the absence of this condition, deviations in work resulted.

7.2. In using the several-tiered administrative system associated with regional government, it was difficult to achieve coordination and cooperation between regional and lower levels in the bureaucracy. Without such coordination, problems in work occurred.

7.3. In implementing policies, the habits and attitudes prevalent among the KMT before 1949 had to be eradicated. Where they persisted, policy execution was impaired.

7.4. In implementing policies, cadres' work style had to conform to CCP work style and embody CCP ideology. When their work style deviated from the prescribed style and when insufficient attention was paid to ideology, policies were wrongly applied.

These propositions show the relationship between personnel and administrative systems in the Southwest and the resultant tensions. Where the tensions were not resolved, deviations in work resulted.

Where regionalism is strong, the reactions of target populations to regime strategies of integration are conditioned by the nature of the strategy used in one of the following two ways:

7.5. When a direct strategy (entailing reduction of local diversity and replacement of local leaders) is applied with great pressure and coercion, the probable political reactions are alienation, passive noncompliance, or rebellion.

7.6. Where an indirect strategy (involving retention of local traditions, autonomy, and political elites) is utilized to the point where no controls are placed on the populace, this populace tends to attempt to attain additional local power. This may be manifested in hoarding resources, subversion of national policy goals, a self-conscious refusal to conform, and the growth of "independent kingdoms."

This says simply that the policies and strategies adopted to integrate the Southwest at times produced adverse reactions, and that these reactions had an important effect on the attainment of integration.

These sixteen propositions suggest that the process of planned national integration in China up to 1954 occurred along several dimensions simultaneously. Moreover, each aspect of the process had an effect on the others. Although the central government was generally the orchestrator in Integration I, events in the localities and the success of Integration II shaped the options of the central government. Finally, the behavior of the cadres and the responses of target population groups also had an important impact on the ultimate success of the overall process.

Thus the propositions indicate that this process of integration consisted of a complicated interaction between various levels of government and between the government and the governed. Such an analysis, of course, fails to state precisely to what degree integration had proceeded by 1954. In attempting to gauge this, it might be useful to review the standard indicators used in the literature.

Evaluation of the Success of Political Integration in the Southwest

Certain numerical indicators show that the Southwest was in fact becoming tied together internally, as well as becoming linked to the national system, between 1950 and 1954. This can be seen in the expansion of transport and communications facilities throughout the Southwest. Developments in these fields meant that the Southwest localities were becoming interconnected, and that the area as a whole was becoming united with other regions across the country. This increase in integration also appeared in the growing number of CCP members in the area over time.

In transport, the total route length of identified railways for the Southwest relative to the nation as a whole for the years 1949, 1952, and 1957 is as follows: in 1949, the Southwest's 244 kilometers represented 1.5 percent of the nation's 17,036 kilometers. By 1952, the 905 kilometers of rail line in the Southwest were 4 percent of the national total of 22,810 kilometers. And by 1957, the 1,786 kilometers of line here were about 6 percent of the 29,176 kilometers nationwide.[4]

Also, from 1950 to 1954, about 2,304 kilometers of new rail line were laid nationally; of this total, 782 kilometers, or more than one-third, were in the Southwest.[5] The crucial Chengtu-Chungking line, 505 kilometers long, had a great impact, both in joining production and marketing centers in the Southwest and in increasing commercial and industrial ties between the Southwest and the rest of the country.

Similarly, whereas 10,268 kilometers of highways were constructed throughout the country in the same four-year period, 5,795 kilometers of these roads, or nearly one-half, were located in the Southwest.[6] According to an article in the April 1954 *Hsin-Hua yüeh-pao*, by that time highways had been restored connecting Szechwan with Shensi, Hunan, Yunnan, Kweichow, and Sikang, respectively; and large-scale new construction had also been undertaken in the area.[7] In 1953 the investment in highway construction in the Southwest was increased by more than 11 percent over the period just after liberation. At that time too, new roads were being built across the Sikang-Tibet Plateau, the Yunnan-Kweichow Plateau, and in the high mountain districts of Szechwan, to reach areas in the interior. The article states that these developments contributed to national economic construction, by increased urban-rural trade, and helped the minorities economically and culturally.

Also, marked improvements were made in air transport. In August 1951 service was begun between Chungking and Hankow and between Chungking and Kunming. Each route boasted one flight a week. By May 1953, flights were increased to seven per week and new routes were set up between Chungking and Peking, Shanghai, and Sian, with connections for Canton and Ti-hua (in the Northwest).[8] These new transport links "shortened the distance within the region and between the Southwest and other areas"; and thus permitted the "people in Chungking to read *Jen-min jih-pao* the day it was published and see the latest

4. Wu Yuan-li, *The Spatial Economy of Communist China* (1967), p. 135.
5. *Ibid.*, pp. 359, 360.
6. *Ibid.*, pp. 72, 73.
7. *Hsin-Hua yüeh-pao* [New China Monthly] (Peking), No. 54 (1954), p. 169.
8. *Survey of China Mainland Press* [hereafter *SCMP*], No. 668 (1953), pp. 23-24.

films, books, and pictures."[9] Surely these achievements in transport and communications provided the physical infrastructure
within which the ideological and political aspects of integration
could occur.

The expansion of the Party in the Southwest illustrated that
political facets of integration were also taking place. Initially the
Southwest was an area with an extremely weak Party structure. As
of the autumn of 1952, only 7 percent of the rural *hsiang* there
had Party organizations.[10] After a membership drive in 1952, and
especially in 1953 and 1954, membership grew as the completion
of land reform and the movement to build cooperatives provided
opportunities to recruit new Party members. By March 1954, the
Southwest had 117,536 rural Party members, and Party branches
had been set up in 63 percent of the more than 20,000 *hsiang* in
the area.[11]

In spite of the fact that more than one-half of the *hsiang* in the
Southwest had Party branches by early 1954, the CCP was still
relatively weak in the area. According to the 1953 census, the
Southwest's population was 98,195,110, or about one-sixth of the
total national population.[12] Since both the Southwest and China
as a whole are overwhelmingly rural, the Southwest rural population is also approximately one-sixth the national rural population.[13] And yet, if its rural Party membership remained roughly
constant between early 1954 and early 1955, the Southwest's
117,536 rural Party members represented only 3 percent of the
national total of rural Party members, estimated in March 1955 as
more than 4,000,000.[14] Still, the growth of Party cadres had to
mean that by 1954 the rural areas in the Southwest had the
personnel to develop effective political and ideological links with
the CCP nationally.

In the three problem areas considered in Chapters Six and

9. *Ibid.*, p. 23.
10. *Hsin-Hua jih-pao* [New China Daily] (Chungking) [hereafter *HHJP*],
August 9, 1952, p. 3; October 23, 1952, p. 1.
11. See *SCMP*, No. 830 (1954), pp. 15-16.
12. Stanford University, China Project, *Southwest China* (1956), 7:55.
13. *Ibid.*, 8:745-746. Here the Southwest rural population is given as about 80
percent of the total Southwest population. And, according to Buck, using the 80
percent figure to represent the proportion of farm to total population nationally
is probably accurate. See John Lossing Buck, Owen L. Dawson, and Yuan-li Wu,
Food and Agriculture in Communist China (1966), pp. 39-40.
14. *Jen-min jih-pao* [People's Daily] (Peking), March 9, 1955, p. 1.

Seven, statistical signs of progress were also published. In counter-revolutionary work, one million bandits had been eliminated
in the Southwest by October 1952.[15] Nearly one-fourth of the
approximately 18,000,000 minority peoples in the Southwest[16]
lived in areas which had been granted regional autonomy by mid-
1954.[17] In trade, the amount of special native products shipped
from the Southwest to other parts of the country had increased
by more than six times between 1949 and late-1952.[18] And in
1952 the amount of local products that the state trading organs
bought up in the Southwest increased by 5.4 times over what had
been purchased in 1950 in the region.[19] By October of that year
there were more than 1,500 new trade organs in the Southwest.[20]

In general, numerical indicators clearly demonstrate that the
Southwest was making great strides in a variety of fields, both in
internal integration and in fitting into the national system. This
progress was apparent in the construction of new transport
facilities and in the creation of nationally homogenous units—
Party branches, autonomous areas, and trade organs, for example. However, these numbers show only that communication and
organizational linkages had been built; they offer no way to infer
the political implications of having roads and enlisting Party
members. Further, these figures give no clue as to the types of
processes that occur during integration. Nor do they specify the
nature of the bureaucratic considerations involved, or give a
sense of the obstacles encountered along the way. Therefore, in
the end, speculation based on the propositions above may be
more productive in understanding and evaluating integration as
a political and administrative process.

Such an evaluation can be sharpened by returning to the
central questions raised here. This book opened with a query as
to why, in a country beset by localism and separatism, regional
forms were used to advance unification and development. What
was the efficacy of such an approach, both in combating regionalism and in promoting national integration? By now it should be

15. *HHJP*, October 1, 1952, p. 3.
16. *SCMP*, No. 716 (1953), pp. 26-27.
17. *SCMP*, No. 813 (1954), pp. 34-35.
18. *Current Background*, No. 218 (1952), p. 24.
19. *HHJP*, September 29, 1952.
20. *Ibid.*

clear that the first question—why regional forms were utilized—
has been answered. To summarize, local diversity—in political,
economic, and cultural forms—could best be countered, if at all,
through parceling out the country in intermediate-size packages.
Administrative structures so delimited were able to apply national policy to roughly similar areas, while being conscious of local
peculiarities. The attempt to gear policy to the particularities in
these areas was ultimately directed toward minimizing local
differences, toward setting up the conditions for economic development through a more or less standardized bureaucratic network in each area. Thus, it is possible to speak of the paradox of
decentralization *for* centralization: the relative decentralization
that marked administration in the first three years after takeover
was decentralization for the purpose of centralization, a reliance
on regional organs to abolish regionalism.

It is more difficult to answer the other questions: whether regionalism was combated and national integration achieved. From
hindsight, it is relatively easy to make statements about probable
national goals, as we have done above. Analyzing whether these
goals were in fact met is a more challenging task. However, it does
seem that, given the fact that many of the forms of separatism in
the Southwest were rooted in subprovincial areas, the regional
organs would have had problems in eradicating regionalism
thoroughly. It is true that the search for "counter-revolutionaries" has never ended in China; and in 1957 there were revolts
among the minorities in the Southwest.[21] While control of trade
has perhaps been more successful than the controls instituted in
the other two problem areas, comparison of such disparate areas
along these lines may not be fruitful. It also may be true,
however, that a mixed strategy, such as the one utilized in
handling trade, is more successful in coming to terms with the
sources of local separatism than a strategy of eliminating them
entirely. As one analyst has suggested, the expedient and realistic
arrangement in developing countries may be "reaching contrac-
tual agreements with centers of local or regional power, even if to
do so implies less than desired by way of central control."[22]

21. See Chapter Seven, pp. 236-237.
22. Joseph La Palombara, "Penetration: A Crisis of Governmental Capacity,"
in Leonard Binder, ed., *Crises and Sequences in Political Development* (1971),
pp. 230-231.

Finally, it is difficult to assess whether national integration was actually achieved in the early 1950s. However, it is clear that the First Five Year Plan entailed a great measure of centralization which would not have been possible without the developmental pattern outlined here. Also, by 1957 some leaders in Peking felt confident enough about the extent of national uniformity to permit the decentralization that led to the Great Leap Forward. Thus, following Mao, one may take a dialectical view of administrative structuring in China, and consider the partial decentralization described from 1949 to 1952 as being *for* centralization; just as the centralization that began in 1952 created the conditions for a new decentralization.

By way of conclusion, we might consider that the twin processes of overcoming regionalism and achieving national integration have two interrelated but analytically distinct components. The first, which corresponds to Integration I, involves increasing the centralized direction of the country from the national capital. The second, then, pertains to combating local-level autonomy and separatism, and is described by Integration II. In this light, we can say that of the two, Integration I was probably more successful than Integration II, as of 1954.

These tentative evaluations of the success of regional government in controlling regionalism and achieving political integration speak to the specific issues of this study as set out in its initial introductory paragraphs. Before bringing this work to a close, some final reflections can further illuminate the study's broader concerns.

Reflections on Regional Government
and Political Integration

This book has implications for the study of regional government in China over time; and for problems of regionalism and integration in other nations in the modern world. What, exactly, do the findings of this study signify about regional government in China generally and about the conditions conducive to its institution? Can we infer from the experience of the early 1950s explanations of the reestablishment of Regional Party Bureaus from 1961-1966? Can we use this data to interpret the functions of the Military Regions still in existence?

First, it is important to note that the period researched here was marked by many special considerations which influenced the form that administration took. Some aspects of that situation have recurred; some may never recur. The problems of economic dislocation in 1949, too complex for a single province to manage, could be dealt with handily through regional organs. Possibly economic problems were again a factor in recreating the Party Bureaus in 1961 after the difficulties of the Great Leap Forward.

On the other hand, other important circumstances have not and quite possibly will not reappear. For example, the ultimate goal of centralization to facilitate the First Five Year Plan was special to that time; so was the strong influence of the Soviet Union, with its model of centralized administration.[23] This goal and model both informed the direction regional government took in the early 1950s. Thus, the end of regional government in 1954 meant greater central control. In 1966, however, the demise of regions was followed by greater decentralization and local control.

Moreover, the majority of the officials appointed to the regions were new to the areas they ruled and unfamiliar with these areas in 1949. However, beginning in 1966 charges of creating "independent kingdoms" were leveled against most regional officials during the Cultural Revolution. As a result, untrammeled regional rule may no longer be considered efficacious in China, once the cadres in the regions have built up networks of local power.

From another angle, though, the successful use of regions within a framework of central control depends upon the "clout" and unanimity of politicians at the center. During the first five years of the PRC, the central government was gradually accumulating strength to control the entire country and could ultimately handle any regional aberrations. Today and in the future, the balance of power may not rest so unequivocally with central officials, and regional government—as under the present Military Regions—may consequently have a very different role to play than the one it had in the past.

Thus, a particular configuration of events, circumstances, and elite goals combined to fashion the form political integration took in China from 1949 to 1954. If it is difficult to use data on this period to make sweeping predictions about a possible reemer-

23. See Chapter One, footnote 29.

gence of regional government, this study still offers conclusions about the meaning of political integration in China.

For the purposes of this work, the term political integration has been defined as entailing control from above, compliance from below, and cooperation among those living close together. Since it was suggested above that the integration achieved by 1954 was adequate to permit attaining the developmental goals of that time, apparently there is a close connection between integration and the fulfillment of nationally set goals. Thus, according to the analysis here, China may be considered integrated politically when goals and policies dictated at the central level are pursued at all levels throughout the country. And this is most likely to be the case whenever administrative, organizational linkages between levels, such as those described in this study, are reliable enough to ensure cooperation in action and consensus in values on a nationwide basis.

We have also shown the intricacies of coordinating a nation the size of China, and the dependence of this coordination on reliable cadres, an efficient bureaucracy, and policies that elicit mass support. The size of the country and the diversity of its regions will probably always prove to be challenges in achieving these requisites to national unity.

Besides making possible certain generalizations about regional government and political integration in China, this work has also presented a comparative perspective on these problems, so that its findings may be extended to other developing nations. In this vein the study has treated China in a comparative way in two regards. First, it views China in a generic sense as a large and diverse nation, and considers its problems of political unification in this light. Here the finding of the efficacy of regional or intermediary structures in integrating the country might well be relevant to other nations with similar developmental problems.

Second, it handles the problem of regionalism and the attempts to combat it within a comparative framework. The propositions put forward on this subject were drawn from materials on a wide range of modernizing nations. These propositions, therefore, ought to lead to greater understanding of the measures taken by many modern governments in facing the pressures of regionalistic enclaves within their territories.

As a case study, however, this work is bound to be limited: some of its findings will hold true for a small class of countries; others will be more generally applicable. The crucial question, then, is: What factors were most salient in determining the particular developmental course the PRC chose to follow in its early years? For when these factors are pinpointed, other cases can be more readily compared with this one.

Among the elements that shaped the pattern here, Mao's ideological commitment to dialectics has been central. This has informed his belief in the need to combine centralism with local initiative in governing the country, and has contributed to the alternation between centralization and decentralization in China over time. Also, the regime's concern with legitimation and mass support dictated the use of a strategy of gradualism in building up central power at the expense of local groups after 1949.

Besides the influence of these values on the integration process in China, certain institutional and structural features of the country also had an impact. Institutionally, the availability of a disciplined, unified Party and army made the central direction of development possible, and helped to strengthen central power in the localities. Structurally, the country is split into fairly distinct economic regions of roughly comparable size. None of these regions has been sufficiently large, rich, or powerful to tip the balance of power between center and region, or between all the regions, permanently in its direction. Finally, a relatively large degree of cultural homogeneity across the country has permitted a transfer of personnel into new regions without grossly disruptive effects. It has also made possible the introduction of uniform programs of social reform across the country.

These factors—ideology, elite goals, institutions, the economic and cultural situation in the regions, and the power balance between center and region—all accounted for the developmental pattern followed in China. Given the presence of at least several of these conditions in other countries, China's solutions to the problems of regionalism and integration as analyzed here might serve as guides in evaluating the success or failure of development elsewhere.

APPENDIX

Key Southwest Great Administrative Region Officials, 1949–1954

(The designations under the headings "Classification" and "Background" are the same as those used in the text and tables in Chapter Five.)

Job	Name	Classification	Background	Province of Origin

I. MAC/AC CHAIRMAN AND VICE CHAIRMEN

Job	Name	Classification	Background	Province of Origin
Chairman	Liu Po-ch'eng 劉 伯 承	Local Red	2nd FA	Szechwan
Vice Chairmen	Teng Hsiao-p'ing 鄧 小 平	Local Red	2nd FA	Szechwan
	Ho Lung 賀 龍	Outside Red	1st FA	Hunan
	Sung Jen-ch'iung 宋 任 窮	Outside Red	2nd FA	Hunan
	Wang Wei-chou 王 維 舟	Local Red	Other	Szechwan
	Hsiung K'o-wu 熊 克 武	Local White	KMT	Szechwan

Job	*Name*	*Classification*	*Background*	*Province of Origin*
	Liu Wen-hui 劉 文 輝	Local White	KMT	Sikang
	Lung Yün 龍 雲	Local White	KMT	Yunnan
	Lu Han 盧 漢	Local White	KMT	Yunnan
	Teng Hsi-hou 鄧 錫 侯	Local White	KMT	Szechwan

II. MILITARY REGION OFFICIALS

Job	*Name*	*Classification*	*Background*	*Province of Origin*
Commander	Ho Lung 賀 龍	Outside Red	1st FA	Hunan
Pol. Commissar	Teng Hsiao-p'ing 鄧 小 平	Local Red	2nd FA	Szechwan
Deputy Comman- ders	Ch'en Keng 陳 賡	Outside Red	2nd FA	Hunan
	Li Ta 李 達	Outside Red	2nd FA	Shensi
Deputy Political Commissars	Sung Jen-ch'iung 宋 任 窮	Outside Red	2nd FA	Hunan
	Chang Chi-ch'ün 張 際 春	Outside Red	2nd FA	Hunan
	Li Ching-ch'üan 李 井 泉	Outside Red	1st FA	Kiangsi
Chief-of-Staff	Li Ta 李 達	Outside Red	2nd FA	Shensi
Deputy Chief-of- Staff	Li Fu-k'o 李 夫 克	?	?	?
Chairman Political Dept.	Wang Hsin-t'ing 王 新 亭	Outside Red	2nd FA	Hupeh
Vice-Chairman Political Dept.	Chang Tzu-i 張 子 意	Outside Red	?	Hunan

Job	Name	Classification	Background	Province of Origin
Industry Department	Tuan Chün-i 段 君 毅	Outside Red	2nd FA	Shantung
Communications Department	Ch'ao Chien-min 趙 健 民	Outside Red	2nd FA	Shantung
Labor Department	Ts'ai Shu-fan 蔡 樹 藩	?	?	Hupeh
Agriculture-Forestry Department	Ch'en T'ieh 陳 鐵	Local White	KMT	Kweichow
Water Conservancy Department	Teng Hsi-hou 鄧 錫 侯	Local White	KMT	Szechwan
Cooperative Affairs Bureau	Hu Chün-ch'üan 胡 浚 泉	?	?	?
Culture-Education Department	Ch'u T'u-nan 楚 圖 南	Local White	Democratic personage	Yunnan
Public Health Department	Ch'ien Hsin-chung 錢 信 忠	?	2nd FA	?
News-Publications Department	Liao Ching-tan 廖 井 丹	?	?	Szechwan
Judicial Department	Tan Mou-hsin 但 懋 辛	Local White	KMT	Szechwan
Public Security Department	Chou Hsing 周 興	Outside Red	1st FA	Kiangsu
Civil Affairs Department	Sun Yü-t'ing 孫 雨 亭	?	1st FA	?

Job	Name	Classification	Background
	III. DEPARTMENT HEADS		
Secretary-General	Sun Chih-yüan 孫 志 遠	Outside Red	1st FA
General Office Manager	Hu Hsing 胡 光	?	?
Personnel Bureau	Tung Hsin-shan 董 新 山	?	?
Finance-Economic Committee	Teng Hsiao-p'ing 鄧 小 平	Local Red	2nd FA
Culture-Education Committee	Ch'u T'u-nan 楚 圖 南	Local White	Democra personag
Nationalities Affairs Committee	Wang Wei-chou 王 維 舟	Local Red	Other
People's Supervisory Commission	Li Hsiao-t'ing 李 筱 亭	Local White	KMT
Political-Legal Committee	Wang Wei-chou 王 維 舟	Local Red	Other
Land Reform Committee	Chang Chi-ch'ün 張 際 春	Outside Red	2nd F.
Supreme People's Court	Chang Shu-shih 張 曙 時	?	?
Finance-Economic Department	Ch'en Hsi-yün 陳 希 雲	?	?
Trade Department	Wang Lei 王 磊	?	Ot

Job	Name	Classification	Background	Province of Origin

IV. PROVINCIAL GOVERNORS AND VICE-GOVERNORS

Szechwan

Governor	Li Ching-ch'üan 李 井 泉	Outside Red	1st FA	Kiangsi
Vice-Governors	Li Ta-chang 李 大 章	Local Red	2nd FA	Szechwan
	Yen Hung-yen 閻 紅 彥	Outside Red	2nd FA	Shensi

Kweichow

Governor	Yang Yung 楊 勇	Outside Red	2nd FA	Hunan
Vice-Governors	Tseng Ku 曾 固	?	?	Kweichow
	Chou Su-yüan 周 素 園	?	?	Kweichow

Yunnan

Governor	Ch'en Keng 陣 賡	Outside Red	2nd FA	Hunan
Vice-Governors	Chou Pao-chung 周 保 中	Local Red	Other	Yunnan
	Chang Ch'ung 張 冲	Local White	Other	Yunnan

Sikang

Governor	Liao Chih-kao 廖 志 高	Local Red	Other	Sikang
Vice-Governors	Chang Wei-chiung 張 爲 炯	Local White	KMT	Sikang
	Lu Jui-lin 魯 瑞 林	Outside Red	2nd FA	Shansi

V. PROVINCIAL MILITARY DISTRICTS

Szechwan

Commander	Ho Ping-yen 賀 炳 炎	Outside Red	1st FA	Hupeh
Political Commissar	Li Ching-ch'üan 李 井 泉	Outside Red	1st FA	Kiangsi

Job	Name	Classification	Background	Province of Origin
Deputy Commander	Fan Ch'ao-li 范 朝 利	?	2nd FA	?
Deputy Political Commissars	Yen Hung-yen 閻 紅 彥	Outside Red	2nd FA	Shensi
	Chung Han-hua 鍾 漢 華	?	?	?
Kweichow				
Commander	Yang Yung 楊 勇	Outside Red	2nd FA	Hunan
Political Commissar	Su Chen-hua 蘇 振 華	Outside Red	2nd FA	Hunan
Deputy commanders	Yin Hsing-ping 尹 光 炳	?	?	?
	P'an Jung 潘 榮	?	2nd	?
Deputy Political Commissar	Wang Hui-ch'iu 王 輝 球	?	2nd	?
Yunnan				
Commander	Ch'en Keng 陣 賡	Outside Red	2nd FA	Hunan
Political Commissar	Hsieh Fu-chih 謝 富 治	Outside Red	2nd FA	Hupeh
Deputy Commanders	Kuo T'ien-min 郭 天 民	Outside Red	Other	Hupeh
	Chung T'ien 莊 田	Outside Red	Other	Kwang-tung
Deputy Political Commissar	Nan Ching-chih 南 靜 之	?	?	?
Sikang				
Commander	Liao Chih-kao 廖 志 高	Local Red	Other	Sikang

Job	Name	Classification	Background	Province of Origin
Political Commissar	Same	Same	Same	Same
Deputy Commanders	Hsiung K'uei 熊 奎	?	?	?
	Liu Yüan-hsüan 劉 元 瑄	?	?	Sikang
Deputy Political Commissar	Kao Te-hsi 高 德 西	?	2nd FA	?

CHINESE TERMS USED IN THIS WORK

ch'ang-chen 場鎮 — market at the township level

che-chiu chin 折舊金 — money set aside to replace depreciated macinery

chen 鎮 — urban township

chou 州 — historical administrative district

ch'u 處 — office

ch'u-chi 初級 — elementary or basic level

chü 局 — bureau

ch'ü 區 — district

ch'uan-pien t'e-pieh ch'ü-ü 川邊特別區域 — Szechwan special border region

chün 軍 — corps (in the army)

fang-ch'ü 方區 — garrison area

hsiang 鄉 — rural administrative unit under the county (or township)

hsiao t'u-ssu 小土司 — minor native chief

hsien 縣 — county

hu-k'ou-tuan 戶口段 — neighborhood

hu kuo chün 護國軍 — National Protection Army

jen-min-pi 人民幣 — currency used by the PRC

k'ang ta 抗大 — Resistance University

ko lao hui 哥老會 — Elder Brothers' Society

lien ta 聯大 — short for Southwest Associated University

liu fa 六法 — literally, six laws; modern Chinese law code in use under the KMT

p'a ma-fan 怕麻煩 — fearing troublesome work

pao 堡 — subdivision of a township

ping-t'uan 兵團   army
pu 部   department
san-fan 三反   three-anti movement
ta yeh 大爺   here, secret society leader
tao 道   historical administrative district
tsung-tu-ch'ü 總督區   governor-general's district
t'u-mu 土目   native headman
t'u-ssu 土司   native chieftain
t'ung-i ling-tao, 統一領導   unified leadership with different
  fen-chi fu-tse 分級負責   levels dividing up responsibilities
wu-fan 五反   five-anti movement
yin-ti-chin-i 因地制宜   to take actions that suit local circum-
                               stances, or local initiative

BIBLIOGRAPHY

Two major sources of data for this study were the Southwest China daily newspaper *Hsin-Hua jih-pao* (New China Daily; Chungking) and the national journal *Hsin-Hua yüeh-pao* (New China Monthly; Peking). The daily paper was sampled such that between two and four months were read for each year from 1950 to 1954. The sample was meant to indicate changing patterns in regional affairs over time. The choice of months to read was based both on the availability of newspapers at The Hoover Institution on War, Revolution and Peace at Stanford University and on my desire to cover significant events.

For the years 1950-1952, the same period during each year was used (October to December for 1950 and 1951; September to December for 1952) in order to include plenary meetings of the Military Administrative Committee and national day reports. In 1953, spring was the crucial period because the transition from the Military Administrative Committee to the Administrative Committee was occurring then. Thus for that year papers from the end of January through the first half of June were read. Since The Hoover Institution has no papers for 1954, materials in the Archives of the Library of Congress, Washington, D.C., were used, and the months January and April read to correspond to the same time of year covered in 1953.

Hsin-Hua yüeh-pao was consulted for important policy articles bearing on regional government and shifts in its workings, and also for articles on the Southwest considered important enough to be published in this national journal. All issues were researched over the period 1949 to 1954.

Other publications utilized from the People's Republic include *Jen-min Jih-pao*, *Jen-min shou-ts'e*, and *Ching-chi chou-pao*. The articles chosen from *Jen-min jih-pao* (People's Daily; Peking) were those dealing either with the Southwest or with important national policies. *Jen-min shou-ts'e* (People's Handbook; Shanghai) was covered for the years 1950 through 1953, both for material on national policies and for lists of personnel in the Southwest administration. Finally, selected articles from *Ching-chi chou-pao* (Economic Weekly; Shanghai) were read.

A third group of sources included periodicals published in Hong Kong containing translations of Chinese documents and varying degrees of interpretive comment. Among these were *Survey of the China Mainland*

269

Press and *Current Background,* prepared by the Union Research Institute; and *China News Analysis* and the *Far Eastern Economic Review.* Also in this category was the U.S. *Joint Publications Research Service,* published in Washington, D.C. All of these were checked systematically for the years 1949 to 1954; and pertinent later issues were also used.

Two other sources on the PRC were Albert Blaustein's *Fundamental Legal Documents of Communist China* (South Hackensack, New Jersey: Fred B. Rothman, 1962); and several biographic dictionaries, both in English and Chinese.

Finally, among the primary sources utilized were several varieties of analytical accounts written by first-hand observers. This category included the reports of U.S. Foreign Service officers reproduced in the *Foreign Relations of the United States, Diplomatic Papers* series on China for the 1940s (Washington: U.S. Government Printing Office, 1957); and reports in Record Group 226 of the Office of Strategic Services from the same period, housed in the National Archives in Washington, D.C. Also some articles in the *New York Times* of the late 1940s were useful in interpreting the ongoing events of that time in the Southwest. And, lastly, a diary prepared by L. Earl Willmott recounting daily happenings in Szechwan in the early 1950s was used.

Secondary sources consulted fell into two broad groupings. The first group contained writings, in both Chinese and English, which describe and analyze society and politics in China, and particularly in the Southwest, during the 1940s and early 1950s. Literature on regional administration in China was also part of this category. Those sources which were particularly useful are listed in the bibliography below.

The other group of secondary sources consisted of social science literature bearing on the themes of the study. This comprised theoretical treatments of such concepts as political development, integration, and regionalism, as well as works on local politics and organization theory. It also included comparative studies showing how problems in these areas have been handled in other countries and in other areas of China.

Despite the fact that a wide range of sources was consulted, much of the available literature on the Southwest in the early 1950s is impressionistic; and for the years after the expulsion of Westerners from China in 1950 and 1951, there is no reliable means of verifying Chinese newspaper accounts. Moreover, the bearing of national events on the situation in the Southwest is never made explicit in the Chinese press. However, within limits, the aims of this work could be met with the sources at hand: to investigate the workings and functions of regional government, its successes and difficulties; and to trace the history of the integration of the Southwest region into the nation as a whole.

The following bibliography is divided into Chinese-language and English-language sources.

Chinese-Language Sources

Chang Chi-ch'ün. "Kuan-yü hsi-nan ch'ü chien-tsu wen-t'i ti pao" [Report on Questions in Rent Reduction in the Southwest], in *Cheng-fu kung-tso pao-kao hui-pien* [Compilation of Government Work Reports]. Peking: Jen-min ch'u-pan she, 1951, pp. 1005-1010.

Chang Hsiao-mei. *Kuei-chou ching-chi* [The Economy of Kweichow]. N.p.: Chung-kuo kuo-min ching-chi yen-chiu so, 1939.

———. *Yün-nan ching-chi* [The Economy of Yunnan]. Chungking: Chung-kuo kuo-min ching-chi yen-chiu so, 1942.

Chang Kuo-hua, "Hsi-tsang hui-tao le tsu-kuo ti huai-pao" [Tibet Returns to the Fatherland's Fold], in *Hsing-huo liao yüan* [Sparks Light up the Prairie]. Peking: Jen-min wen-hsüeh ch'u-pan she, 1958, 10: 525-543.

Chang Wen-shih. *Yün-nan nei-mu* [Behind the Scenes in Yunnan]. Kunming: Kuan-ch'a ch'u-pan she, 1949.

"Ching-chien hsing-cheng chi-kou, t'i-kao kung-tso hsiao-lü" [Simplify Administrative Organs, Raise Work Efficiency]. *Hsin-Hua yüeh-pao*, No. 53 (1954), pp. 21-22.

Chou Fang, *Wo kuo kuo-chia chi-kou* [My Country's State Organs]. Peking: Chung-kuo ch'ing-nien ch'u-pan she, 1955.

Chung-kung jen-ming lu pien-hsiu wei-yüan-hui [Who's Who in Communist China Compilation Commission]. *Chung-kung jen-ming lu* [Who's Who in Communist China]. Taipei: Chung-Hua min-kuo kuo-chi kuan-hsi yen-chiu so, 1967.

Fang Chün-kuei, "Chung-kung ti yeh-chan chün" [The Chinese Communists' Field Armies]. *Chung-kung wen-t'i* [Problems in Chinese Communism] (Taipei), No. 1 (1954), pp. 46-51.

Hsin-Hua jih-pao [New China Daily] (Chungking). October-December 1950; October-December 1951; September-December 1952; January-June 1953; January and April 1954.

Hsin-Hua yüeh-pao [New China Monthly] (Peking). November 1949-August 1954.

Huang Chen-hsia. *Chung-kung chün-jen chih* [Mao's Generals]. Hong Kong: Tang-tai li-shih yen-chiu so, 1968.

Huang Fu-chung. "Hsi-nan ch'eng-hsiang kuan-hsi ti hsin mien-mao" [The New Appearance in Urban-Rural Relations in the Southwest]. *Ching-chi chou-pao* [Economic Weekly] (Shanghai) 12, No. 18 (1951), pp. 16-17.

"Hui-i t'ao-lun t'ung-kuo er-shih-lui hsiang ren-ming; Mao chu-hsi shuo-ming pi-hsü t'ung-i ho yin-ti chih-i yao hu-hsiang chieh-ho" [Conference Discusses and Passes Twenty-Six Appointments; Chairman Mao Explains that We Must Combine Unity and Local Initiative]. *Jen-min jih-pao*, December 4, 1949, p. 1.

Jen-min jih-pao [People's Daily] (Peking). Selected issues, 1949-1954.

Jen-min shou-ts'e [People's Handbook]. Shanghai: Ta-kung pao, 1950, 1951, 1952, 1953.

Li I-jen, ed. *Hsi-k'ang tsung-lan* [A General Survey of Sikang]. Shanghai: Cheng-chung shu-chü, 1947.

Li P'ei-t'ien. "Lung Yün Lu Han en-ch'ou chi" [The Affection and Enmity between Lung Hün and Lu Han]. *Hsin-wen t'ien-ti* [News World] (Hong Kong), Nos. 777-785 (1963).

Li Ta, "Chieh-fang ta hsi-nan chih chan" [The Campaign to Liberate the Great Southwest], in *Hsing-huo liao-yüan* [Sparks Light up the Prairie]. Peking: Jen-min wen-hsüeh ch'u-pan she, 1958, 10: 475-485.

Liang Po-ming. "Chung-kung chün-ch'ü piao-chieh" [Chinese Communist Military Regions]. *Chung-kung wen-t'i* [Problems in Chinese Communism] (Taipei), No. 1 (1954), pp. 36-45.

Liu Chin. *Ch'uan K'ang i-shou ch'ien-hou* [Before and After Szechwan and Sikang Changed Hands]. Hong Kong: Freedom Press, 1956.

Sung Chung-k'an. *Ssu-ch'uan ko-lao-hui kai-shan chih shang-chüeh* [Consideration of the Reform of Szechwan's Ko Lao Hui]. Chengtu: Ssu-ch'uan ti-fang shih-chi wen-t'i yen-chiu so, 1940.

"T'ung-i ling-tao, fen-chi fu-tse shih ts'ai-cheng kung-tso ti cheng-ch'üeh fang-chen" [Unify Leadership, Divide Responsibility among Levels is the Proper Direction in Finance Work]. *Hsin-Hua yüeh-pao*, No. 18 (1951), p. 1358.

Wang Wei-tsu. "Hsi-nan kung-shang-yeh i nien lai ti chin-pu ts'e-hsieh" [Emphasizing a Year of Progress in Southwest Industry and Commerce]. *Ching-chi chou-pao* [Economic Weekly] (Shanghai) 12, No. 8 (1951), pp. 17-18.

"Wei shem-ma yao t'ung-i kuo-chia ts'ai-cheng ching-chi kung-tso?" [Why Should We Unify National Financial and Economic Work?] *Hsin-Hua yüeh-pao*, No. 6 (1950), pp. 1329-1330.

Wei-ta Fa-shih (pseudonym). *Chung-Kuo pang-hui* [Chinese Secret Societies]. Chungking: Shuo-wen she, 1949.

English-Language Sources

"The Abolition of Regional Administrations in China." *Far Eastern Economic Review* 17, No. 4 (1954), pp. 101-102.

Ake, Claude. *A Theory of Political Integration.* Homewood, Illinois: Dorsey Press, 1967.

Almond, Gabriel, and G. Bingham Powell. *Comparative Politics: A Developmental Approach.* Boston: Little, Brown and Company, 1966.

"An Observer in Sikang." *Office of Naval Intelligence Review* 4, No. 2 (1949), pp. 28-37.

Ashford, Douglas. *National Development and Local Reform: Political Participation in Morocco, Tunisia, and Pakistan.* Princeton: Princeton University Press, 1967.

————. *Perspectives of a Moroccan Nationalist.* Totowa, N.J.: Bedminster Press, 1964.

Asiaticus. "How Communist China Is Governed." *Far Eastern Economic Review* 11, No. 23 (1951), pp. 728-733.

Bailey, F. G. *Stratagems and Spoils.* New York: Schocken Books, 1969.

Barnard, Chester I. "A Definition of Authority," in Robert K. Merton, ed., *Reader in Bureaucracy.* Glencoe: Free Press, 1952, pp. 180-185.

Barnett, A. Doak. *China on the Eve of Communist Takeover.* New York: Praeger, 1963.

————. *Communist China: The Early Years, 1949-1955.* New York: Praeger, 1965.

Bates, Robert H. "Ethnic Competition and Modernization in Contemporary Africa." *Comparative Political Studies* 6, No. 3 (1973), pp. 457-484.

Bernatzik, Hugo Adolf, *AKHA and MIAO.* New Haven: Human Relations Area Files Press, 1970.

Bertsch, Gary K. *Nation-Building in Yugoslavia.* Beverly Hills: Sage Publications, 1971.

Bertsch, Gary K., and M. George Zaninovich. "A Factor-Analytic Method of Identifying Different Political Cultures." *Comparative Politics* 6, No. 2 (1974), pp. 219-243.

Binder, Leonard. "Crises of Development," In Leonard Binder, ed., *Crises and Sequences in Political Development.* Princeton: Princeton University Press, 1971, pp. 3-72.

————. "National Integration and Political Development." *American Political Science Review* 58, No. 3 (1964), pp. 622-631.

————, ed. *Crises and Sequences in Political Development.* Princeton: Princeton University Press, 1971.

Black, Cyril. *The Dynamics of Modernization.* New York: Harper and Row, 1966.

Blau, Peter, and Richard Scott. *Formal Organizations.* San Francisco: Chandler, 1962.

Blaustein, Albert P. *Fundamental Legal Documents of Communist China.* South Hackensack, N.J.: Fred B. Rothman and Company, 1962.

Bloch, Karl. "Warlordism." *American Journal of Sociology* 43, No. 5 (1938), pp. 691-703.

Bondurant, Joan V. *Regionalism Versus Provincialism: A Study in Problems of Indian National Unity.* Berkeley: University of California Press, 1958.

Boorman, Howard L., ed. *Biographic Dictionary of Republican China.* 4 vols. New York: Columbia University Press, 1967.

Bridgham, Philip. "Factionalism in the Central Committee," in John W.

Lewis, ed., *Party Leadership and Revolutionary Power in China*. Cambridge: Cambridge University Press, 1970, pp. 203-235.

Brunnert, H. S., and V. V. Hagelstrom. *Present Day Political Organization of China*. Revised by N. Th. Kolessoff, and translated by A. Beltchenko and E. E. Moran. Taipei: Book World Company, n.d. Reprint of a 1912 edition.

Buck, John Lossing, Owen L. Dawson, and Wu Yuan-li. *Food and Agriculture in Communist China*. New York: Praeger, 1966.

Carter, G. M., ed. *National Unity and Regionalism in Eight African States*. Ithaca: Cornell University Press, 1966.

"Central People's Government Council Decision on the Abolition of Regional First-Grade Administrative Machinery and Changes in Provincial and Municipal Structures." *Survey of China Mainland Press*, No. 832 (1954), pp. 8-10.

"Chairman Mao Discusses Twenty Manifestations of Bureaucracy," in "Selections from Chairman Mao." U.S. *Joint Publications Research Service*, Translations on Communist China, No. 90 (1970), pp. 40-43.

Chamberlain, Heath B. "Transition and Consolidation in Urban China," in Robert A. Scalapino, ed., *Elites in the People's Republic of China*. Seattle: University of Washington Press, 1972, pp. 245-301.

———. "Transition and Consolidation in Urban China: A Study of Leaders and Organizations in Three Cities, 1949-1953." Ph.D. dissertation, Stanford University, 1971.

Chang, A. S. "An Analysis of Administrative Regions in China." *Far Eastern Economic Review* 14, No. 2 (1953), pp. 41-44.

Chang Li-men. "Special Features in the Changes of Administrative Areas in China." *Extracts from China Mainland Magazines*, No. 57 (1956), pp. 1-14.

Chao Kuo-chün. *Economic Planning and Organization in Mainland China: A Documentary Study (1949-1957)*. Cambridge: Harvard University Press, Center for East Asian Studies, 1960.

Ch'en, Jerome, ed. *Mao*. Englewood Cliffs, New Jersey: Prentice-Hall, 1969.

Chesneaux, Jean. "The Federalist Movement in China, 1920-1923," in Jack Grey, ed., *Modern China's Search for a Political Form*. London: Oxford University Press, 1969, pp. 96-137.

———, ed. *Popular Movements and Secret Societies in China, 1840-1950*. Stanford: Stanford University Press, 1972.

Chi Ch'ao-ting. *Key Economic Areas in Chinese History as Revealed in the Development of Public Works for Water Control*. London: George Allen and Unwin, 1936.

China News Analysis (Hong Kong). Selected issues, 1950-1954.

"Chinese Reds Plan Six Regional Rules." *New York Times*, September 12, 1949, p. 15.

Chou Fang. "Explaining Changes in the Organic Structure and Functions of People's Governments in the Administrative Regions." *Survey of China Mainland Press,* No. 494 (1953), pp. 36-38.

Coleman, James S. "The Development Syndrome: Differentiation-Equality-Capacity," in Leonard Binder, ed., *Crises and Sequences in Political Development.* Princeton: Princeton University Press, 1971, pp. 73-100.

Coleman, James S., and Carl J. Rosberg, Jr. *Political Parties and National Integration in Tropical Africa.* Berkeley: University of California Press, 1964.

Compton, Boyd, trans. *Mao's China: Party Reform Documents.* Seattle: University of Washington Press, 1952.

"Conditions in Yunnan and Kunming." *Far Eastern Economic Review* 5, No. 23 (1948), pp. 601-602.

Connor, Walker, "Nation-Building or Nation-Destroying?" *World Politics* 24, No. 3 (1972), pp. 319-355.

Cónquest, Robert. *The Soviet Political System.* New York: Praeger, 1968.

Cressey, George B. *China's Geographic Foundations.* New York: McGraw-Hill, 1934.

————. *Land of the 500 Million.* New York: McGraw-Hill, 1955.

da Silva, Milton M. "Modernization and Ethnic Conflict: The Case of the Basques." *Comparative Politics* 7, No. 2 (1975), pp. 227-251.

de Beauclair, Inez. *Tribal Cultures of Southwest China.* Taipei: Orient Cultural Service, 1970.

"Decision on Changes in the Structure and Tasks of the People's Governments of the Administrative Regions." *Current Background,* No. 245 (1953), pp. 9-11.

de Francis, John. "National and Minority Policies." *Annals of the American Academy of Political and Social Science,* No. 277 (1951), pp. 146-155.

Deutsch, Karl W. *Political Community and the North Atlantic Area: International Organization in the Light of Historical Experience.* Princeton: Princeton University Press, 1957.

Dickinson, Robert E. *Regional Ecology: The Study of Man's Environment.* New York: John Wiley and Sons, 1970.

Dingle, Edwin John, ed. *The New Atlas and Commercial Gazeteer of China.* 2nd ed. Shanghai: North China Daily News and Herald, n.d.

Donnithorne, Audrey. *China's Economic System.* New York: Praeger, 1967.

Downs, Anthony. *Inside Bureaucracy.* Boston: Little, Brown and Company, 1967.

Duchacek, Ivo D. *Comparative Federalism.* New York: Holt, Rinehart and Winston, 1970.

"Economic Geography of Southwest China." U.S. *Joint Publications Research Service,* No. 15069 (1962). Translation of a Chinese language monograph, Sun Ching-chih, ed., "Hsi-nan ti-fang ching-chi ti-li." Peking: K'o-hsüeh ch'u-pan she, 1960.

Emerson, Rupert. *Malaysia: A Study in Direct and Indirect Rule*. Rev. ed. Kuala Lumpur: University of Malaya Press, 1964.

———. "Nation-Building in Africa," in Karl W. Deutsch and W. J. Foltz, eds., *Nation-Building*. New York: Atherton, 1963, pp. 95-116.

Enloe, Cynthia H. *Ethnic Conflict and Political Development*. Boston: Little, Brown and Company, 1973.

Etzioni, Amitai. "A Basis for Comparative Analysis of Complex Organizations," in Amitai Etzioni, ed., *A Sociological Reader on Complex Organizations*. 2nd ed. New York: Holt, Rinehart and Winston, 1969, pp. 59-76.

———. *Modern Organizations*. Englewood Cliffs, N.J.: Prentice-Hall, 1964.

———. *Political Unification*. New York: Holt, Rinehart and Winston, 1965.

Falkenheim, Victor C. "Provincial Leadership in Fukien, 1949-1966," in Robert A. Scalapino, ed., *Elites in the People's Republic of China*. Seattle: University of Washington Press, 1972, pp. 199-244.

Fei Hsiao-t'ung. *Earthbound China: A Study of Rural Economy in Yunnan*. Chicago: University of Chicago Press, 1945.

———. "Minority Groups in Kweichow Province." *Current Background*, No. 150 (1952).

Fisher, Jack C. *Yugoslavia—A Multinational State: Regional Difference and Administrative Response*. San Francisco: Chandler, 1966.

Foltz, W. J. "Building the Newest Nations: Short-run Strategies and Long-run Problems," in Karl W. Deutsch and W. J. Foltz, eds., *Nation-Building*. New York: Atherton, 1963, pp. 117-131.

Foreign Relations of the United States. Diplomatic Papers: China, 1943, 1944, 1945, 1946. Washington: U.S. Government Printing Office, 1957.

Furniss, Norman. "The Practical Significance of Decentralization." *Journal of Politics* 36, No. 4 (1974), pp. 958-982.

Garavente, A. "The Long March." *China Quarterly*, No. 22 (1965), pp. 89-124.

Geertz, Clifford. "The Integrative Revolution," in Clifford Geertz, ed., *Old Societies and New States*. London: Free Press of Glencoe, 1963, pp. 105-157.

Ginsburg, Norton S. "China's Administrative Boundaries." *Far Eastern Economic Review* 10, No. 4 (1951), pp. 103-108.

———. "China's Changing Political Geography." *Geographic Review* 42, No. 1 (1952), pp. 102-117.

Gittings, John. *The Role of the Chinese Army*. London: Oxford University Press, 1967.

Gluckman, Max. "Inter-Hierarchical Roles: Professional and Party Ethics in Tribal Areas in South and Central Africa," in Marc J. Swartz, ed., *Local-Level Politics*. Chicago: Aldine Press, 1968, pp. 69-93.

Gooch, R. K. *Regionalism in France*. New York: Century Press, 1931.

Gordon, L. "Economic Regionalism Reconsidered." *World Politics* 13, No. 2 (1961), pp. 231-253.

Haas, Ernst B. *The Uniting of Europe: Political, Social and Economic Forces*. Stanford: Stanford University Press, 1958.

Hall, John C. S. "Opium Prohibition and the Chinese Communist Party." Canberra: Australia National University Research School of Pacific Studies, Contemporary China Center, Seminar Series, 1975.

———. "The Opium Trade in Yunnan Province, 1917-1937." Canberra: Australia National University, *Papers on Far Eastern History*, September 10, 1974, pp. 1-28.

———. "The Yunnan Provincial Faction, 1927-1937." Manuscript. Canberra, 1974.

Han Su-yin. *Birdless Summer*. New York: G. P. Putnam's Sons, 1968.

Harding, Harry, Jr. "The Organizational Issue in Chinese Politics." Ph.D. dissertation, Stanford University, 1973.

Harrison, Selig S. *India: The Most Dangerous Decades*. Princeton: Princeton University Press, 1960.

Hedtke, Charles H. "The Genesis of Revolution in Szechuan." Paper presented at the Research Conference on the Chinese Revolution of 1911, Wentworth-by-the-Sea, New Hampshire, August 1965.

Herberle, R. "Regionalism: Some Critical Observations." *Social Forces* 21, No. 3 (1943), pp. 280-286.

Hess, Robert L. "Ethiopia," in G. M. Carter, ed., *National Unity and Regionalism in Eight African States*. Ithaca: Cornell University Press, 1966, pp. 441-538.

Ho Kan-chih. *A History of the Modern Chinese Revolution*. Peking: Foreign Languages Press, 1959.

Hosie, Alexander. *Three Years in Western China*. London: George Philip and Son, 1890.

Hough, Jerry. *Soviet Prefects*. Cambridge: Cambridge University Press, 1969.

Huang Chen-hsia, personal letters, dated June 16, 1973, and July 10, 1973.

Hughes, T. J., and D. E. T. Luard. *The Economic Development of Communist China, 1949-1960*. 2nd ed. London: Oxford University Press, 1961.

Jackman, Robert W. "Political Parties, Voting and National Integration: The Canadian Case." *Comparative Politics* 4, No. 4 (1972), pp. 511-536.

278   REGIONAL GOVERNMENT AND POLITICAL INTEGRATION

Johnson, William R. "Revolution and Reconstruction in Kweichow and Yunnan." Paper presented at the Research Conference on the Chinese Revolution of 1911, Wentworth-by-the-Sea, New Hampshire, August 1965.

Kao Ying-mao. "The Urban Bureaucratic Elite in Communist China," in A. Doak Barnett, ed., *Chinese Communist Politics in Action*. Seattle: University of Washington Press, 1969, pp. 216-267.

Kapp, Robert A. *Szechwan and the Chinese Republic*. New Haven: Yale University Press, 1973.

Klein, Donald W., and Anne B. Clark. *Biographic Dictionary of Chinese Communism, 1921-1965*. 2 vols. Cambridge: Harvard University Press, 1971.

"Kweichow of the Fatherland." U.S. *Joint Publications Research Service*, No. 10761 (1961). Translation of portions of *Tsu-kuo ti Kuei-chou*. Kweiyang: Kuei-chou jen-min ch'u-pan she, 1955.

"Kweichow Province." *China News Analysis*, No. 329 (1960).

Lang, Nicholas R. "The Dialectics of Decentralization: Economic Reform and Regional Inequality in Yugoslavia." *World Politics* 27, No. 3 (1975), pp. 309-335.

La Palombara, Joseph. "Penetration: A Crisis of Governmental Capacity," in Leonard Binder, ed., *Crises and Sequences in Political Development*. Princeton: Princeton University Press, 1971, pp. 205-232.

Lerner, Daniel. *The Passing of Traditional Society*. Glencoe: Free Press, 1964.

Lewis, John W. *Leadership in Communist China*. Ithaca: Cornell University Press, 1966.

———. "Memory, Opportunity and Strategy in Peasant Revolutions: The Case of North China." Paper presented for the Research Conference on Communist Revolutions, St. Croix, 1973.

———. "Revolutionary Struggle and the Second Generation in Communist China." *China Quarterly*, No. 21 (1965), pp. 126-147.

Liao T'ai-ch'u. "The Ko Lao Hui in Szechuan." *Pacific Affairs* 20, No. 2 (1947), pp. 161-173.

Lieberman, H. R. "On Conditions in North China; Territory Divided into Six Administrative Regions." *New York Times*, April 4, 1949, p. 3.

Lieberthal, Kenneth. "The Suppression of Secret Societies in Post-Liberation Tientsin." *China Quarterly*, No. 54 (1973), pp. 242-266.

Lin Yueh-hua. *The Lolo of Liang Shan*. New Haven: Human Relations Area Files Press, 1961.

Love, Joseph L. "An Approach to Regionalism." No place, no date.

Mao Tse-tung. *Selected Works*. New York: International Publishers, 1954-1956.

———. *Selected Works*. Peking: Foreign Languages Press, 1961.

McColl, Robert W. "The Development of Supra-Provincial Administrative Regions in Communist China, 1949-1960." *Pacific Viewpoint*
4, No. 1 (1963), pp. 53-64.

"The Meaning of the Recent Reorganization of Government Organs
to Meet Economic Construction." *Survey of China Mainland Press*,
No. 460 (1952), pp. 29-30.

Melson, Robert, and Howard Wolpe. "Modernization and the Politics
of Communalism: A Theoretical Perspective." *American Political
Science Review* 64, No. 4 (1970), pp. 1112-1130.

Merton, Robert K. "Bureaucratic Structure and Personality," in Robert
K. Merton, ed., *Reader in Bureaucracy*. Glencoe: Free Press, 1952,
pp. 361-371.

Michel, Franz. "Regionalism in Nineteenth-Century China." Introduction to *Li Hung-chang and the Huai Army: A Study in Nineteenth-
Century Chinese Regionalism*, by Stanley Spector. Seattle: University
of Washington Press, 1964.

Modern Military Records Division. Record Group 226 (Office of Strategic Services Research and Analysis Branch). National Archives,
Washington, D.C.

Moseley, George V. H. *The Consolidation of the South China Frontier*.
Berkeley and Los Angeles: University of California Press, 1973.

——. "The Frontier Regions in China's Recent International Politics," in Jack Grey, ed., *Modern China's Search for a Political Form*.
London: Oxford University Press, 1969, pp. 299-329.

New China's Economic Achievements. Peking: China Committee for the
Promotion of International Trade, 1952.

Nixon, Charles R. "Self-Determination: The Nigeria/Biafra Case."
World Politics 24, No. 4 (1972), pp. 473-497.

Nye, J. S., Jr. "Comparative Regional Integration: Concept and Meas-
urement." *International Organization* 22, No. 4 (1968), pp. 855-880.

——. *Pan-Africanism and East African Integration*. Cambridge: Harvard
University Press, 1965.

——. "Patterns and Catalysts in Regional Integration," in J. S. Nye,
Jr., ed., *International Regionalism: Readings*. Boston: Little, Brown and
Company, 1968, pp. 333-349.

"Organic Law of the New Regional Government Councils." *Current
Background*, No. 170 (1952), pp. 19-22.

Organski, A. F. K. *The Stages of Political Development*. New York: Alfred
A. Knopf, 1965.

Perkins, Dwight H. *Market Control and Planning in Communist China*.
Cambridge: Harvard University Press, 1966.

Pye, Lucian W. *Aspects of Political Development*. Boston: Little, Brown
and Company, 1966.

"Regional Administration in Communist China." *Current Background,* No. 245 (1953), pp. 1-11.

[Republic of China.] Office of Military History. *Liu Po-ch'eng: A Chinese Communist Leader.*Taipei: n.p., 1971.

Reshetar, John S., Jr. *The Soviet Polity.* New York: Dodd, Mead and Company, 1971.

Rice, Edward E. *Mao's Way.* Berkeley and Los Angeles: University of California Press, 1972.

Rigg, Robert B. *China's Fighting Hordes.* Harrisburg: Military Service Publishing Company, 1951.

Rustow, Dankwart. *A World of Nations: Problems of Modernization.* Washington, D.C.: Brookings Institute, 1967.

Schapiro, Leonard. *The Government and Politics of the Soviet Union.* London: Hutchinson University Library, 1967.

Schneider, Peter, Jane Schneider, and Edward Hansen. "Modernization and Development: The Role of Regional Elites and Noncorporate Groups in the European Mediterranean." *Comparative Studies in Society and History* 14, No. 3 (1972), pp. 328-350.

Schram, Stuart, *Mao Tse-tung.* Harmondsworth, England: Penguin Books, 1966.

Schurmann, Franz. "China's 'New Economic Policy'—Transition or Beginning." *China Quarterly,* No. 17 (1964), pp. 65-92.

———. *Ideology and Organization in Communist China.* Berkeley and Los Angeles: University of California Press, 1966.

Schwartz, Benjamin. *Chinese Communism and the Rise of Mao.* Cambridge: Harvard University Press, 1966.

Segal, Aaron, "The Integration of Developing Countries: Some Thoughts on East Africa and Central America." *Journal of Common Market Studies* 5, No. 3 (1967), pp. 252-282.

Selznick, Philip. "Coöptation: A Mechanism for Organizational Stability," in Robert K. Merton, ed., *Reader in Bureaucracy.* Glencoe: Free Press, 1952, pp. 135-139.

———. *Leadership in Administration: A Sociological Interpretation.* Berkeley: University of California Press, 1957.

Sewell, W. G. *I Stayed in China.* South Brunswick, N.J.: H. S. Barnes, 1966.

Sharp, Walter R. "Procedural Vices: La Paperasserie," in Robert K. Merton, ed., *Reader in Bureaucracy.* Glencoe: Free Press, 1952, pp. 407-410.

Sherwood, Frank. "Devolution as a Problem of Organizational Strategy," in Robert T. Daland, ed., *Comparative Urban Research: The Administration and Politics of Cities.* New York: Sage Publications, 1969, pp. 60-87.

Shie I-yuan. "China's Administrative Divisions." *Survey of China Mainland Press,* No. 737 (1954), pp. 28-31.

Simon, Herbert A. *Administrative Behavior*. 2nd ed. New York: Mac-Millan, 1960.

———. "Decision-Making and Administrative Organization," in Robert K. Merton, ed., *Reader in Bureaucracy*. Glencoe: Free Press, 1952, pp. 185-194.

"The Situation in Kunming." *Far Eastern Economic Review* 9, No. 5 (1950), pp. 135-136.

Skinner, G. W. "Aftermath of Communist Liberation in the Chengtu Plain." *Pacific Affairs* 24, No. 1 (1951), pp. 61-76.

———. "The City in Chinese Society." Paper prepared for the Research Conference on Urban Society in Traditional China, Wentworth-by-the-Sea, New Hampshire, August 1968.

———. "Marketing and Social Structure in Rural China." *Journal of Asian Studies* 24, No. 1 (1964), pp. 3-43.

Skinner, G. W. and Edwin A. Winckler. "Compliance Succession in Rural Communist China: A Cyclical Theory," in Amitai Etzioni, ed., *A Sociological Reader on Complex Organizations*. 2nd ed. New York: Holt, Rinehart and Winston, 1969, pp. 410-438.

Sklar, R. L., and C. S. Whitaker. "Nigeria," in G. M. Carter, ed., *National Unity and Regionalism in Eight African States*. Ithaca: Cornell University Press, 1966, pp. 7-150.

Smedley, Agnes. *The Great Road: The Life and Times of Chu Teh*. New York: Monthly Review Press, 1956.

Spencer, J. E. "Kueichou: An Internal Chinese Colony." *Pacific Affairs* 13, No. 2 (1940), pp. 162-172.

———. "The Szechuan Village Fair." *Economic Geography* 16, No. 1 (1940), pp. 48-58.

Stanford University. China Project. Subcontractor's Monograph HRAF-30 Stanford-4. Vols. 7 and 8: *Southwest China*. New Haven: Human Relations Area Files Press, 1956.

Steiner, H. A. "New Regional Governments in China." *Far Eastern Survey* 19, No. 11 (1950), pp. 112-116.

"Strengthen the Centralized Nature of our State Work to Meet the Large-Scale Economic Construction." *Survey of China Mainland Press*, No. 455 (1952), pp. 3-5.

Sutton, Donald Sinclair. "The Rise and Decline of the Yunnan Army, 1909-1925." Ph.D. Dissertation, Cambridge University, 1970.

Swartz, Marc. "The Political Middleman," in Marc J. Swartz, ed., *Local-Level Politics*. Chicago: Aldine Press, 1968, pp. 199-203.

———, ed. *Local-Level Politics*. Chicago: Aldine Press, 1968.

"Szechuan." U.S. *Joint Publications Research Service*, No. 15308 (1962). Translation of a Russian-language book by Ye. A. Afanas'yeskiy. Moscow: Publishing House of Oriental Literature, 1962.

Teiwes, Frederick. "A Review Article: The Evolution of Leadership

Purges in Communist China." *China Quarterly*, No. 41 (1970), pp. 122-135.

Teng Hsiao-p'ing. "Report on the Revision of the Constitution of the Chinese Communist Party," in *Eighth National Congress of the Chinese Communist Party*. Peking: Foreign Languages Press, 1956, 1:171-228.

Thomas, S. B. "Government and Administration in China Today." *Pacific Affairs* 23, No. 3 (1950), pp. 248-270.

————. *Government and Administration in Communist China*. Rev. ed. New York: Institute of Pacific Relations, 1955.

————. "Structure and Constitutional Basis of the Chinese People's Republic." *Annals of the American Academy of Political and Social Science*, No. 277 (1951), pp. 46-55.

Thompson, James D. *Organizations in Action*. New York: McGraw-Hill, 1967.

Thompson, Victor A. *Modern Organization*. New York: Alfred A. Knopf, 1961.

Thornton, Richard C. "The Structure of Communist Politics." *World Politics* 24, No. 4 (1972), pp. 498-517.

Tullock, Gordon. *The Politics of Bureaucracy*. Washington, D.C.: Public Affairs Press, 1965.

U.S. Consultate General. Hong Kong. *Current Background* (Hong Kong). June 1950-December 1954.

U.S. Consultate General. Hong Kong. *Survey of China Mainland Press* (Hong Kong). November 1950-December 1954.

Vance, R. B. "Region." *International Encyclopedia of the Social Sciences*. New York: Crowell, Collier, MacMillan, 1968, 13:377-382.

Van Slyke, Lyman, ed. *The Chinese Communist Movement: A Report of the United States War Department, July, 1945*. Stanford: Stanford University Press, 1968.

Vassal, Gabrielle M. *In and Around Yunnan Fou*. London: William Heinemann, 1922.

Verba, Sidney. "Sequences and Development," in Leonard Binder, ed., *Crises and Sequences in Political Development*. Princeton: Princeton University Press, 1971, pp. 283-316.

Vogel, Ezra. *Canton Under Communism: Programs and Politics in a Provincial Capital 1949-1968*. Cambridge: Harvard University Press, 1969.

Walker, Richard L. *China Under Communism: The First Five Years*. New Haven: Yale University Press, 1955.

Wakeman, Frederic, "The Secret Societies of Kwangtung, 1800-1856," in Jean Chesneaux, ed., *Popular Movements and Secret Societies in China, 1840-1950*. Stanford: Stanford University Press, 1972.

Wang Gungwu. "Comments," in Ho Ping-ti and Tsou Tang, eds.,

China in Crisis. Chicago: University of Chicago Press, 1968, 1:264-270.

————. *The Structure of Power in North China during the Five Dynasties*. Kuala Lumpur: University of Malaya Press, 1963.

Watts, Ronald. *Administration in Federal Systems*. London: Hutchinson Educational Press, 1970.

Weiner, Myron. "Political Integration and Political Development." *Annals of the American Academy of Political and Social Science*, No. 358 (1965), pp. 52-64.

————. "National Integration versus Nationalism." *Comparative Studies in Society and History* 15, No. 2 (1973), pp. 248-254.

Whitney J. B. R. *China: Area, Administration and Nation Building*. Chicago: University of Chicago. Department of Geography. Research Paper No. 123, 1970.

Whitson, William W. with Chen-hsia Huang. *The Chinese Communist High Command: A History of Communist Military Politics, 1927-1971*. New York: Praeger, 1973.

————. "The Field Army in Chinese Communist Military Politics." *China Quarterly*, No. 37 (1969), pp. 1-30.

Whyte, Martin King. "Bureaucracy and Modernization in China: The Maoist Critique." *American Sociological Review* 38, No. 2 (1973), pp. 149-163.

Wiens, Harold J. *China's March Toward the Tropics*. Hamden, Connecticut: Shoe String Press, 1954.

Wilbur, Martin. "Military Separatism and the Process of Reunification under the Nationalist Regime, 1922-1937," in Ho Ping-ti and Tsou Tang, eds., *China in Crisis*. Chicago: University of Chicago Press, 1968, 1:203-276.

Wilensky, Harold L. *Organizational Intelligence*. New York: Basic Books, 1967.

Willmott, L. Earl. "Tentative Manuscript for Diary of a Revolution." Unpublished manuscript. No place, no date.

Wu Yuan-li. *The Spatial Economy of Communist China*. New York: Praeger, 1967.

Zolberg, Aristide R. "Patterns of National Integration." *Journal of Modern African Studies* 5, No. 4 (1967), pp. 449-467.

INDEX

Administrative Committee, 1, 36, 37, 106, 107, 242-243, 245. *See also* Military Administrative Committee
abolition, 209
buffer role, 239-240
in Southwest, 1952-1954, 119-131
  and central government, 120-125
  and provinces, 129-130
  and Regional Party, 125-129
  membership, 140, 141-142 tables, 146 table
Africa, integration strategy in, 7, 167
Air transportation, 250-251
Ake, Claude, on ethnic divisions, 9n
Anti-Japanese War, 22-23, 57, 79, 80
Autumn Harvest uprising (1927), 21

Bandits, policy toward, 85, 95-96, 103
Barnard, Chester I., on power and compliance, 233-234
Base areas, CCP administration and, 21-23
Binder, Leonard, on political modernization, 6
Blau, Peter, on organizational conflict, 212
Budget procedures, MAC role in, 112-113
Bureaucracy, tensions within, 214-226
  "bureaucratism," 218
  "bureaupathological" behavior, 212
Burma, 52, 66, 83, 84

Cadres, Party, 211, 214-226
  behavior, 211, 214-215
  bureaucratic tensions, 214-226
  deviations in dealing with
    counter-revolutionaries, 228-229
    minorities, 229-230
    trade, 230-233
  integration failures and, 239-240
  by region, 213n
Canton (Kwangtung province), 87, 201, 250
Center-region interaction, 93-107
Central America, integration strategy in, 7
Centralization, 38-39
  Soviet model for, 26n, 255
Central People's Government Council, 36, 38, 89, 115, 136

Chamberlain, Heath B., on classification of local leaders, 140, 147, 149, 150
Chang Chi-ch'ün, 149
Chang Chün, 57-58, 79
Chang Kuo-hua, 97, 161
Chang Kuo-t'ao, 143
Ch'ang-ch'un (Kirin province), 62
Chao Er-feng, 53
Chao-t'ung (Yunnan province), 52
Chekiang province, 22
Ch'en Ch'eng, 61, 78
Chengtu (Szechwan province), 52, 68, 84, 88, 174, 216
Chengtu-Chungking Railway, 92, 96, 100, 197, 250
Chengtu Plain, 49
Ch'en Hsi-lien, 159n, 161
Ch'en Keng, 161
Ch'en Yi, 157
Chi Ch'ao-ting, 19
Chia-ling River, 49, 65
Chiang Kai-shek, 46, 56-59, 62, 63, 78, 79, 80
Ch'in dynasty, 18
China topographical map, 46
Chinese Communist Party (CCP)
  administrative reform doctrines, 23-25
  Central Committee, 22, 23, 28, 41, 121, 126, 136
    Seventh Central Committee, Third Plenum, 93-94, 175, 176
    Seventh Central Committee, Fourth Plenum, 40, 105-106
  expansion of membership, and integration, 251
  ideological errors, 223-226
  liberation policy for Southwest, 157-158
  Regional, 90, 125-129
  and regional experience before 1949, 21-25
  role in integration, evaluation of, 257
Ch'ing dynasty, 20, 53, 73, 74, 75
Ching-kang-shan, 21
Chou Fang, 27-28, 37-38
Chou Period, 18
Chu Hsiao-ling, 59